WITHDRAWN

Literacy
for Young
Children

D1403916

To my uncle, Colonel Wilfred A. Steiner, who asked me,
"Have you written a book yet?"

—Priscilla L. Griffith

To my mother, Lois Beach, who taught me how to read and to love reading.

—Sara Ann Beach

To Bev Cox, whose passion for emergent literacy is inspirational.

—Jiening Ruan

To Mrs. Geraldine Jones, for giving me a child care job at age
eighteen and starting my career.

—Loraine Dunn

Literacy
for Young
Children

A Guide for Early
Childhood Educators

Priscilla L. Griffith
Sara Ann Beach
Jiening Ruan
Loraine Dunn

CORWIN PRESS
A SAGE Company
Thousand Oaks, CA 91320

For information:

Corwin Press
A SAGE Company
2455 Teller Road
Thousand Oaks, California 91320
www.corwinpress.com

SAGE India Pvt. Ltd.
B 1/I 1 Mohan Cooperative
    Industrial Area
Mathura Road, New Delhi 110 044
India

SAGE Ltd.
1 Oliver's Yard
55 City Road
London EC1Y 1SP
United Kingdom

SAGE Asia-Pacific Pte. Ltd.
33 Pekin Street #02–01
Far East Square
Singapore 048763

Printed in the United States of America

Library of Congress Cataloging-in-Publication Data

Literacy for young children: a guide for early childhood educators/
Priscilla L. Griffith . . . [et al.].
        p. cm.
Includes bibliographical references and index.
ISBN 978-1-4129-5199-9 (cloth)
ISBN 978-1-4129-5200-2 (pbk.)
    1. Language arts (Preschool)—United States. 2. Reading (Preschool)—United States. 3. Literacy—Study and teaching (Preschool)—United States. I. Griffith, Priscilla L. (Priscilla Lynn), 1946– II. Title.

LB1140.5.L3L58 2008
372.6—dc22   2007040295

This book is printed on acid-free paper.

08   09   10   11   12   10   9   8   7   6   5   4   3   2   1

Acquisitions Editor:	Stacy Wagner
Managing Editor:	Jessica Allan
Editorial Assistant:	Joanna Coelho
Production Editor:	Veronica Stapleton
Copy Editor:	Gretchen A. Treadwell
Typesetter:	C&M Digitals (P) Ltd.
Proofreader:	Dennis Webb
Indexer:	Sheila Bodell
Cover Designer:	Karine Hovsepian

Table of Contents

Acknowledgments

Corwin Press gratefully acknowledges the following peer reviewers for their editorial insight and guidance:

Emma McGee Barnes
Literacy Facilitator
Hawk Ridge Elementary School
Charlotte, NC

Kara L. Burrows-Johnson
Prekindergarten Teacher
P. M. Akin Elementary School
Wylie, TX

Teresa P. Cunningham
Principal
Laurel Elementary School
Laurel Bloomery, TN

Addie Gaines
Principal
Kirbyville Elementary School
Kirbyville, MO

Gail Hardesty
Early Reading First Mentor
Chicago Public Schools Early Childhood Department
Chicago, IL

Ann Ketch
PreK–5 Literacy and Language Arts Coordinator
Des Moines Public Schools
Des Moines, IA

Karen Stuard
First Grade Teacher
Northville Public Schools
Northville, MI

About the Authors

Priscilla L. Griffith is the Ruth G. Hardman Chair in Education and a professor in the Department of Instructional Leadership and Academic Curriculum at the University of Oklahoma where she teaches undergraduate and graduate level literacy education courses. Priscilla has worked in language and literacy and teacher education for over three decades. She has applied her expertise in these areas as an editor of professional journals including *The Reading Teacher* and *Action in Teacher Education*, as a consultant for school districts, and as a classroom teacher. She has worked with PreK teachers in Early Reading First classrooms. In addition, Priscilla works regularly with teachers as Director of the Oklahoma Writing Project, a site of the National Writing Project. She is a past president of the Florida Reading Association and the Oklahoma Reading Association. Priscilla received her PhD from the University of Texas at Austin.

Sara Ann (Sally) Beach is a Professor of Literacy Education at the University of Oklahoma where she is coordinator of the reading program and teaches undergraduate and graduate literacy courses. She has a master's degree from Texas A&M University and a PhD in Reading from the University of California, Riverside. Her professional experiences include teaching children from kindergarten through fifth grade and teaching teachers around the world to use reading and writing as a tool for thinking. She has worked with preschool teachers on Early Childhood Professional Educator and Early Reading First grants. Her research focuses on children's development as literate people and the classrooms that provide opportunities for becoming critically literate.

Jiening Ruan is Associate Professor of Reading/ Literacy Education in the College of Education at the University of Oklahoma. She also directs the university's Reading Clinic and its Reading Specialist Certification Program. She holds master's degrees in Elementary Education and Reading Education from Indiana University of Pennsylvania and a PhD in Curriculum and Instruction with an emphasis on Language and Literacy Education from Purdue University. Her current teaching responsibilities include both graduate and undergraduate courses in reading and literacy education at the University of Oklahoma. Her research interests focus on literacy development of children from diverse backgrounds and the effectiveness of technology integration in literacy education.

Loraine Dunn is an Early Childhood Education faculty member at the University of Oklahoma where she teaches early childhood classes, oversees the child development laboratory, and makes student teaching placements. Recently she was part of a team that developed the Early Steps to Literacy project funded by an Early Childhood Educator Professional Development grant from the U.S. Department of Education. Loraine began her career teaching in a child care center serving children living in poverty. Later she served as the education coordinator for a Head Start program and taught kindergarten in a small rural school. After obtaining her master's degree in Child Development from Iowa State University, Loraine spent several years teaching children and adults in university child development laboratories. Since earning her PhD in Child Development and Family Studies from Purdue University, her research has focused on child care program quality, developmentally appropriate practice, and children's learning and development.

Introduction

Why Early Literacy?

L et's begin by contemplating the question of "Why early literacy?" from a historical perspective. At one time, learning to read and write was linked with entering first grade. In fact, many educators believed there was a magical moment when children were "ready" to learn to read. This belief was reinforced by one influential study published in the *Elementary School Journal* (Morphett & Washburne, 1931) in which it was determined that children needed to reach a "mental age" of six and a half years in order to be successful with reading in first grade.

However, research starting in the mid 1960s has led us in another direction when thinking about what children know about written language before they begin formal schooling. Much of the research through the 1960s, 1970s, and 1980s pointed to reading and writing as conjoined developmental processes that started well before children entered first grade. Throughout the chapters in this book you will get a flavor for this early research as we develop the theoretical underpinnings for the information we present about early literacy instruction.

While much of this research focused on how young children develop an understanding of reading and writing, less of it focused on specific instructional strategies teachers in early childhood classrooms might use to foster the understandings and literacy development of young children. However, over the last two decades teachers and researchers have begun to think about early literacy from an instructional perspective. In part, this has resulted from a focus on literacy at the national level. The lenses for this focus are multifaceted and include a nationally funded research center, an important policy statement, two high-profile research reports, and two influential pieces of legislation.

- The Center for the Improvement of Early Reading Achievement (CIERA) was funded by the Office of Educational Research and

Improvement from the period of 1997–2002. The purpose of this research center was to study ways to improve reading achievement in the early elementary years.

• In April 1998, the International Reading Association and the National Association for the Education of Young Children published the joint position statement *Learning to Read and Write: Developmentally Appropriate Practices for Young Children.* This statement helped bring light to the teacher's role in supporting the early literacy development of young children (Neuman, Copple, & Bredekamp, 2000).

• "Reading is essential to success in our society" (p. 1) begins the Executive Summary of *Preventing Reading Difficulties in Young Children* (Snow, Burns, & Griffin, 1998). This work resulted from a committee established by the National Academy of Sciences at the behest of the United States departments of Education and of Human Services. The committee charge was to study the effectiveness of interventions for young children at risk of having problems learning to read. Among the recommendations was ensuring high-quality preschool and kindergarten programs that support language and literacy development.

• In 1998, the U. S. Congress passed the Reading Excellence Act. As a result of this act, the term "scientifically based reading research" was introduced. SBRR, as it is sometimes called, is defined in the bill as the "application of rigorous, systematic, and objective procedures to obtain valid knowledge relevant to reading development, reading instruction, and reading difficulties" (Office of Elementary and Secondary Education, 2003).

• In 2000, the report of the National Reading Panel was released. This report, commissioned by the U.S. Congress, was prepared by a group of "leading scientists in reading research, representatives of colleges of education, reading teachers, educational administrators, and parents" (NICHD, 2000, pp. 1–1). The Panel reviewed studies in the areas of alphabetics (phonemic awareness and phonics), fluency, and comprehension (including vocabulary). On January 8, 2002, President Bush signed into law the No Child Left Behind Act. This law reauthorized the Elementary and Secondary Education Act of 1965, and it added two new reading initiatives: Reading First and Early Reading First.

The result of these national initiatives is an emphasis on closing the gap: closing the achievement gap and closing the gap between best and current practices in early childhood.

Head Start is the nation's oldest and largest nationally-funded program designed to close gaps in achievement of children at risk of school failure. National studies following two cohorts of Head Start children (1997–1998 and 2000–2001) have indicated that "all 4-year-old children who entered Head Start both in the fall of 1997 and fall of 2000 were considerably below grade level in vocabulary, emergent reading, writing ability, and letter identification" (Stahl & Yaden, 2004, p. 143). In addition, the performance of Spanish-speaking children was behind the performance of both the U.S. population of preschool children and English-speaking preschoolers (Stahl & Yaden, 2004). Yet we know from studies of early childhood development and literacy learning (Shonkoff & Phillips, 2000; Snow, Burns, & Griffin, 1998) that children who begin schooling with rich preschool experiences are more likely to be successful in their early school achievement than children who have less rich experiences.

Early Reading First is one of the federal government's "closing the gap" initiatives aimed at children before they enter kindergarten, and since its inception in 2001, billions of dollars have been invested in sites around the United States to improve the quality of child care and to bring the emphasis on early literacy into prekindergarten classrooms. The goal of Early Reading First is to create early childhood centers of excellence that will provide preschool children with rich literacy experiences. Many of the recommendations in this book come out of our work in Early Reading First classrooms. In the next section, we provide information about the Early Reading First initiative.

EARLY READING FIRST

Early Reading First (ERF) seeks to foster development in early language, cognitive, and prereading skills so that children, and particularly children from low-income families, enter kindergarten prepared for continued school success. Specific program goals include the following:

• To enhance the early language, literacy, and prereading development of preschool-age children, particularly those from low-income families, through strategies and **professional development** that are based on scientifically based reading research.

• To provide preschool-age children with cognitive learning opportunities in **high-quality language and literature-rich environments** so that the children can attain the fundamental knowledge and skills necessary for optimal reading development in kindergarten and beyond.

- To demonstrate language and literacy activities based on scientifically based reading research that supports the age-appropriate development of:
  - ○ Oral language (vocabulary, expressive language, listening comprehension)
  - ○ Phonological awareness (rhyming, blending, segmenting)
  - ○ Print awareness
  - ○ Alphabetic knowledge

- To use **screening assessments** to effectively identify preschool-age children who may be at risk for reading failure.

(These Early Reading First program goals are quoted directly from the Early Reading First Web site at http://www.ed.gov/programs/earlyreading/index.html. The emphasis within the goals, in bold, is ours.)

Early Reading First legislation has an impact on teacher training, curriculum development, and student assessment as one sees in the language woven through the ERF goals. This book addresses each of these components of ERF.

DEVELOPMENTALLY APPROPRIATE PRACTICE

Standards aimed at accountability are a force in education today even at the preschool level (Dunn & Kontos, 2003). Frequently, however, literacy educators find themselves navigating the tension around instruction informed by standards, including SBRR teacher-directed instruction, and what they consider developmentally appropriate practice in early childhood classrooms. However, there need not be a disconnection between these two forces, both of which can inform instruction in early childhood classrooms. Our approach in discussing aspects of instruction in early literacy classrooms is that teachers must be informed decision makers who understand their children and purposefully provide learning experiences (Bredekamp & Copple, 1997; Dunn & Kontos, 2003). In fact, we believe teachers' practical and professional knowledge is at the heart of decision making and is what ties together what we teach and how we teach it in an era of standards and accountability (Griffith & Ruan, 2003). Below we provide a discussion of developmentally appropriate practice that forms the foundation for the literacy practices we present in this book.

Developmentally appropriate practice requires that teachers use knowledge about child development to inform practice (Bredekamp & Copple, 1997). We also know that literacy does not just emerge naturally (Neuman, Copple, & Bredekamp, 2000). In this book, we rely on what we know about scientifically based and developmentally appropriate practice for literacy instruction in early childhood classrooms based on the following principles:

- Literacy includes both reading and writing.
- Oral language development is the foundation for literacy development.
- Reading and writing develop concurrently along a continuum from emergent to standard behaviors.
- There is no one method of instruction that is effective for all learners.
- Literacy experiences must build on prior knowledge.
- Literacy experiences must occur in meaningful contexts.

OVERVIEW OF THIS BOOK

This book is designed to meet the needs of early childhood teachers in PreK and kindergarten classrooms, as well as literacy coaches working at this level. Throughout the book we include vignettes of four children representing diverse backgrounds and different levels of accomplishment to illustrate the nature of early literacy development and how PreK teachers can align their instruction to support each individual child. The reader is introduced to these children in Chapter 1, and subsequent chapters contain vignettes about these children. Each chapter also includes sections addressing theory to practice, assessment and instruction, centers, diversity, and a chapter summary. For further reference, an appendix contains a list of appropriate Web sites. Chapters address the following topics: child development, oral language, phonological awareness, the alphabetic principle, writing, comprehension, sharing books with children, integrating literacy across the curriculum, literacy in the real world, and bringing developmentally appropriate literacy instruction together in the classroom.

Children's Development and Literacy Learning

1

From the time that they are born, children begin to learn about language, both oral and written. They learn how language is used. They learn what written language looks like as it surrounds them in the environment in the form of signs, billboards, labels on food, newspapers, magazines, and junk mail and on computers and television. Children also see adults using print in their daily lives to make lists, read recipes, read books and magazines, and write notes. The use of print is so wide-ranging in our society that children begin to learn about how it works from a very early age. We call this early learning emergent literacy.

Emergent literacy means that literacy learning begins at birth and unfolds throughout a child's early years. It also means that to become literate, children develop and bring together complex subsystems of resources. Specifically, children use linguistic, cognitive, social, and cultural experiences as they interact with print and make meaning from print (Clay, 2001). Each child follows a unique developmental path as he or she develops these resources and learns how to bring them together. Thus, emergent literacy is the developmental process of becoming a proficient reader and writer. It includes the skills and knowledge that children develop and the behaviors that they demonstrate before they are able to read and write like adults. This knowledge and these skills are the resources children use and build on as they have interactions with and around print. They then build up an understanding of what it means to read and write as well as develop listening and speaking abilities. Children's literacy development is not necessarily evident in how conventional or adult-like their reading and writing appear. Instead, it is evident in the literate behavior they exhibit. Literate behavior is what children do when they exhibit an action or performance that, on the surface, looks like something an adult engaged in a literacy

> Emergent literacy is the developmental process of becoming a proficient reader and writer.

activity might do. Examples of literate behaviors demonstrated by preschool children include holding a book and turning its pages, talking about a book, or pretending to write.

HOW CHILDREN DEVELOP AND LEARN

Literate behavior emerges through normal child development and learning. The experiences young children have at home and at school can either facilitate or slow the literacy learning process. Experiences that allow children to construct their own ideas or theories about how the world works are an important part of the process. Knowledge construction is the essence of learning—personally making sense of the world. Current views of learning and development describe children as active meaning-makers rather than as sponges that absorb information (Miller, 2002). In early childhood education, this process is often called active learning.

This view of children as active participants in the learning process is known as constructivism. The theories of both Piaget and Vygotsky are considered constructivist although each approaches the learning process in different ways (Shapiro, 2002). Short descriptions are provided here to show how the practices advocated in this book help children construct their own knowledge.

Piaget's Adaptation Process

Piaget, a Swiss psychologist, stated that development and learning occur through an interactive process between the child and the environment with both influencing each other (Miller, 2002). As the environment provides experiences, the child responds and in so doing has an impact on the environment. Specifically, as children have experiences in the world, they try to make sense of these experiences through their existing knowledge. Sometimes they can fit a new experience into their existing knowledge, allowing the new information to be assimilated. An example is three-year-old Joshua on a field trip to a local arboretum. He tromps along intent on making "giant steps," not paying attention to the teacher asking him to look up at the banana trees. Finally he looks up and discovers them himself saying, "Look at those big *leaves*!" Joshua has assimilated the huge banana leaves into his existing knowledge of trees and leaves.

In other cases, the new experience simply does not fit and so children must change or adjust their knowledge to accommodate the new information. The experience of one of the authors at age two provides an example. Loraine was with her mother in a city park. She ran up to a fence to pet the pretty swan on the other side. She thought the swan would be happy to be petted, just like her neighbor's dogs. Instead the swan honked and tried to bite her fingers, forever changing Loraine's conception of swans from nice to mean. This change in understanding illustrates accommodation. Piaget said that the processes of assimilation and accommodation always occur together and comprise the process of adaptation or learning.

Vygotsky's Social Interaction

Another prominent theory that gives the child an active role in her own development is that of the Russian psychologist Vygotsky. While Piaget concentrated on the individual experiences of children and an internal process through which knowledge is actively constructed, Vygotsky described development as a social process. While interacting with others, children create understanding, or knowledge, that is shared between them. Thus, active knowledge construction occurs in the social world. As children become sure of their knowledge, it becomes their own and they are able to use it independently.

Vygotsky says that children construct this shared understanding in the zone of proximal development or the ZPD (see Box 1.1). The ZPD represents the difference between the child's actual, or achieved developmental level, and her potential developmental level. The actual level of development includes knowledge and skills the child has mastered and can do independently. Potential development refers to things the child can do or achieve with the help of someone with a higher skill level. This helper is often called "the more skilled other" and may be either another child or an adult. The more skilled other helps the child move forward by supporting or scaffolding his learning process (Miller, 2002). For example, a teacher might help three-year-old Jacob who is working on a new, difficult puzzle by turning a piece around and saying, "try it this way," or suggesting he look for yellow pieces to match the yellow of the sun in the corner, or even by moving some pieces away and others closer. These strategies all provide a scaffold to help Josh solve the problem of what piece goes where. Thus, for Jacob, the skills for completing the puzzle are part of his social interactions with the teacher in the zone of proximal development. He will need many experiences like this to master puzzle problem-solving strategies, but over time, Josh will eventually be able to use these strategies independently, making them part of his actual developmental level.

Box 1.1   Theoretical Terms

Theorist	Concept	Definition
PIAGET	**Assimilation**	Making new information fit into existing knowledge and understandings
	Accommodation	Changing existing knowledge and understanding to fit new information
	Adaptation	How learning occurs The simultaneous processes of assimilation and accommodation
VYGOTSKY	**Shared Understanding**	Knowledge shared between interaction partners Knowledge developed in social situations
	Zone of Proximal Development	The distance between what a child can do independently and what she can do with the help of someone who has greater knowledge and skills
	Scaffolding	Providing assistance to help a child perform or understand at a more advanced level

CHILD DEVELOPMENT: THE FOUNDATION FOR LITERACY

While the theories of Piaget and Vygotsky explain how children learn, child development research provides information on children's competencies in various developmental areas. Three areas of development are particularly important for children's emerging literacy: language development, cognitive or intellectual development, and physical-motor development. Physical motor development will be addressed first, followed by language development and then finally cognitive development.

Physical-Motor Development

Development of the small muscles, or fine motor development, and maturation of the brain, affect children's ability to manipulate writing tools and to focus their eyes on printed material. At birth, babies wrap their fingers tightly around anything that touches their palm, often an adult's finger. This reflex action quickly fades away around three to four months, allowing for purposeful grasping. Eye-hand coordination remains crude during the first year of life though, so babies often miss the object they reach for. While toddlers can use a pincer grasp—their thumb and forefinger—to pick up objects around the end of the first year, crayons are still held in a fist-like grip. In fact, writing remains a challenging task for toddlers as it involves both controlling the writing tool and keeping the paper still (Berger, 2006). There is wide variability in the age at which children demonstrate a mature pencil grasp. Most children master it toward the end of the preschool years but a few others continue to struggle into elementary school. However, by age four, eye-hand coordination is sufficiently developed for easy writing and drawing— although the writing does not look like adult writing (Trawick-Smith, 2006).

> By age four, eye-hand coordination is sufficiently developed for easy writing and drawing.

Language and Communication

Because literacy includes speaking and listening, children's learning of oral language and the conventions of speech are important to their literacy learning. Language development begins early in infancy as babies begin to communicate through cries, grunts, and facial expressions. Around two or three months of age, cooing begins wherein babies make repeated vowel sounds that vary in pitch in a sing-song fashion. Cooing changes into babbling around six months. Babbling adds consonant sounds to the vowels of cooing resulting in vocalizations such as "gaga" and "mama." The onset of babbling also marks the time when sounds not used by the native language of the infant's culture begin to disappear from her vocalizations. This indicates she is learning the phonology, or sounds, of her language system (Hoff, 2006; Puckett & Black, 2005).

> Language development begins early in infancy.

A few months later, as the child moves from infancy to toddlerhood, vocalizations take on the rhythm and cadence of speech with accompanying facial expressions and an expectation that others will respond. It seems that if one could listen closely enough, intelligible words would be heard. This phenomenon is known as expressive jargon and indicates intelligible speech is right around the corner. Loraine's experience with twenty-month-old Abby illustrates how adult response to a child's vocalization validates the child's attempt to communicate. While Abby has many words in her vocabulary, such as "pink," "baby," "mine," and of course "*No!*" she is not yet using multiword sentences. She pats Loraine's leg, and jibbers and jabbers earnestly. Using the context of the ongoing activity, Loraine responds saying, "Yes, I know you want to go, but we have to wait for Austin [her older brother] to find his shoes." Abby shrugs her shoulders, says "hruumph," and dashes off yelling "Austin!" Her message was received and she set off to urge her brother to hurry.

Responding to children as though their behaviors communicate meaning is important for language and literacy development. By engaging children as communicative partners, adults help them to see themselves as speakers, readers, and writers. Evidence of this important process is seen very early in life as children begin to understand that language and communication are social enterprises requiring turn-taking (Jaffe, Beebe, Feldstein, Crown, & Jasnow, 2001). This understanding develops over time as the children have repeated experiences in which adults make turn-taking happen. Specifically, while a baby makes cooing or babbling sounds, his mother listens, waits for a pause, and then responds. The baby repeats his vocalization, and his mother again makes a vocal response. Through the repetition of this sequence, the baby learns that turn-taking is a part of communication—each partner in the interaction waits and listens to the other, then adds his or her own vocal contribution.

> Language and communication are social enterprises requiring turn-taking.

Clearly, the young child develops the idea that speech has meaning and communicates messages. She focuses her efforts on the sound system of her own language as her understanding (or receptive language) and production (or expressive language) skills grow. Vocabulary development proceeds somewhat slowly over the toddler period, with the average child knowing 500 words by age two. However, during the preschool years vocabulary growth literally explodes as the child learns about ten new words per day. This rapid increase in vocabulary development is possible because of fast mapping in which children map new words to similar concepts they already understand, allowing them to learn a word after hearing it only once (Berger, 2006; Puckett & Black, 2005).

> During the preschool years, vocabulary growth literally explodes.

Along with the development of receptive (listening) and expressive (speaking) language comes the child's learning of the structure of grammar, or syntax of language. Syntax refers to the ability to combine words together in an order to communicate a message—the creation of meaningful sentences. Along with syntax, children learn that specific sounds can have meaning and when added to words they change the meaning. Examples are adding "ed" for past tense or "s" for plural. These meaningful units of sound are called morphemes (Hoff, 2006). One indication that a child is learning about syntax and morphemes is the child's application of the rules to the exceptions. Past tense and plural words take on the delightful preschool forms of "eated," "goed," and "feets" (Puckett & Black, 2005).

Family income has consistently been related to children's language and cognitive development. The vocabulary development of preschool children growing up in poverty is typically behind that of children living in families with higher incomes. The difference is quite dramatic as seen in a recent national study of children entering kindergarten. Seventy-six percent of children receiving public assistance scored at or below the 50th percentile on a standardized literacy test which included a vocabulary assessment. In contrast, children whose families were not receiving government aid were equally likely to score above or below the 50th percentile: 47 percent scored at or below and 53 percent scored above the 50th percentile (West, Denton, & Germino-Hausken, 2000).

> Seventy-six percent of children receiving public assistance scored at or below the 50th percentile on a standardized literacy test.

The number of challenging factors, or risks, present in the home magnifies the effect of poverty such that children living in the worst circumstances have the poorest language development. Taylor and colleagues (Taylor, Dearing, & McCartney, 2004) noted that children living in families experiencing long-term poverty with mothers who had little education and were clinically depressed had lower vocabulary scores than children whose families were experiencing only short-term financial problems.

Chapter 3 includes more detailed information on teaching strategies to facilitate the language development of children living in poverty. However, language development is only one area in which children of low-income families differ from other children. As they enter elementary school, their scores on assessments of a variety of academic skills are typically behind that of middle-class children (see Ryan, Fauth, & Brooks-Gunn, 2006 for a review). Fortunately, high quality preschool programs can help with this problem. This means it is extremely important for programs serving low-income families to offer a stimulating learning environment with many opportunities for learning language and literacy concepts as well as other academic skills.

Cognitive Development

Language and cognitive development are tightly intertwined. Both Piaget and Vygotsky emphasize the importance of the child's ability to use symbols. Vygotsky places great importance on the psychological "tools" children use in their interactions with the world (Miller, 2002). He stated that language is the most important tool a child can use to interact with others, learn about the world, and solve problems. Oral language is a symbol system that uses a word or phrase to represent an actual object or idea. It is a symbolic tool that enables learning to occur. Written language or print is an even more abstract symbol system than oral language, because it takes oral language and turns it into a second symbol system—that of the specific forms of letters.

> Language is the most important tool a child can use to learn about the world.

One of the most significant developmental events for literacy learning is the emergence of symbolic or representational thinking. According to Piaget, symbolic thinking is the ability to use one object to represent another. Early examples of this skill are seen during the toddler years as children rock baby dolls and speak into toy telephones. In the preschool years, symbolic thinking blossoms in two important ways. One is elaborate and organized pretend play and the other is the understanding that marks made on paper can represent specific things. Thus, symbolic thinking plays a critical role in the development of both reading and writing as it brings meaning to marks on paper.

In contrast to this remarkable ability to think symbolically, there are limitations to the typical thinking patterns of preschool children. The primary limitation is that children reason from specific to specific; they do not see the relationships in between. Many preschool teachers have encountered children such as four-year-old Kara when she stamps her foot and says, "I live in Lafayette, *not* Indiana!" This inability to take relationships into account may not be resolved until age eight. Being oblivious to relationships like this results in interesting writing behaviors. Robert, age four, sees no problem with writing letters or words backwards and gets frustrated with his mother who does. For Robert, the meaning of the letter symbol is not tied to its orientation in space or its relationship to other symbols. He is very focused on his own point of view. For the third letter of his name, he wrote a "b" and expects everyone to know that it is a "b" even if he writes it backwards like "d" or upside down like a "p."

INTRODUCING REBECCA, JUAN, MICHAEL, AND ANNIE

All children in preschool classrooms are different. They come from different cultural backgrounds that support diverse ways of using language and literacy. They live in different types of communities that value different literacy practices. They learn to use language in different communities of practice (Wenger, 1998). Some children come to preschool not speaking English as a first language or speaking English using a nonmainstream dialect. Some come with learning differences. All of these children, however, are in our classrooms and all come to those classrooms with conceptions and beliefs about literacy. We would like to introduce you to four such children who attend diverse types of preschool settings. These children are composites of children that we have known in preschool classrooms. We will use these children throughout the rest of the book to illustrate both the theory and the practice we describe.

Rebecca, a four-year-old African American girl from a middle-class family who lives in a suburban area, attends a half-day preschool affiliated with a local church. Her teacher's name is Kathi. It is the custom in this program, as in many others, for children to use the teacher's first name. Rebecca bustles around the preschool classroom during centers time, chatting with her friends as they play in the different centers. She is a talkative child when she is with her friends or with familiar adults. Her parents have always taken time to talk with her and answer her questions. From the time she was a baby, they have cuddled her on their laps and read books with her, first pointing to the pictures and talking about them and later reading the stories while asking for her input. She has seen her parents writing on the computer as well as making lists and using writing for other daily tasks. She often makes her own list when she accompanies her mother to the store. In the classroom, she writes in her own journal in the writing center daily, often visits the library area and "reads" to her friends, and likes to find her own and her friends' names in various places around the classroom. At least one parent volunteers in the classroom each week, reading to children, taking dictation in different centers, or helping children make the daily snack.

Juan attends a Head Start classroom situated in an ethnically diverse neighborhood in a large metropolitan area. Because this program follows a more traditional practice regarding teacher names, Juan addresses his teacher as "Mr. Gonzalez." Juan's parents immigrated to the United States from Mexico in their teens and became migrant farm workers. Once they had married and started a family, they settled in the city in order to provide their children with the education that they did not have. Neither parent had gone beyond the third grade, and when they came to the United States, neither spoke English with any fluency. They now work hard to support their growing family. Because of their circumstances, Juan has not had very much exposure to literacy at home and extended conversations are not the norm. Literacy at home is limited to religious bulletins and bills. At the Head Start classroom, Juan spends much of centers time in the block area building or at the sand table. He seldom responds to questions during group time, but sits quietly listening.

Michael is enrolled in a child care center in a small town. Ashley is the lead teacher in his classroom. Both of Michael's parents work in a factory in the nearby metropolitan area, his father on the assembly line and his mother as a secretary. They drop Michael off each morning at 7 a.m. and pick him up at 6 p.m. On weekends, to make ends meet, his father also works at the nearby discount store. Michael is an active, energetic boy who loves to play outside and enjoys finding out how things work. In the classroom, he often can be found in the block area building a structure or at the sand or water table experimenting with the manipulatives there. He seldom goes to the writing center or the library area. He usually doesn't stay very long in one place, and during group time, he is always moving around or shouting out answers to questions about the stories being read.

Annie attends a full-day Head Start program in the small rural community in which her family lives. Her teacher's name is Mrs. Jones. Annie's family lives outside of the community and earns their living as share croppers. Her family has lived in the area for generations and has been unable to break the cycle of poverty. Neither parent completed high school, dropping out as soon as possible. Neither parent had good experiences in school and had difficulty learning to read and write. Therefore, there is little mainstream literacy use at home. Her family speaks the nonstandard dialect of the area. Annie has few friends in the preschool classroom. The other children do not want to play with her because of her poor hygiene and dirty clothes. She often speaks out inappropriately at group time.

FOUNDATIONS FOR LEARNING TO READ

This book explains how teachers can help children like those just introduced become readers and writers. To do this, we must define literacy and explain how it develops. We define literacy as reading, writing, and oral language use in a particular culture. Reading is constructing meaning using print. It involves breaking the code, that is, matching letters to oral language, and constructing meaning. Children construct meaning using the words chosen by the author, their knowledge and experiences, the purpose for the specific reading task, and the social and cultural context in which the reading occurs. Writing involves using print to construct a message that communicates to others. Writing includes *both* writing letters and words onto a page *and* composing the meaning of the message. Reading and writing are intertwined processes. Learning about one contributes to learning about the other. Both are woven together with oral language. To learn to read and write easily, children need to develop experience in oral language, phonological awareness, alphabetic principle, concepts about print, and comprehension (see Figure 1.1). Box 1.2 defines each of these terms. As children experience each of

> Reading and writing are intertwined processes.

these foundational aspects of literacy, they begin to understand how print and language work together as well as conventions of written language use. All of these understandings develop *simultaneously* over time. Therefore, it is important for preschool age children to have experiences with *both* reading and writing, as illustrated in Box 1.3.

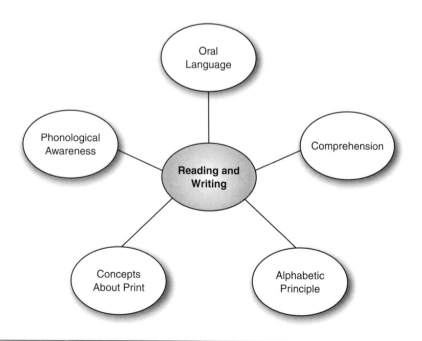

Figure 1.1　Important Foundations for Learning to Read

Box 1.2   Definition of Literacy Terms

Concept	Definition
ORAL LANGUAGE	Ability to use spoken language to make oneself understood Knowledge of vocabulary; ability to use more and more complex sentence structures Ability to engage in appropriate conversations
PHONOLOGICAL AWARENESS	Sensitivity to the sounds in speech, including recognizing rhymes and alliteration (same beginning sounds); being able to blend sounds together to form words; being able to break words down into the sounds that make them up
ALPHABETIC PRINCIPLE	Written language is made up of symbols we call letters and these letters or groups of letters match the words we say in a systematic way.
CONCEPTS ABOUT PRINT	Print works in specific ways; it can be talked about and manipulated, and is stable—it stays the same over time.
COMPREHENSION	Ability to make meaning from print using prior experiences, making predictions, connections, and inferences about the structure of the text

Box 1.3   Key Understandings and Abilities

Oral Language Ability

- **Vocabulary knowledge.** Children build up a dictionary of words and word meanings or descriptions of concepts that form the basis of understanding how things go together and how to interpret ideas.
- **Ability to understand and use more complex sentence structure.** More complex sentence structures include more relationships between words and concepts and more cognitively challenging talk, talk about nonpresent topics, generalizations, the future and past, and human motivations.

- **Ability to have an extended conversation.** In a conversation, a speaker and a listener exchange ideas, taking turns. A listener responds immediately to what a speaker has said, and can ask questions to clarify and extend understandings.

Understanding About Print and Language

- **Reading and writing serve many of the same functions that oral language does.** These purposes include revealing or asserting one's needs and wants; connecting with oneself and with others; and creating, comprehending, and expanding one's knowledge about the world (Christie, Enz, and Vukelich, 2003).

- **Written language conveys meanings but without the cues oral language has.** When making predictions about the meaning of a story the reader does not have vocal and body language cues. The content of the story is not about events happening now. The reader must make inferences, use prior experiences, make connections, and construct an understanding without being able to ask questions directly of the author.

- **Language is something that can be talked about and manipulated as well as used to communicate.** This metalinguistic awareness enables a child to step back from a message to begin to see the structure of language. As children become metalinguistically aware, they begin to learn the labels we use to talk about language, labels such as "word," "sentence," "sound," and "letter."

- **Language can be broken up into parts and pieces, and those pieces can be manipulated.** These pieces include breaking sentences up into the words that make them whole and breaking words into their different parts, including being able to count syllables in words, to identify and form rhyming words, to recognize words that begin with the same sound, to segment sounds in words or blend sounds to form words.

- **Print is stable and can be revisited over time.** Print does not disappear after it is used. Since it is stable, it can be used to help people remember what was said or what they would like to tell others. It can be used to communicate with others who are not present.

- **There are specific ways that print works.** These concepts about print include that we read and write from left to right, top to bottom, and front to back; that writers leave a space between words to set them apart from each other; and that punctuation gives cues to the reader about what is going on.

(Continued)

(Continued)

> ■ **Written language is made up of symbols or letters, and those symbols match the sound of oral language in a systematic way.** Children need to understand that each symbol or letter has particular characteristics, that these characteristics cannot be changed or the resulting symbol is not the same letter, that the letters all have names, and that these letters, either by themselves or in a group, represent particular speech sounds.

Rebecca, Juan, Michael, and Annie all began to develop their oral language skills at home before they came to their different preschool classrooms. However, because they each come from a different home setting, they have had different exposure to words and conversations. It is likely that Juan, Michael, and Annie have had fewer conversations with adults, have been exposed to fewer words and experiences since their families are struggling either to break the cycle of poverty or to just make ends meet (Snow, Tabors, & Dickinson, 2001). Because they potentially have a smaller lexicon or dictionary of words, they may not have built up the store of concepts that are networked together in conceptual structures (Duchan, 2004). These conceptual structures give children the basis to learn new information, understand how things go together, and interpret ideas. All of these things are important for comprehending stories and books.

Rebecca's middle-class family has more time to engage in conversations and more resources to provide her with a myriad of experiences, including reading to her from different books and taking her to places such as the zoo and the natural history museum. Her parents have modeled complex sentence structures in many types of verbal communication. Examples include discussing what they are seeing on everyday outings and asking Rebecca questions about the motivations of characters in stories. They have also asked her to make generalizations about what she saw at the museum, and have given her information about the animals seen there and when and where they lived. This cognitively challenging talk (Dickinson, 2001b) has helped Rebecca use decontextualized language, that is, language about people or events that are not present (Watson, 2001) as she has conversations with adults.

All four children have been exposed to both talk and print in their environments. They have begun to develop key understandings about how print and oral language work, the relationship between talk and print, and the conventions of print use. Juan and Michael often demonstrate their understanding of the functions of language as they inform the other children in their classrooms not to touch their constructions. At their teachers' prompting, both boys have begun to leave signs on their unfinished block constructions that say, "Don't touch! Under construction." Annie also demonstrates that she understands how print can be used to connect with others as she plays and talks to imaginary companions and the dolls in the housekeeping center, reading soup can labels as she asks the dolls and imaginary friends what they would like her to cook for them for lunch and then making a list of what to buy at the store.

All four children understand that in a conversation, a speaker communicates something and the listener responds to what the speaker has said. They know that language is an important mode of communication in their lives. Juan has conversations with his parents about the religious activities they participate in each weekend. Michael enjoys talking to the children around him about what he is doing as he experiments with the funnels and water wheels at the water table. Annie knows she may respond to the teacher's questions during group time. Rebecca often asks questions to clarify her understanding and responds at length to questions from adults or peers. She uses voice tone, gestures, and body language to get her message across and as cues to build her own understanding. Because books have been read to her from the time she was a baby, she also knows that books do not always have those cues to help her make predictions about what is happening in a story. She has built up an understanding that the content of books can be about events that are not realistic and that are not occurring in the immediate context. She has become familiar with book language, which uses different structures than conversations, and is decontextualized from the immediate setting.

Because of her exposure to mainstream literacy in her home, Rebecca has also begun to demonstrate metalinguistic awareness (the ability to pay attention to the characteristics of words separate from their meanings), phonological awareness, concepts about print, and alphabetic principle knowledge. While the other three children have a bit of understanding of these things as well, Rebecca's knowledge base is the most comprehensive. She often talks to herself in the writing center about what she is writing. For example, when making a card to send to her grandmother who has just had surgery, she said, "I better write some words on the front to tell her to get better. Then I better put some different words inside. I think I'll write a E first then a R and then a B." She continues talking to herself, naming the letters as she writes them down. As she completes the cover of the card, she reads it to herself, saying, "Get better soon." She then opens the card, and repeats the process, writing a variety of letters in a left-to-right, top-to-bottom fashion. As she finishes writing, she again reads the card to herself. "Dear Grandma, I hope you get better.

I hope it doesn't hurt too much where they cut you. I love you." She then writes her name at the bottom of the page, slowly stretching out the sounds in her name and writing a letter for each sound she hears. When she is finished writing her name, she shows the card to her teacher who asks Rebecca to read it to her. Rebecca responds, "I drawed a picture of my grandma in a bed 'cuz she is in the hospital and these letters say 'get better soon.' And then I wrote 'Dear grandma. I hope you get better soon. I hope you don't hurt too much where they cut you. Love, Rebecca.' Do you think she will like it?"

Rebecca's reading of her card demonstrates that she knows that print is stable. While the words that she read to herself after she finished writing and the words she read to her teacher are not exactly the same, the message she conveys is consistent both times. She demonstrates metalinguistic awareness by talking about what she is doing to construct the message and using terms such as "word" and "letter." She demonstrates her understanding of concepts of print by distinguishing between the picture she has drawn and words that she has written, and by writing from left-to-right and top-to-bottom. She demonstrates alphabetic principle knowledge when she names the letters as she writes them and combines that knowledge with phonological awareness as she stretches out her name, saying the sounds and writing the letters.

Annie, Michael, and Juan also demonstrate their understanding of print and language in how they interact with print. Michael and Juan know that print is stable as they put signs on their block constructions and make sure to tell the children around them that the sign says not to touch their block constructions. Annie demonstrates her concepts of print as she writes her grocery list in the housekeeping center, writing from left-to-right and top-to-bottom and as she points to the words on a can of food and tells the doll what kind of soup it contains.

SUPPORTIVE CLASSROOM ENVIRONMENTS

Although Annie, Michael, Rebecca, and Juan live in different communities and attend different types of preschools, all of their teachers know that children learn about literacy at both home and school. The teachers realize that children construct their first understandings of language and literacy as they interact with their families. These understandings develop as children observe and participate in the print and language practices used by their parents and older siblings (Gee, 2001; Rogoff, 1990). Active participation at home and at preschool supports the development of each child's ways of thinking, talking, knowing, and acting in connection with print. This process is sometimes called an apprenticeship in thinking

(Rogoff, 1990). Through this apprenticeship, children learn and begin to demonstrate the behaviors of literate people.

The children's teachers know that there are two key elements to support children's literacy learning: (1) the environment in which they are immersed, and (2) the adults who plan and support children's active participation in that environment. While the resources available in each classroom are different, there are similarities across them. All four classrooms have an environment that is rich in literacy materials—including a wide variety of books and writing materials as well as both functional and environmental print. The teachers also provide opportunities for children to engage in activities incorporating oral language and literacy play.

The books in all four classrooms can be found in a comfortable and inviting library as well as in other learning centers (Roskos & Neuman, 2001). The books are easily accessible so that children can refer to them during centers time or sit down with one in the library. The writing materials are also easily accessible in both a dedicated writing center and other learning centers. Additionally, children can experiment with writing using different writing tools (such as pencils, markers, chalk) and writing surfaces (such as paper, blank books or journals, chalkboard).

The children see functional and environmental print all around them. Functional print is print that is part of every day activities in a particular setting (Christie, Enz, & Vukelich, 2003). Functional print demonstrates how literacy is used in everyday life for different purposes. For example, in each of the four classrooms children use a sign-in system to indicate they have arrived. Printed labels describe the play materials on shelves. Alphabet charts, posters, and stories written by the class are displayed on the walls and in the library.

Environmental print is print that is found in the everyday environment of the children. In the housekeeping area, children find many materials containing environmental print. Examples include phone books, food cans and boxes, junk mail, and fast food menus. When the housekeeping center is transformed into another setting such as a veterinarian's office, the center contains magazines and posters. In addition, children fill out forms, write prescriptions, and hand out bills for services rendered. They also read magazines and signs about pet food and pet care. Enriching play centers with this type of environmental and functional print extends children's literacy interests and allows them to practice the literate behaviors that they see the important adults in their lives use (Makin, 2003; Roskos & Neuman, 2001; Yaden, Rowe, & MacGillivray, 2000).

The teachers in these classrooms know that while having a variety of materials is important, it is just as important for the children in their classrooms to have activities available that encourage interaction with the materials. One important activity all of the teachers provide is interactive book reading. The goal of interactive book reading is to involve the children in the book, encouraging them to extend the ideas, make predictions, discuss aspects of the story, and tie the book to their own experiences. In this co-constructive reading (Dickinson, 2001a), the teacher and the children co-construct the meaning of a book using cognitively challenging talk.

Cognitively challenging talk is part of the interactional environment of the classroom. It takes children beyond the here and now and out of the context of their own lives, helping them to develop comprehension skills and strategies (Yaden et al., 2000). Asking children to think and talk about things that are not present requires them to decontextualize. This means they must glean meaning from words without the benefit of situational cues, facial expressions, or gestures. Teachers can engage children in cognitively challenging talk through complex, elaborate conversations. Other important aspects of cognitively challenging talk include using rare words (words children do not know) and asking open-ended questions (Dickinson, 2001b; Dickinson & Tabors, 2001). Much of teacher talk is brief and simple; elaborate and open-ended exchanges with children do not occur very often (Dunn, 1993). Therefore teachers should consciously think about using cognitively challenging talk in the classroom. See Box 1.4.

> Cognitively challenging talk takes children beyond the here and now.

Box 1.4   Cognitively Challenging Talk

Cognitively challenging talk:

- Is decontextualized
  - takes children out of the current situation, asks children to think and talk about things that are not present or events that happened in the past
  - conveys meaning through words instead of the context, gestures, or facial expression
- Includes the use of rare words
  - words that children do not know
- Involves extended, complex conversations
- Uses open-ended questions and elaborative comments
- Includes information children do not know

The teachers of our four preschool children provide many opportunities for cognitively challenging talk between children and adults as well as opportunities for children to talk to each other. Extended conversations occur as children play together in centers, when the teacher joins their conversations in a learning center, or while the teacher leads small and large group discussions. Using cognitively challenging talk, the teachers address topics and events that may not be immediately present, such as asking children what they did over the weekend or to remember an experience from the previous day. They ask open-ended questions that encourage children to elaborate on what they are saying. They often ask "Why?" or "What do you think?" to encourage higher-order thinking and to extend the conversation. They include information that children may not know and words not in the children's vocabulary.

Mrs. Jones, Mr. Gonzalez, Kathi, and Ashley are active figures in their classrooms. They pay attention to what the children do and say as they participate in the life of the classroom. They understand the literacy practices of the community outside of the classroom so they can then build on what the children bring with them. They carefully and intentionally plan a curriculum that blends opportunities for children to use literacy to learn about their world with opportunities to learn literacy (Dickinson, McCabe, & Clark-Chiarelli, 2004; Hall, 2003). They model their own thinking, reading, and writing processes so that children see these tasks as an important part of life (Hall, 2003). For example, Mr. Gonzalez might think aloud about his interpretation of a story or Kathi might talk about her experiences related to a topic during an interactive book reading. Ashley might model writing a list of tasks that need to be accomplished in the classroom, or Mrs. Jones might model the writing of a sign reminding others that a painting is wet. They also enter play as coplayers, extending the use of literacy items in the center beyond what the children are doing. For example, Kathi might enter the doctor's office play as a nurse and hand the "doctor" a prescription pad to write down the medicine the "patient" needs to take.

Children learn by having meaningful experiences that allow them to create new understandings about the world. But what is a meaningful experience? A look into classrooms serving preschool-age children reveals a confusing array of interpretations. Common practices range from permissive and unstructured environments in which children play as they choose, to structured seat-work with traditional worksheets and flash card drills, to specific learning centers requiring children to explore specific materials and concepts. It is this latter strategy that is most likely to produce meaningful experiences that lead to learning. This book provides information on how teachers can create goal-directed learning experiences that actively engage children in meaningful, authentic experiences that lead to becoming readers and writers. It will help you understand each of the important precursors to learning to read successfully and how to support children's learning of each one. Finally, it will help you plan your curriculum, bring the community into the classroom, and help parents support literacy learning.

SUMMARY

This chapter focuses on the developmental processes of language and literacy development. Children begin to learn about print from birth through the environment around them. We refer to this learning about reading and writing as emergent literacy. The learning process is described as active—children construct their own knowledge through experiences in the world. Piaget's and Vygotsky's views of learning and development are explained to provide a framework that can help us understand literacy learning. Piaget described learning as an adaptation process which includes assimilation of information, the process of fitting new information into existing knowledge, and accommodation, the process of restructuring existing knowledge. Vygotsky described learning as a social process. From Vygotsky we have the term "zone of proximal development," or learning that is actual to a child with the help of someone at a higher skill level.

Three areas of development that are crucial to a child's literacy learning are physical-motor, language, and cognitive or intellectual. Fine motor development is needed for children to manipulate writing tools and focus on print. Language development begins in infancy with cooing and babbling, and by the time a child is in preschool she will be learning nearly ten new words a day. However, language learning includes more than vocabulary development. It also includes acquiring conversational turn-taking skills, understanding that the purpose of language is communication, and developing knowledge about how words are put together to form sentences (syntax of language). Language development is closely tied to cognitive development. The development of symbolic thinking, an aspect of cognitive development, is important to literacy learning because language is symbolic. Children explore the symbolic nature of language in their play when they use the props in their play (i.e., toy telephone) to represent real objects in their environment. In this chapter, we also introduced the four children who will be featured in subsequent chapters of this book as we describe how early childhood classrooms can become centers of excellence.

Language Development and Diversity

2

The children in Michael's preschool classroom love nursery rhymes. Ashley, Michael's teacher, introduced the nursery rhyme *One, two, three, four, five* (Cousins, 1989) to the children the day before, during their math lesson. Ashley had written it on large chart paper so that all the children could see and follow along while she read it, pointing to each word. She also had a prop fish to show the children. They were laughing and giggling when Ashley, in a very dramatic way, acted like she was bitten by the fish.

Today, Ashley and her children revisited the nursery rhyme. She started by rereading the entire rhyme with dramatic intonation and expression as she had done the day before. She then invited the children to join her in a rereading. After this shared reading, she invited the children to respond. She asked the children what happened in the nursery rhyme. They discussed that in the story the character was bitten by a fish. Then she gave the children a chance to share personal experiences by telling whether they had ever been bitten by a dog, or by anything else, and what they did in response to the incident. She then asked them to share their ideas about what to do if they ever got bitten by a fish. The children were excited about being able to help solve the problem and offered a wide range of answers, such as letting the fish go just as it was described in the nursery rhyme or putting it in the classroom fish tank. One child said to put it back in the ocean to live with his mommy. Michael, who was typically disengaged, was fascinated by the nursery rhyme because he liked numbers and ocean creatures. He shouted out that he wouldn't let the fish go but instead he would fry the fish for dinner. Ashley accepted all their answers. She told the children that there were different ways of handling the same situation.

(Continued)

(Continued)

> She listed different alternatives on the chart paper and asked the children to vote for their favorite alternative. She recorded their votes by each alternative.
>
> In this vignette, we see that Ashley used the nursery rhyme as a springboard for engaging the preschoolers in active listening and speaking. The children were able to use oral language in playful ways. Language was also used as a tool for their learning of math and problem solving skills.

ROLE OF ORAL LANGUAGE IN LITERACY DEVELOPMENT

Oral language includes both receptive (listening) and expressive language (speaking), and vocabulary is a critical part of both. The more vocabulary children have, the better they can listen and understand other people's messages as well as express themselves through speech output. It is also important to note that oral language development involves children's development of communicative competence (i.e., when, where, and what to say in different situations). Figure 2.1 shows the components of oral language.

Language is a tool for learning (Vygotsky, 1978). While young children learn about language, they also learn through language. Oral language is "a foundation for reading acquisition" (Snow, Burns, & Griffin,

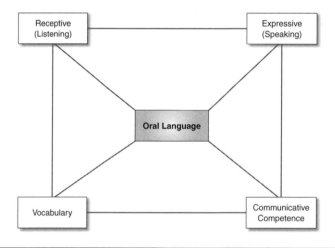

Figure 2.1   Components of Oral language

1998, p. 79). Children use language to interact with parents, teachers, and peers, and it is through this interaction, particularly with more knowledgeable others in the zone of proximal development, that children gain the knowledge and skills necessary for their future success in literacy. Meanwhile, teachers use language to deliver instruction, assess, and scaffold/mediate student learning. The majority of a school day is filled with oral interaction or activities that require active use of speaking and listening. The importance of supporting preschool children's oral language cannot be overemphasized in preschool classrooms.

> The importance of supporting preschool children's oral language cannot be overemphasized.

Oral language development lays the foundation for literacy development. According to Snow et al. (1998), preschool children's oral language development predicts how successful they will be in their future reading achievement. Children whose oral language is well developed tend to have a better chance to become successful readers because vocabulary knowledge influences reading comprehension. A reader who understands the words she is encountering in a book has a better chance of making sense out of the text. I (Griffith) can read, understand, and thoroughly enjoy a romance novel whose setting is the NASCAR circuit. However, I would be much less successful reading technical manuals about engine repair because I lack any in-depth vocabulary knowledge about words related to that topic (e.g., transmission, torque, piston). In fact, I even experienced difficulty generating words to apply to the example! Hart and Risley (1995) postulated that it is difficult for children who are delayed in their language development to ever catch up.

Let's put language development in the perspective of other aspects of literacy development we will address in this book. In Chapter 1, we introduced the important foundations for learning to read. Among these are concepts about print, phonological awareness, the alphabetic principle, and oral language. Throughout this book we refer to various concepts about print, including understanding that we read left to right, top to bottom, that a word in print is bounded by blank space on the page, and that letters are the components for writing our thoughts on a page. These ideas are arbitrary conventions of written English. They are important for children to understand, but with print experiences children quickly grasp these ideas. Phonological awareness is an understanding of the structure of spoken language. It includes skills such as being able to rhyme words and to segment and blend the sounds of spoken language. We know that with specific, purposeful instruction these are skills children can acquire.

Understanding the alphabetic principle revolves around knowing letters and grasping the mapping principle of letters as the concrete representation of sounds when we write our thoughts. This is a concept children grasp once the acquisition of letter knowledge comes together with phonological awareness. The common characteristic of concepts of print, phonological awareness, and the alphabetic principle are that these are finite domains of information. Yet oral language, which is the basis on which each of these finite domains of knowledge is built, is not a finite domain. As we indicated in Chapter 1, in the preschool years vocabulary literally explodes, and because it is an infinite domain of knowledge, it never stops growing. That is due to the complex nature of language acquisition. It involves both knowing language and knowing how to learn about language. Being attuned to word meanings not known—as in a child asking "What does that word mean?"—is equally as important as knowing word meanings.

WHAT DOES RESEARCH SAY ABOUT HOW CHILDREN ACQUIRE LANGUAGE?

Language development involves both nature and nurture. Children are born with an innate mechanism and ability to acquire language (Chomsky, 2002). However, that mechanism has to be activated by experiences in the environment. Newborn babies attend to the aural input from their mothers. As they grow older, babies constantly attempt to communicate with their parents or caregivers by attending to inputs that are meaningful to them and producing sounds, sometimes only intelligible to themselves.

By and large, language use is rooted in our desire to communicate ideas and to get things done. In other words, language use is functional. Halliday (1975; 1996) has identified seven major functions of language (see Figure 2.2): to satisfy material needs; to control people's behavior; to get along with others; to express personal identity; to learn about the world; to create an alternative reality (pretend); and to communicate information. (We discuss these functions again in Chapter 9 as we discuss how children learn to use literacy in the real world.) Careful observation of how preschool children use oral language to realize the various functions can provide a teacher with insights about children's language development. Of course not all functions are demonstrated by all children at the same time. Tracking children's progress over a period of time, providing modeling, and planning activities to allow them to gain experience with the various functions of language is an important part of a classroom focus on oral language development.

> Language use is rooted in our desire to communicate ideas and to get things done.

1. Instrumental function. To satisfy material needs. (e.g., "I want . . .")

2. Regulatory function. To control other people's behavior. (e.g., "Do as I tell you.")

3. Interactional function. To get along with others. (e.g., "me and you," "me and my mother")

4. Personal function. To express self and personal identity. (e.g., "Here I come.")

5. Heuristic function. To learn and explore the world. (e.g., "Tell me why.")

6. Imaginative function. To create an alternative reality. (e.g., "Let's pretend.")

7. Representational function. To communicate content. (e.g., "I've got something to tell you.")

Figure 2.2   Functions of Language

SOURCE: From Halliday, M. A. K., Relevant models of language. In B. A. Power & R. S. Hubbard (Eds.), *Language development: A reader for teachers,* copyright © 1996, pp. 36–41. Englewood Cliffs, New Jersey: Merrill, an imprint of Prentice Hall.

According to Holdaway (1979), language acquisition is a process that involves multiple stages and multiple individuals. His well-known developmental model for language learning includes four stages.

1. *Observation of demonstrations.* At this stage, the child is a spectator who observes how people around him/her use language in authentic and purposeful ways. These people serve as models of language use for the child.

2. *Participation.* At this second stage, the child is invited to participate in various events of interest (e.g., learning to talk). The adult collaborates with the child and explains, instructs, or demonstrates how to express what he/she wants and what to do.

3. *Role playing or practice.* This third stage is a critical trial and error period where the child is given opportunities to practice the language and other learning skills without direction or observation. The child also learns to self-regulate, self-correct, and self-direct his/her own learning efforts.

4. *Performance.* At this last stage, the child feels competent and voluntarily demonstrates his/her learning and accomplishment. The child is able to independently use language to communicate and to accomplish his/her goals.

Although originally developed to explain language acquisition, this model can be applied to literacy learning and other types of learning. Teachers who are in tune with children's developmental trajectory have a better chance of helping them move on to the higher levels of language competency.

BENCHMARKS OF ORAL LANGUAGE DEVELOPMENT FOR PRESCHOOL CHILDREN

After reviewing the preschool standards in thirteen states in the United States, Schickedanz (2004) compiled a list of preschool standards, including standards for oral language. She categorized the standards into five major areas: gestural expression, verbal expression, vocabulary and background knowledge, listening (attention to and comprehension of talk), and phonological awareness, which we address in Chapter 3. Building upon Schickedanz's (2004) preschool standards we have constructed a list of oral language indicators structured around the components of oral language depicted in Figure 2.1. These indicators are listed in our Preschool Oral Language Acquisition Checklist in Figure 2.3. Please note this checklist is not a hierarchy of skills. Of course, teachers can develop their own checklist based on their state or district standards.

Preschool Oral Language Acquisition Checklist

Student Name: _____

Date: _____

	First Observed	Sometimes	Often
Expressive Language Indicators			
Use gestures in combination with speech to communicate			
Express feelings, thoughts, and needs verbally			
Speak in sentences			
Identify common objects with correct vocabulary			
Ask questions, explain, and give directions			
Help generate and maintain scripts in sociodramatic play			
Generate words and phrases related to a topic of study			

Use language elements:
 	
    Inflectional endings
 	
    Pronouns
 	
    Irregular past-tense verbs			

Ask "wh" questions			
Receptive Language Indicators			
Respond to name when called			
Discriminate between different environmental sounds			

	First Observed	Sometimes	Often
Answer yes or no questions			
Attend to stories read aloud			
Follow directions:			
Two to three steps			
Complex directions			
Respond to verbal cues from partners in sociodramatic play			
Listen actively to acquire new information:			
5–10 minute blocks of time			
10–15 minute blocks of time			
Relate own comments to topic			
Respond appropriately to "wh" questions			
Demonstrate verbal memory for short rhymes			
Vocabulary Indicators			
Use new words encountered in stories in retellings			
Use new words from book or other contexts in conversations			
Ask for names of unfamiliar objects and their parts			
Use descriptors			
Ask for the meaning of unfamiliar words			
Understand relationships among objects			
Understand processes and properties associated with objects, animals, and plants			
Communicative Competence Indicators			
Use language to maintain relationships with others			
Participate in conversation			
Exhibit awareness of conversational etiquette:			
Take turns in conversation			
Use appropriate voice tones and responses			
Initiate and lead a conversation			

Figure 2.3 Preschool Oral Language Acquisition Checklist

SOURCE: Incorporates indicators from Schickedanz, J. A., A framework and suggested guidelines for prekindergarten content standards, *The Reading Teacher*, 58 (1), copyright © 2004, pp. 95–97.

ASSESSING ORAL LANGUAGE DEVELOPMENT

Teacher observation is the most common method of assessing preschool children's oral language development. As with any assessment, the goal is to inform short-term and long-term instruction. Because children experience spurts in their language development during preschool years, frequent assessment (approximately four times a year) is critical to understanding of each child's language development.

> Teacher observation is the most common method of assessing preschool children's oral language development.

For teachers interested in doing more thorough assessments of oral language acquisition, several formal assessments are also available for your use. These assessments are for the purpose of screening only, should a teacher suspect that a child might be delayed in oral language acquisition.

- *Get It, Got It, Go: Picture Naming Test* is a test battery developed by the Center for Early Education Development at the University of Minnesota and funded by the U.S. Department of Education. Its Picture Naming Test is developed specifically to assess preschool children's expressive language.
  - This instrument presents to a child images of objects printed on 8" × 5" index cards, one at a time. The objects are commonly found in preschoolers' natural environments (i.e., home, classroom, community). The child is asked to name the pictures as fast as possible. After exactly one minute, the examiner stops the activity and counts the total number of pictures named correctly. This test is not appropriate for children who come from a different linguistic background and are just starting to learn English.
  - The Get It, Got It, Go: Picture Naming Test, including a set of stimulus cards and the instruction for test administration, is available for free downloads from the "Get It" section of the official Web site of Get It, Got It, Go (http://ggg.umn.edu). There is no charge for teachers to maintain assessment results online at the "Got It" section of the Web site. Teachers can enter individual student scores, get score recording forms, and compare the performance of a child with the children in the reference group.
- *Peabody Vocabulary Test (PPVT-4)* is a widely-used, norm-referenced instrument for measuring receptive vocabulary of

people ranging in age from two to ninety. It can also be used as a screening test of verbal ability. This test is individually administered. When administering the test, the teacher will call out a word and have the child point to the object on the page. The test kit has two forms (Form A and Form B) for reliable testing and retesting. Items are arranged in seventeen sets of twelve items each for more efficient and accurate application of basal and ceiling rules. PPVT-4 is easy and quick to administer. (The test takes about ten to fifteen minutes to complete.) The results provide information on age-based standard scores, percentile scores, and age equivalents.

- *Preschool Language Scale (PLS-4)* is a standardized norm-referenced test for assessing both receptive and expressive language of children birth through age six years and eleven months. The test provides developmental milestones for teacher reference. This instrument includes an English basic kit, English value pack with manipulatives, an examiner's manual, picture manual, and record forms. Test administration requires approximately twenty to forty-five minutes. Teachers can obtain scores on Total Language, Auditory Comprehension, Expressive Communication, Standard Scores, Percentile Ranks, and Language Age Equivalents by using the test.

RESEARCH-BASED INSTRUCTIONAL STRATEGIES SUPPORTING ORAL LANGUAGE DEVELOPMENT

Show and Tell is a favorite time in Kathi's classroom. The children get a chance to share with the class something they have brought from home. Many of these sharings develop into a story about the item. Rebecca listened carefully when her friend Rachel showed the class a snake skin her father had found in a field around their house. Rachel explained to the class what her father had told her about snakes shedding their skin. Since Rebecca's dog had recently killed a small snake in her back yard, when it was her turn to talk, she told the class, "Jack got a snake and he shaked and shaked it but Mommy said come in and leave him alone."

Teachers' support of children's oral language development is ongoing and occurs in explicit and implicit ways. We will focus on three aspects: classroom environment, storybook reading, and oral language activities.

Classroom Environment

Since oral language lays the foundation for future success in literacy development, it is of utmost importance that teachers devote much attention to support children's language development through a supportive classroom environment. We want children to feel safe to take risks using language and to be encouraged to use language in meaningful and purposeful ways.

> We want children to feel safe to take risks using language and to be encouraged to use language in meaningful and purposeful ways.

Oral language and literacy development are inseparable. A high quality oral language environment is also an environment rich in print, reading and writing materials, and literacy-related activities. When oral language activities are thoughtfully planned and integrated into other modes of literacy learning (reading, writing, and viewing), young children tend to make more rapid progress in their development in all areas including oral language development. Kathi supports the language use of the children in her classroom in various ways throughout the day. Figure 2.4 comprises a list of some things Kathi does to support oral language use.

In 1995, Betty Hart and Todd Risley published the results of a longitudinal study on children's language learning in their home environments. This book, *Meaningful Differences in the Everyday Experiences of Young American Children*, revealed some dramatic differences in the language experiences of children from professional as compared to low-income homes. Hart and Risley received permissions from families to observe in forty-two homes. These homes included thirteen families categorized as upper socioeconomic status (SES), ten categorized as middle SES, thirteen categorized as lower SES, and six families on welfare. Observations began when the children were seven to nine months old and continued for two and a half years. Their observers made monthly hour-long observations, but they did not interact with the children during the observations.

Let's look at the meaningful differences. By age three, the children in professional homes heard more than 30 million words as compared to the children in welfare homes who had heard about 10 million words by age three. The children in professional homes heard more different words of all kinds, more complex (multi-clause) sentences, and received affirmative feedback at the rate of more than thirty affirmations per hour. In terms of vocabulary and sentence complexity exposure, children in the welfare homes experienced less than half of what working-class children experienced in each hour of their lives. On average they heard eleven prohibitions per hour. Hart and Risley concluded that children in professional homes were being

Kathi supports oral language use:

- Greetings: She greets children individually when they arrive in the classroom, and she encourages the children to exchange a greeting with her and their classmates.
- Show and Tell: Children are encouraged to talk about and expand on their experiences outside the classroom. During Show and Tell, children can bring something from home, or something interesting they have found in their yard or neighborhood to show the class. Kathi has found that these items from outside the classroom serve as props to stimulate the children's talk. At the beginning of the year, she models this by bringing items from her own home. She makes a point to have her examples reflect items most children could also bring. Examples of Show and Tell items that children have brought include rocks, a bird nest, leaves, flowers, and a pasta server. Once, a child brought an unusually shaped piece of colored glass, and Kathi accepted and applauded the unusual find. From time to time, Kathi notes children who have not ever participated in Show and Tell. She tries to bring them into the process by asking them to share something she found with the class. This works best for her when she shows the child the item the day before and allows him/her to take it home for some preliminary thought and perhaps practice.
- Story Rereadings: Kathi reads many stories to children in a shared book format using a big book (book with enlarged print). Frequently, these stories contain repetitive language patterns and rhyming text. As the book is shared through the week, children begin to remember parts of the text, and she urges the children to chime in with the reading when they feel comfortable.
- Story Discussions: Kathi encourages children to participate in conversations about books. This is a time when they are able to practice their conversation turn-taking skills. She accepts all of the children's responses, and she often repeats and expands on the responses using a variety of conversation stretchers (e.g., adding details or explaining terms). These conversation are joyous times that include Kathi modeling her own wonderings about the story and celebrating the children's language with comments such as "What a wonderful way to put that. Yes it does look like popcorn." Kathi displays books she has read to the class throughout the classroom. She finds ways to extend story discussions in smaller groups by casually entering a small group of children with a comment such as "I was just thinking about this book the other day . . ." as a way to engage a small group discussion.
- Writing and Reading: Kathi co-constructs all sorts of text with children (e.g., lists, stories, paragraphs of information). These constructions, written on big pieces of chart paper, are read as a group following the recording and then displayed as part of the environmental print in the classroom. She has seen children, usually in pairs, engaged in conversation around a co-constructed chart.
- Language Play: Kathi finds ways in both small and large groups to engage children in language in playful ways. This includes singing songs that incorporate finger plays and body movement, playing games with directions and problem solving (e.g., Simon Says and I Spy), and listening to and repeating tongue twisters and rhymes. Songs and music are a daily activity. In the dramatic play center, she provides various writing tools and paper, and she encourages the children to create directions, signs, and labels to go with their play.

Figure 2.4   Ways to Support Oral Language Use Throughout the Day

prepared to participate in a culture concerned with symbols and analytic problem-solving, whereas children in the welfare homes were being prepared to participate in a culture of conformity to established norms.

Hart and Risley's findings have implications for the classroom environment in preschool and kindergarten settings. For many children who served in Head Start and Early Reading First settings, oral language development in the classroom is very much an issue of trying to "close the gap." These researchers described characteristics of quality interactions with children that teachers can try to emulate. Specifically, the more we talk to children, the more words they will hear over time. It is important to talk to children beyond what is required to manage or provide care. Equally as important is to remain involved through the day with casual talk about classroom activities. Recommendations from Hart and Risley's study are summarized in Figure 2.5.

Just Talk

- Ramble on.
  - o The more we talk to children, the more words they will hear over time.
- Talk to children beyond what is required to manage or provide care.
- Remain involved through casual talk about activities.

Listen

- Focus on what children have to say in order to encourage more child talk.
- Listen to add information, encourage commenting, and prompt elaboration.

Be Nice

- Maintain a positive emotional tone.
- Name the right behaviors rather than commenting on children's misbehavior.
- Use more affirmative language than prohibitions.
  - o An effective form of affirmative language is an approval with a repetition.

Give Children Choices

- Use yes/no and wh-questions to instruct children.
  - o "Have you put the blocks away?"
  - o "Which color are you going to use on that?"

Tell Children About Things

- Name, repeat, and restate to help children understand.
- Put words to what children seem to be thinking or feeling.
- Tell children what is worth noticing or remembering.
- Tell children about what to expect and how to cope.

Figure 2.5   Characteristics of Quality Interactions with Children

SOURCE: From Hart, B. & Risley, T. R., *Meaningful differences in the early experience of young American children*, copyright © 1995. Baltimore: Brookes.

Storybook Reading

Preschool teachers making children's oral language development an important priority involve their children in abundant book reading experiences. They constantly read books aloud to their children. These books should include nursery rhymes, alphabet books, fairy tales/folktales, informational books, and other developmentally appropriate books that can expand the children's vocabulary, conceptual knowledge, and world knowledge. Teacher read-alouds have been supported by research as one of the most important activities that promote language and literacy development. The benefits include active listening, oral language comprehension, and vocabulary development. We discuss sharing books with children in depth in Chapter 7. However we want to present three types of book reading activities that have a specific application to language development.

> Preschool teachers making children's oral language development an important priority involve their children in abundant book reading experiences.

Dialogic reading is a version of shared picture book reading that has research support for developing children's oral language (Lonigan, Anthony, Bloomfield, Dyer, & Samwel, 1999; Lonigan & Whitehurst, 1998; Wasik & Bond, 2001; Whitehurst, Epstein, Angell, Payne, Crone, & Fischel, 1994). The strengths of dialogic reading are the nature of the interaction (dialogue through teacher prompts) and the gradual transfer of interaction from one in which the teacher dominates to one in which the child does more of the talking.

The goal of dialogic reading is for children to become active participants in a book reading session and to move from being a listener to a storyteller during the book reading. Dialogic reading is implemented best in small groups or can be carried out with an individual child. Two acronyms help a teacher recall the steps in dialogic reading. The first is CROWD which refers to the prompts an adult uses in a dialogic reading session. These prompts are for the purpose of the child to engage in dialogue about the book and do not have to occur in any particular order. (Note: All illustrations of CROWD are based on *Bunny Cakes* by Rosemary Wells):

- *Completing.* The adult invites the child to fill in the blank at the end of a sentence. For example, the adult would pause at the end of the reading of "Max made her an earthworm birthday _____" to allow the child to complete the sentence by supplying the word "cake."
- *Recall.* The adult asks questions about the book that has just been read. For example, "How did this story begin? How did it end?"

- *Open-ended.* The adult encourages the child to tell what is happening in a picture. For example, one of the illustrations in *Bunny Cakes* is of a table with a bottle of milk tipped over and milk pouring on the floor. The illustration before hints at what is about to happen because the milk bottle is just beginning to topple over. The adult might say, "Let's look at this milk bottle. What is about to happen?"
- *"Wh."* The adult asks "Wh" questions about the pictures in the book. For example, the setting of *Bunny Cakes* is two different places, the kitchen and the grocery store. Looking at the picture of the first time Max went to the grocery store, the adult might ask, "Why did Max have to go to the grocery store?" Of course the answer is because he dropped the carton of eggs, all the eggs broke, and he had to get more.
- *Distancing.* The adult relates the story to the child's experiences outside the book. For example, the adult might say, "Max was trying to help his sister Ruby bake a birthday cake. How do you help with cooking at home?"

The prompts in dialogic reading are used through a reading technique called PEER: the adult invites the child to comment about something in the story using one of the CROWD *prompts.* The adult *evaluates* and *expands* the child's response. The adult *repeats* the prompt. Through the PEER cycle and by employing CROWD prompts, the child becomes increasingly familiar with the book and is better prepared to engage in more extensive talk around the story. Detailed information about dialogic reading is available at the What Works Clearinghouse. (To obtain a free report with a description of this instructional procedure go to the What Works Clearinghouse Web site at http://www.whatworks.ed.gov. Use the navigation bar to access "All Available Reports" under the category of Products. Select "Early Childhood Education" and then "Dialogic Reading.")

Hickman, Pollard-Durodola, and Vaughn (2004) describe a variation of storybook reading that has application for oral language development in preschool and kindergarten classrooms. In this version of storybook reading, the teacher selects one or two high utility words for special study. High utility words, sometimes called Tier 2 words (Beck, McKeown, & Kucan, 2002), are words that a reader might encounter across a variety of reading materials. According to Beck et al. (2002) instruction about the meaning of high utility words is very beneficial to children's long-term reading development. To illustrate, Hickman et al. (2004) suggest "privacy," "artistic," or "semicircle" as possible high utility words from the book *Lilly's Purple Plastic Purse.*

Hickman et al. (2004) recommend a five-day cycle that incorporates instruction in high utility vocabulary, read-aloud with a guided comprehension discussion, rereading with a focus on vocabulary, and story summarization. Steps for the high utility vocabulary instruction that are applicable to preschool and kindergarten classrooms are as follows:

1. Introduce the new story in the usual manner, including pointing out the title and author/illustrator and making predictions (characters, setting, what might happen) about the story.

2. Introduce one or two high utility words that will be in the story. Depending upon the maturity of the group, the children can be shown these words in print on index cards. Provide an explanation of the meaning of the word using the context of the story, and give children practice pronouncing the words.

3. Take a picture walk through the story to enhance the prediction process, and provide additional context for the high utility words. A picture walk is a process of turning through the pages of a book and using the pictures to get an advanced idea of the story.

4. Read the story with a focus on enjoyment and comprehension.

5. Review the meanings and pronunciations of the high utility words and encourage the children to discuss the story with a focus on their predictions and the parts of the story they enjoyed.

6. On subsequent rereadings of the story, remind the children of the high utility words. During a first rereading, the teacher can stop at each high utility word, review and clarify the meaning, and check for understanding of the word. During subsequent rereadings, the teacher can remind the children of the high utility words and ask that they raise their hands when they hear the word being read.

7. Identify these high utility words during the reading of other stories, to provide a long-range follow-up, and talk about their meanings in the various contexts.

It is also important that teachers engage children in grand conversations (Tompkins, 2006) after read-alouds. A grand conversation is very similar to dinner table talk in which children respond to other children's comments and engage in turn-taking. A grand conversation works best in a circle arrangement where everyone can see everyone else's face. During grand conversations, children should be given opportunities to make connections between the text and their own personal experiences, between the text and other known texts, and between the text and the world. Teachers should structure the environment so that children feel comfortable and confident to express their ideas and thoughts in a supportive and friendly environment. If carefully structured, daily teacher read-alouds and the subsequent grand conversation can effectively contribute to preschool children's oral language development.

Oral Language Activities

Most preschool teachers use a variety of oral language techniques and activities in their classrooms. Show and Tell, storytelling and retelling, and singing and playing are all important, common language activities. In all activities, teachers should give clear directions and repeat if necessary to make sure that the children understand the message. It is also important to allow preschool children enough time to process the information before responding to requests or directions. In guided learning activities, teachers can engage children in listening and responding to the books and nursery rhymes that have been read aloud to the class and provide language models and scaffolds. Teachers can also encourage children to practice active listening and speaking with each other in play centers and other learning centers.

Storytelling is an important oral language activity in every preschool classroom. Young children have a natural tendency to share their stories with other people around them. Storytelling helps to build expressive language, receptive language, oral language comprehension, story structure, and vocabulary. When children are required to listen and allowed to respond to each other's experience, they are learning to be a user of oral language.

Language Experience Activity (LEA) is one of the most desirable activities for oral language development. LEA was originally used as a reading method based on a language-reading connection philosophy: What I can say, I can write (or someone can write for me). What I can write, I can read. During an LEA activity the children are engaged in discussion of a common experience, and the teacher serves as a scribe to record their ideas. We recommend that this occur in small writing groups working with the teacher or a teacher aid. The ideal configuration of such a group is one with children having a common interest and heterogeneous language skills. LEA includes the following steps:

1. *Preparing for an LEA story.* Select a common experience to base the discussion and recording of ideas. For example, the group might discuss and write about a trip to a fire station. Basing the LEA story around an experience ensures that the children have ideas to discuss.

2. *Engaging in language activity.* Encourage the children to share their experience—what they saw, what they liked the best, what they are wondering about. This step is very important because it develops language each child needs to contribute to the group story.

3. *Taking dictation from the group.* Each child contributes a line to the story. Many teachers connect the child's name to the contribution. For example, "He let me wear his hat. (Roger)." There is controversy about whether the teacher should record the child's exact syntax or edit for standard syntax. The reasoning behind recording the child's exact syntax is that in subsequent rereadings, the child will read the story as originally dictated to the teacher. However, in a PreK or kindergarten classroom, the primary goal of LEA is to develop oral language. We recommend a negotiation between the teacher and the child to scaffold the child to a higher level of language functioning. (Note: This concept is an application of Vygotsky's zone of proximal development.)

4. *Reading the story.* The teacher reads the story to the group, modeling expression and phrasing, and commenting on various points of interest.

5. *Rereading the story.* If applicable and based on the interest and development of each child, students can reread the line they contributed. This might occur over several days in casual interactions with the teacher.

6. *Extending the activity.* The LEA story should be available in the classroom for discussion and independent reading. LEA can be used for teaching concepts about print, identifying letters and sounds, identifying sight words, and using learned high utility words in a new context.

Simon Says is excellent for developing the speaking skills of preschool children, including English language learners. Simon Says does not require any special materials or preplanning, so it is ideal as a sponge activity to utilize the short amounts of extra time that inevitably come up through the day. There are various ways of playing the game. Some basic steps are as follows:

1. The teacher models how to play the game by standing in front of the class and modeling commands. It is usually a good idea to start with body parts that most children know. Examples of commands are "Touch your head," "Touch your nose," "Touch your leg," and "Touch your ear." Words associated with movements also work well with this game. Examples are "Jump," "Hop," "Sit down," and "Stand up."

2. The teacher tells the class that they have to listen carefully to the commands. They should only perform the action when the command follows the words "Simon Says." Otherwise, they will be out of the game. The last one in the game is the winner.

3. After the children are familiar with the game, a child can be chosen or volunteer to be "Simon."

LANGUAGE DIVERSITY

Diverse English vernaculars such as African American Vernacular English (AAVE) and Chicano English are spoken by people in predominantly African American and Hispanic communities. These vernaculars tend to bear certain undeserved stigmas and are considered inferior languages by some people. Unfortunately, such stigmas may also be attached to people who speak nonstandard English. However, these nonstandard English vernaculars deserve more respect from educators. Linguists have found that these vernaculars are rule-governed and systematic, as is standard English (Labov, Cohen, Robins, & Lewis, 1968).

> Linguists have found that nonstandard English vernaculars are rule-governed, as is standard English.

Under no circumstance should teachers look down upon children who speak nonstandard English vernaculars/dialects nor consider the children to be inadequate in their language development. Children coming from a family background where a vernacular is spoken come into the classroom with challenges but also with rich linguistic resources upon which teachers can build. Preschool teachers should maintain a positive attitude about these children and try to help them adjust to the language of schooling. We do not support correcting children's language, but instead modeling through responses in standard English. Preschool teachers who understand the major language patterns (syntax and wording choices) of these common vernaculars can provide more effective scaffolding for children speaking diverse dialects and help them make the necessary transition from speaking the vernaculars to standard English when they are at school. The most important considerations for teachers are to respond to the content of children's talk, to model standard English, and to encourage oral language use by establishing an environment in which children feel comfortable taking risks.

> Do not correct children's language, but instead model through responses in standard English.

As the number of immigrants continues to increase, more and more preschool classrooms will have children such as Juan in this book, whose first language is not English. When Juan started preschool, he almost never talked. When asked questions, he would either nod or shake his head. Other times, he would present no response. His teacher, Mr. Gonzalez, is bilingual himself. He understood that like many other English language learners, Juan was going through a silent period in his English language development. Mr. Gonzalez was always positive and patient toward Juan. Sometimes, Mr. Gonzalez would switch to Spanish to ensure that Juan understood his directions and instructions. Two months into the school year, Juan started to respond in English in simple telegraphic words or phrases such as "yes," "no," or "I like," along with gestures. Other times, he would converse with Mr. Gonzalez or other children using a mix of English and Spanish, a common linguistic phenomenon with second language learners called code-switching (Romaine, 1994).

To meet the challenge of working with English language learners (ELLs) such as Juan, knowledge about second language development is critical. ELLs tend to go through a silent period when there is limited language output in English. We cannot assume that during this silent period children do not understand English. Frequently the development of their receptive English language skills precedes the development of their expressive skills. For some children, such a period can be short; for others, it can be long. Teachers have to be patient and offer a positive and risk-free environment for these children to experiment with their new language. It is important that we do not confuse this phenomenon, which is caused by the child's limited exposure to English, with other language delays caused by cognitive or developmental problems. Misdiagnosis of language problems can do more harm than good to ELLs.

The good news is that several language assessments in the children's native language, Spanish in particular (e.g., Pre-IDEA Proficiency Test Spanish and Preschool Language Scale, Fourth Edition, Spanish Edition), are available for teachers who want to have an accurate assessment of the child's language skills or ability. Teachers can also seek help from other bilingual professionals. Having conversations with the family members about the child's first language development can also help determine if the delay is caused by true language problems or a lack of exposure to the new language.

To support the language development of ELLs, many effective practices that teachers use with first language learners are equally applicable. Abundant exposure to reading and writing activities, and to books and environmental print can lay the foundation for English as a second language and for children's future language and literacy development.

In addition, several techniques can help preschool teachers work more effectively with ELLs:

1. Teachers should construct an environment where the children feel safe trying out their new language. Teachers should value children's first language and convey such a message to the class by having class members learn a few of the words and expressions in the ELL child's first language. Involving parents in this learning conveys a valuing of the language and culture of the ELLs in the classroom. A parent might be invited to the class to help children learn vocabulary related to a theme being studied in the classroom.

2. When possible, teachers should introduce books that integrate into a story words in languages other than English. *Fiesta Fiasco* (Paul, 2007) is an example of a story in which Spanish words are integrated into a story primarily written in English.

3. When communicating with children who are learning English as a second language, teachers should use comprehensible input and articulate every sound and word clearly. Comprehensible input is oral language accompanied by gestures and concrete objects to augment the meaning of the message.

4. When giving instructions and teaching content, teachers should use graphics, concrete objects, and gestures. These techniques for making input comprehensible can reduce information load for ELLs and alleviate their anxiety.

5. Allow ELLs to use code-switching to facilitate their learning. For example, they can use a mix of English and their first language for Show and Tell and storytelling.

6. Parents should be encouraged to speak and read to their children in their first language, and it is important for them to understand their important role in helping ELLs maintain and develop their first language. Teachers can explain to parents that their child will naturally learn to code-switch as they are acquiring their second language. I (Griffith) am reminded of Dat, who was born in the United States, although his parents are from Vietnam. Whenever I went into his mother's store, Dat easily spoke to me in English, but when addressing his mother he used Vietnamese. Although probably an implicit understanding, at the young age of four, Dat was aware that he had to vary his language depending on the person to whom he was speaking.

7. Teachers can coordinate family literacy nights, with which we have had much success at our Early Reading First sites. The three components that seem to have made these nights a success are food, child care, and an interpreter. We spend a lot of time in socializing, a lot of time "bragging" on children, and a short amount of time with a planned presentation such as the demonstration of storybook reading techniques.

It is important for teachers of young children to recognize that there are factors other than diverse vernacular or second language learning that can have a negative impact on children's language development. When a child shows signs of language delay, it is important that preschool teachers attend to the possible factors that can lead to such delay. The main factor is hearing impairment, which can be caused by chronic ear infection or other auditory problems. Other cognitive conditions such as neurological problems and autism can also lead to language delay. A child with apparent signs of language delay should be seen by a speech pathologist in order to obtain accurate diagnosis of the problem(s). Appropriate language intervention and therapy can then be provided to the child after the problems are identified. Immediate attention from teachers and parents can prevent the child from developing further language problems and reading difficulties.

SUMMARY

In this chapter, we discuss the importance of oral language development. We also address major components, functions, and theories of its development and present some benchmarks of preschool oral language development. We recommend to you both informal and formal measures of oral language development. Several instructional activities targeting oral language development are also provided. We also discuss issues related to supporting children from diverse language backgrounds and children with special needs.

Phonological Awareness Development in Preschool Children

3

After listening to a story about monkeys jumping on the bed, Rebecca's teacher heard her laughing with other children at the sand and water table as she played with the words in the story. "Look, here is one of those monkeys jumping on the bed. Off the bed. Hit his head. I hope he isn't dead. Dead head on the bed. Fred the dead head on the bed. Fred is a dead head monkey—mookey, wookey, dookey, donkey, wonkey, monkey."

Rebecca's ability to play with language in this way is above average for most PreK children. Her ability indicates that she has a high level of phonological awareness which will help her be successful in learning to read in kindergarten and first grade.

WHAT IS PHONOLOGICAL AWARENESS AND WHAT IS ITS ROLE IN LITERACY DEVELOPMENT?

Since the 1980s, terms such as phonological awareness, phonemic awareness, and phonics have appeared prominently in books on reading instruction. These rather similar words deserve some discussion. What you may notice first about these three terms is the common morpheme "phon" which refers to sound. Each of these words refers to some level of understanding about sounds in spoken English.

Phonological awareness is an umbrella term that refers to sensitivity to speech sounds (Stanovich, 2000). There are two levels of phonological awareness, a beginning awareness level and a more advanced level called phonemic awareness. The beginning awareness level includes sensitivity to large units of sound such as words, sylla- bles, and syllable parts (e.g., the onset and rime of a syllable). Children at the begin- ning awareness level are acquiring abilities such as being able to rhyme words or to categorize words by beginning sounds.

> Phonological awareness is an umbrella term that refers to sensitivity to speech sounds.

Beginning phonological sensitivity precedes the more sophisticated sensitivity of phonemic awareness. Specifically, phonemic awareness is sensitivity to language at the level of individual sounds in words (Stanovich, 2000). According to the National Reading Panel, the two phone- mic awareness skills that have the greatest impact on learning to read are segmenting and blending (National Institute of Child Health and Human Development [NICHD], 2000).

> Phonemic awareness is sensitivity to language at the level of individual sounds in words.

Phonics may be the most familiar of the three terms. Phonics is a method of teaching reading in which children learn about the relation- ship between letters and sounds in order to recognize words (Mesmer & Griffith, 2005/2006). There has been much discussion about the value of phonics instruction, and today most read- ing programs include some level of explicit, systematic phonics instruction.

English is considered an alphabetic language. The written word is a model of the spoken word in that letters follow one another on paper in the same succession that sounds do in time in the spoken word (Elkonin, 1973, p. 558). Because of the

> Phonics is a method of teaching reading in which children learn about the relationship between letters and sounds in order to recognize words.

relationship between letters and sounds in our language, learning to use phonics skills is valuable for children as they move along a path of word learning that ends with being able to recognize most words instantly by sight. Along this path, phonics serves two purposes. First, phonics helps beginning readers obtain an approximate pronunciation for an unfamil- iar written word. This approximate pronunciation is then checked for a match with the reader's store of known spoken words and with the con- text (Anderson, Hiebert, Scott, & Wilkinson, 1985). Second, as readers are using phonics skills to identify unfamiliar written words, they are storing in their long-term memory a representation for the word. The representa- tion may begin as boundary letters and then, over time, the full represen- tation of the word becomes established. As readers use phonics skills to "sound out" a word, the letters in the spelling of the word become bound to the sounds in the pronunciation of the word. Eventually the middle step—phonics—drops out for most readers with most words. Just seeing the spelling activates a connection directly to the pronunciation and the meaning of the word (Ehri, 1994, p. 339). However, phonics serves as an important aid in the process of learning words by sight.

In order to take advantage of phonics instruction, children need an understanding of the structure of spoken language. They need to understand that every utterance is a stream of sounds that can be broken down into smaller and smaller parts, that is, into words, into the syllables within words, and ultimately into the individual sounds in words. Shaywitz (2003) has referred to this as understanding the segmental nature of spoken language. This understanding will prevent confusion about what the sounds are that we as teachers are telling children the letters represent. That, of course, leads us into a discussion of the relationships between phonological awareness, phonemic awareness, and phonics, as illustrated in Figure 3.1. Figure 3.2 contains a set of definitions for terms related to phonological awareness that you will encounter in this and later chapters.

WHAT DOES RESEARCH SAY ABOUT HOW CHILDREN ACQUIRE PHONOLOGICAL AWARENESS?

It is important for teachers to understand that phonemic awareness, not the beginning awareness levels of rhyme and sound categorization, is the critical ingredient in learning to read. However, this does not mean that activities involving this beginning level of sensitivity to speech sounds should be abandoned, as they are the precursors to phonemic awareness. Research suggests that there is a developing progression from awareness of large sound segments (e.g., words in sentences, syllables in words, rhymes) to awareness of small sound elements (e.g., individual sounds in words) (Goswami, 2002). In fact, activities that deal with large sound segments are quite developmentally appropriate for prekindergarten and kindergarten-aged children. It is important to point out that the levels of awareness are not discrete stages. For example, at the time that children are consolidating their awareness of individual words in sentences, they might also be developing an understanding that longer words can be segmented into individual syllables (e.g., literacy has four syllables).

The acquisition of language begins at birth and continues through a lifetime. As children acquire spoken language, their focus is quite naturally on meaning, as the primary motivation for learning

Phonological Awareness

Beginning Awareness Precedes Phonemic Awareness

Children with beginning sensitivity to large sound units . . .	Children with phonemic awareness, sensitivity to small sound units, . . .
• are able to rhyme words. • are successful with sound categorization activities (e.g., identifying words that begin/end with the same sound). • can segment a sentence into words. • can segment a word into syllables. • can segment a syllable into its onset and its rime.	• can segment a word into its individual phonemes (e.g., segmenting *boat* into /b/ /o/ /t/). • can blend individual sounds to form a word (e.g., blending *boat* into /b/ /o/ /t/). • are able to manipulate sounds to form new words (e.g., substituting the /b/ at the beginning of *bat* with a /k/ to form the new word *cat).*

**Phonological Awareness Is the Foundation that
Children Need to Take Advantage of Phonics Instruction**

Phonics
. . . is a way of teaching reading that focuses on the relationship between letters
and sounds.
. . . enables children to read unfamiliar words.
. . . helps children store sight words in long-term memory.

Figure 3.1   The Relationship Between Phonological Awareness, Phonemic
Awareness, and Phonics

language is communication with other individuals. This level of language learning is part of children's genetic structure (Chomsky, 2002) and occurs automatically (Shaywitz, 2003). However, beyond meaning, language has form and structure. Shifting attention from the meanings of words to a focus on their form and structure is difficult, but necessary, for children to become literate (Adams, Foorman, Lundberg, & Beeler, 1998). In the classroom, we can help children in their acquisition of phonological

We can help children in their acquisition of phonological awareness by interacting with literature containing text that plays with the sounds in language.

Those PHon Words

	. . . and other important terms
phoneme——a speech sound; the smallest unit of language that distinguishes one word from another, e.g., /b/ distinguishes big from pig **phonemic awareness**——awareness of the sounds that make up spoken words **phonetics**——the study of the nature, production, and transcription of speech sounds **phonics**——a way of teaching beginning reading and spelling that stresses the relationship between letters and sounds **phonological awareness**——awareness of the constituent sounds of words: syllables, onsets and rimes, and phonemes **phonology**——the study of speech sounds and their functions in a language	**alphabetic principle**——the idea that written spellings systematically represent spoken words; the basis for the spelling system of the English language **orthography**——correct or standardized spelling according to established usage in a given language **grapheme**——the written representation of a phoneme, e.g., "ph" is the grapheme that represents the first sound in the spoken word "phone" **syllable**——the unit of pronunciation; must have a vowel sound **onset**——the part of the syllable that comes before the vowel sound, e.g., the letters "str" represent the onset in the spoken word "string"; not every syllable has an onset **rime**——the vowel sound of a syllable and all the consonant sounds following it, e.g., the letters "ook" represent the rime in the spoken word "book;" every syllable has a rime **alliteration**——the repetition of initial consonant sounds in neighboring words, e.g., the wind in the willows **assonance**——the repetition of a vowel sound in neighboring words that do not rhyme, e.g., The fox got the top spot. **rhyme**——two or more words that sound alike at the end because they share the same rime, with or without the same spelling, are said to rhyme, e.g., cat/hat or mail/tale

Figure 3.2   Definitions for Terms Related to Phonological Awareness

awareness by interacting with literature containing text that plays with the sounds in language, exploring written language through writing, and playing language games. Activities of this type enable children to focus beyond meaning to the form of spoken language.

INDICATORS OF CHILDREN'S DEVELOPMENT OF PHONOLOGICAL AWARENESS

According to Goswami (2002), phonological awareness is reflected in children's ability to reflect on and manipulate the sounds that make up spoken words and may emerge as a result of processes related to language acquisition. According to Catts (as cited in Ericson & Juliebo, 1998), children whose language problems persist past age five may be at risk of developing phonological awareness deficiency. Figure 3.3 lists warning signs related to phonological awareness that might indicate a young child is at risk of later reading difficulties.

By age three, many children have knowledge of nursery rhymes, and determining if words rhyme is a phonological awareness skill that most children can perform at age three or four (Ericson & Juliebo, 1998). Benchmarks at the end of kindergarten include generating rhymes and segmenting words into syllables. Typically, by the end of Grade 1 children have acquired a level of phonemic awareness that enables them to segment and blend sounds in individual words.

> Determining if words rhyme is a phonological awareness skill that most children can perform at age three or four.

Early Warning Signs of Difficulty Acquiring Phonological Awareness

- Delay in speaking beyond the general developmental rule of first words by one year and phrases by eighteen months to two years (Shaywitz, 2003)
- Difficulties in pronunciation beyond five to six years of age (Shaywitz, 2003)
- Insensitivity to rhyme (Shaywitz, 2003) which may include:
  o not comprehending or enjoying rhyming books (Ericson & Juliebo, 1998)
  o being unable to detect or produce rhyming words (Ericson & Juliebo, 1998)
- Difficulty detecting or producing patterns of alliteration (Ericson & Juliebo, 1998)
- Difficulty tapping out the words in a sentence or the syllables in a word (Ericson & Juliebo, 1998)
- Difficulty learning the names and/or the sounds of the letters of the alphabet (Shaywitz, 2003)

Figure 3.3   Early Warning Signs of Difficulty Acquiring Phonological Awareness

ASSESSING PHONOLOGICAL AWARENESS

Sound instruction starts from the knowledge of the learning strengths and needs of our students. The students that we work with come from different family backgrounds, and their exposure to language and literacy activities could vary greatly both in the amount and the quality of exposure.

Now that we understand the importance of developing phonological awareness in preschool children, it is helpful to look at some methods that could allow us to assess their development in this area. These methods range from informal teacher observation to formal commercially published instruments.

Teacher Observation

Careful and systematic observation while the teacher and the children are engaged in daily authentic language, reading, and writing activities is the most powerful form of assessment of preschool children's phonological awareness. Making careful and systematic observation is essential to our ability to effectively determine where individual children fall in the development continuum and to make good instructional decisions to support their growth (Clay, 2002).

To facilitate preschool teachers in making systematic observations and monitoring student progress in phonemic awareness, we have developed a checklist of benchmarks based on our research and work with preschool children (see Figure 3.4). The benchmarks are presented in a developmental continuum.

Let us take another close look at Rebecca, a child with well-developed phonological awareness considering her age. For example, when Rebecca names the rhyming words "bed and head" in her favorite nursery rhyme *10 Little Monkeys Jumping on the Bed,* we know that she has the ability to rhyme words. When she makes up the silly tongue twister, "Rebecca rides in a round rocking rocket," we know that she is able to categorize words that begin with the same sound. When she repeats a sentence one word at a time and counts seven words in the sentence "ten little monkeys jumping on the bed," we know that she can segment a sentence into words. When she claps three times according to the number of beats she hears in a word like "elephant," we know that she has learned the concept of syllables. Similarly, if she tells us that she knows there are a /k/ sound and an /at/ sound in the word "cat," we know that she can segment a syllable into its onset and rime.

We recommend that preschool teachers make a conscious effort to observe each child two to three times each semester and use the checklist (see Figure 3.4) to monitor each child's progress. This checklist could also provide teachers with valuable information on the selection of

---

Phonological Awareness Checklist

Name: _____ Date: _____ Age: _____

School: _____ Recorder: _____

Emergent Stage

_____ 1. Segment spoken words in sentences.

_____ 2. Count the number of syllables in a word.

_____ 3. Identify words that rhyme.

Developing Stage

_____ 1. Produce rhyming words.

_____ 2. Segment syllables in a word.

_____ 3. Blend syllables in a word.

_____ 4. Determine words with same beginning sound.

Advanced Stage

_____ 1. Segment a syllable by onset and rime.

_____ 2. Blend onset and rime.

_____ 3. Determine words with same ending sound.

_____ 4. Distinguish medial sounds in words.

_____ 5. Represent beginning sounds using invented spelling.

_____ 6. Represent ending sounds using invented spelling.

_____ 7. Segment words into phonemes.

Figure 3.4   Phonological Awareness Checklist

phonological awareness activities targeting specific benchmarks for the whole class, small group, or individual children.

In addition to classroom observations, teachers may find it helpful to devise their own informal assessments to monitor children's progress in phonological awareness. To assist, we provide several examples in Figure 3.5 of informal assessments teachers might develop for use with their students. The Phonological Awareness Checklist in Figure 3.4 can also be used as a guide when developing informal assessments. Some teachers assess phonological awareness at the word or sub word level such as rhyme, syllable segmentation, and onset-rhyme segmentation. Others assess phonological awareness at the phoneme level such as segmenting and blending phonemes in words.

The Yopp Rhyme Test assesses phonological awareness at the word level. This individually administered test was developed by Hallie Yopp (Yopp, 1987, 1988) to assess children's ability to detect rhymes. The test is adapted from early work by Calfee, Chapman, and Venezky (1972). The test consists of a list of 20 pairs of words, half of them rhyming pairs (e.g., joy-boy and farm-car). The teacher first explains what rhymes are and provides examples of words that rhyme. Next the teacher asks the child to tell if the word pairs rhyme when read to the child. For each correct answer, the child gets one point. An average kindergarten child can obtain a score of 14 out of 20.

The Yopp-Singer Test of Phoneme Segmentation assesses phonological awareness at the phoneme level. This individually administered test was also developed by Hallie Yopp with contribution from Harry Singer (Yopp, 1995) to assess children's ability to segment phonemes, the most difficult phonemic awareness task. Children who are able to obtain high scores may be considered phonemically aware. The test consists of a list of 22 one-syllable words. The teacher asks the child to break the word apart and identify sounds in the order they occur in the spoken word. For each correct answer, the child gets one point. An average kindergarten child can obtain a score of 12 out of 22.

Rathvon (2004) has categorized phonological awareness assessments based on whether the assessment is at the word and sub word level or the phoneme level. Figure 3.5 summarizes various types of assessments with information for teachers to use to develop their own informal classroom assessments.

Because of the critical role that phonological awareness plays in children's literacy development, many formal assessment instruments, including commercially published instruments, have been developed and therefore are available for teachers to use. Below we describe two widely used research-based instruments. Each is user-friendly and available at no cost to teachers.

Got It, Get It, Go Rhyming Test and Alliteration Test

As referenced in Chapter 2, Got It, Get It, Go is a project of the Center for Early Education Development at the University of Minnesota. It is funded by the U.S. Department of Education. This project provides three tests that assess expressive language (through Picture Naming test) and phonological awareness (through Rhyming and Alliteration tests) of preschool children (ages three–five).

The Rhyming Test is used to assess preschool children's ability to identify rhyming words. The test kit contains a set of stimulus cards and a step-by-step instruction for test administration. On each card, there is a target

Phonological Awareness Assessments

Assessments at the Word and Sub Word Level

Recognizing Rhymes

Develop a list of twenty pairs of one-syllable words, ten rhyming pairs and ten nonrhyming pairs, and some extra practice pairs. Examples of rhyming pairs are cat-rat, big-dig, goat-coat; examples of nonrhyming pairs are cook-big, can-bug, ball-fat. We recommend that all pairs contain three phonemes with the consonant-vowel-consonant sound pattern. Nonrhyming pairs such as train-truck and can-come that begin with the same consonant sound or consonant blend (e.g., c- and tr-), ball-pull that end with the same consonant sound (e.g., -l), or hat-hit that differ by only the medial vowel (e.g., short a and short i) can be included to make the task more difficult.

Directions to the child: I am going to tell you two words, and I want you to tell me if they rhyme. Cat and hat are two words that rhyme. But not all words rhyme. Star and play do not rhyme. Now let's practice. I will say two words and you tell me if they rhyme. Make-cake. Do make and cake rhyme? (Confirm with the child that yes they do rhyme, or no they do not rhyme.) Let's practice one more time. Bake-fox. Do bake and fox rhyme? (Again provide confirmation or correction.) Okay, let's keep going. (Present the word pairs in random order and have the child indicate by saying "yes" or "no" whether the words do or do not rhyme.)

Record the child's answer as "yes" or "no" beside each pair of words on a sheet of paper that contains the list of word pairs.

Producing rhymes

Develop a list of ten one-syllable rhyming pairs such as can-man, big-pig, and trip-slip; and some extra practice pairs.

Directions to the child: I am going to say two words that rhyme. I might say can-man. Then I want you to tell me another word that rhymes. It can be a real word or a made-up word. So if I said can-man, you could say pan because can, man, and pan all rhyme. Or if I said can-man, you could say gan even though gan is not a real word because can, man, and gan all rhyme. Now let's practice. Big-pig. You tell me another word that rhymes. (Confirm with the child that the word he/she said does rhyme or provide correction by giving an example of a third word that does rhyme.) Okay, let's keep going. (Present the other rhyming word pairs and let the child provide a third rhyming word.)

Record the child's response beside each pair of words on a sheet of paper that contains the list of word pairs.

Syllable awareness

Develop a list of ten two- and three-syllable words such as mitten, rocket, acrobat, banana, and some practice words.

Directions to the child: Listen as I say a word. Mitten. Now I am going to say the word again, and this time I am going to clap as I say each syllable. Mitten has two syllables (or you can say beats if you are not sure the child knows the meaning of syllable), so this time when I say mitten I will clap as I say each syllable (or beat). Watch and listen. Mit (and clap at the same time) ten (and clap at

the same time). Now you do it with me. (Repeat with the child) mit (and clap at the same time) ten (and clap at the same time). Okay, let's try another one. (This time provide the practice in the same way, but use a three-syllable word such as "acrobat.") Okay, let's keep going. I will say a word and then you say the word and clap for each syllable.

On a sheet of paper that contains the list of words, simply check off whether the child was or was not able to clap the syllables.

Onset and Rhyme Blending

Develop a list of ten one-syllable words such as cup, train, spring, and some practice words. Try to include some words that begin with two- and three-consonant blends in the list (e.g., train begins with a two-consonant blend and spring begins with a three-consonant blend).

Directions to the child: I am going to say a word that you know, but I am going to say it in parts. I want you to put the parts together and say the whole word. Let's practice. If I said /k/ - /up/, you would say "cup." (Be sure to say the sounds, not the letters. For example, do not say the letter "c." Say the sound /k/, that the letter "c" represents in the word "cup.") Let's practice. If I said /tr/ - /ain/, then what would you say? (Confirm that the child's answer is correct, or provide correction by telling the child that when you put the parts together the word is "train.") Okay, let's keep going. I will say the word in parts, and you put the parts together and say the whole word.

On a sheet of paper that contains the list of words, simply check off whether the child was or was not able to blend the onset and rhyme.

Assessments at the Phoneme Level

Beginning Consonant Awareness

Develop a list of ten pairs of one-syllable words that begin with the same consonant sound (e.g., big-bat, man-moon, tip-tag), and some pairs for practice. In this case it is better if the pairs begin with single consonant sounds rather than with consonant blends.

Directions to the child: I will say two words that start with the same sound. I might say big and bat. Then you will tell me another word that starts with the same sound as big and bat. You can tell me a real word or a made-up word, just as long as the word you say begins with the same sound as big and bat. Let's practice. If I said big and bat, then you could say ball because ball begins with the same sound as big and bat. Listen, big-bat-ball. Or you could say bip, even though bip is not a real word because bip begins with the same sound as big and bat. Listen, big-bat-bip. But, could you say pack? (Wait for an answer) No you could not say pack. Listen big-bat-pack. Pack does not begin with the same sound as big and bat. Let's try another one. Man-moon. Now you tell me another word that begins like man and moon. (Confirm that the child's answer is correct, or provide correction by telling the child a word that does begin like man and moon.) Okay, let's keep going. I will say two words, and you tell me another word that begins the same.

On a sheet of paper that contains the list of word pairs, record the child's answer.

Phoneme Blending

Develop a list of ten one-syllable words such as be (contains two phonemes) and pack (contains three phonemes even though it is spelled with four letters), and some practice words. Do not include words longer than three phonemes.

(Continued)

(Continued)

Directions to the child: I am going to say a word that you know, but I am going to say it in parts. I want you to put the parts together and say the whole word. Let's practice. If I said /b/ - /ee/, you would say "be." (Be sure to say the sounds, not the letters. For example, do not say the letter "b." Say the sound /b/, that the letter "b" represents in the word "be.") Let's practice. If I said /p/ - /a/ - /k/, then what would you say? (Confirm that the child's answer is correct, or provide correction by telling the child that when you put the parts together the word is "pack.") Okay, let's keep going. I will say the word in parts, and you put the parts together and say the whole word.

On a sheet of paper that contains the list of words, simply check off whether the child was or was not able to blend the sounds.

Phoneme Segmentation

Develop a list of ten one-syllable words such as go (contains two phonemes) and phone (contains three phonemes even though it is spelled with five letters), and some practice words. Do not include words longer than three phonemes.

Directions to the child: I am going to say a word that you know, and I want you to break the word apart. You are going to tell me each sound in the word in order. For example, if I say "go," you should say "/g/-/o/." (Be sure to say the sounds in go and not the letters.) Let's practice. Phone. What are the sounds in phone? (Confirm that the child's answer is correct or provide correction by telling the child the three sounds in phone.) Okay, let's keep going. I will say a word, and you break the word apart.

On a sheet of paper that contains the list of words, record what the child said. Later you can determine whether the child can break a word into its phonemes, or whether the child is breaking the word into parts larger than individual sounds. For example, a child might be able to segment a word into onset and rhyme, but not into individual phonemes. Other times a child might break a word into another configuration, such as /fo/ - /n/, but again not into individual sounds.

Figure 3.5   Phonological Awareness Assessments

photo or line drawing at the top and a set of three photos or drawings in a row at the bottom, one of which rhymes with the target photo/drawing. The children are asked to point out the picture that sounds the same as or rhymes with the target picture. This task lasts for a total of two minutes. The score each child obtains is the number of pictures the child correctly identifies within the two minutes.

The Alliteration Test is used to assess preschool children's ability to identify words with the same beginning sound. The test kit contains a set of stimulus cards and a step-by-step instruction for test administration. On each card, there is a target photo or line drawing at the top and a set of three photos/drawings in a row at the bottom, one of which starts with the same sound as the target picture. The children are asked to point out the picture with the same initial sound as the target picture. This task also lasts for a total of two minutes. Again, the score each child obtains is the number of pictures the child correctly identifies within the two minutes.

Both tests, including the stimulus cards and instruction for test administration, are available for free downloads from the "Get It" section of the official Web site of Get It, Got It, Go (http://ggg.umn.edu). This project also helps teachers maintain assessment results online for free. Once the tests are completed, you can go to the "Got It" section of the site and enter individual's scores, get score recording forms, and compare the performance of a child with the children in the reference group.

Dynamic Indicators of Basic Early Literacy Skills (DIBELS)—Initial Sound Fluency and Phonemic Segmentation Fluency

DIBELS is a battery of early literacy tests developed by literacy researchers at the University of Oregon. The Initial Sound Fluency Subtest is used to assess children's ability to rapidly recognize and produce initial sounds in orally presented words. The child is asked to identify the picture from the set of four that starts with the same target sound. The child is also asked to produce the beginning sound of an orally presented word that matches one of the pictures. Each correctly identified initial sound receives a point. The final score is the number of correct initial sounds per minute.

The Phonemic Segmentation Fluency subtest is used to assess children's ability to rapidly segment orally presented three- and four-phoneme words into phonemes. Each correctly segmented sound receives a point. The final score is the total number of correct sound segments per minute.

Both are timed, one-minute tests. Test kits can be purchased for a minimal cost from the University of Oregon or downloaded for free from the official DIBELS Web site (http://dibels.uoregon.edu).

RESEARCH-BASED INSTRUCTIONAL STRATEGIES SUPPORTING PHONOLOGICAL AWARENESS

Because phonological awareness lays the foundation for literacy development, preschool teachers are responsible for providing children with effective instructional and learning activities so that they can be on their way to becoming successful literacy learners.

To help preschool children develop phonological awareness, our priority should be on establishing an environment

> Phonological awareness lays the foundation for literacy development.

rich in opportunities that encourage active oral language development, exploration of written language through reading and writing activities, and playful interaction with language.

Teacher read-aloud of children's favorite nursery rhymes, poems, and songs with words that rhyme and children's innovation of their own versions of the text should be a frequent routine in preschool classrooms. A list of read-aloud books for developing phonemic awareness is identified by Yopp (1995). These books are ideal for young children's playing with language.

Many of the books read to children during the course of a school day incorporate elements of playful language including repetition of syllables, rhyme, alliteration (repetition of initial consonant sounds across several works), and assonance (repetition of vowel sounds within words). Whenever possible, teachers should intentionally give children opportunities to supply the rhyming words and words with the same beginning sounds during read-alouds or shared reading activities. Figure 3.6 contains examples of these language-play elements.

Playful Text	Language-Play Elements
Waves wash across the ship. Waves slosh. Sheep slip. (Shaw, 1989)	Alliteration – waves/wash, ship/sheep, slosh/slip Rhyme – ship/slip
They make a mask with glue and tape And a monster suit with a shiny cape (Shaw, 1997)	Assonance – make/tape, glue/suit Alliteration – make/mask/monster Rhyme – tape/cape
Moonberry Starberry Cloudberry sky Boomberry Zoomberry Rockets shoot by. (Degen, 1983)	Manipulation of syllables – moonberry/starberry/cloudberry Assonance – moon/boom and zoom/shoot Rhyme – boomberry/zoomberry, sky/by
A leaf, a tree, a green bean green. (Serfozo, 1988)	Assonance – leaf/tree/green and bean
Ma was busy cookin' in the kitchen makin' taters when a possum come a-knockin' at the door. (Van Laan, 1990)	Repetition of syllables –in' Alliteration – cookin'/kitchen Assonance – makin'/taters
A cake for tea. . . A cape for me. . . (Hutchins, 1976)	Manipulation of phonemes – cake/cape, tea/me (Note: This is also involves assonance and rhyme.)

Figure 3.6 Text That Plays With Language

We use many of the skills of reading in a different form when we write. Teacher modeling of writing is a powerful tool for helping preschoolers develop beginning literacy skills. When you model writing, or serve as a scribe for children to write, you are giving children the opportunity to see how we go from thought to saying words to writing them (Clay, 1975). Eventually, in the writing center, children can face head-on the problem of mapping spoken language onto written language. Serendipitous to this is a heightened awareness of sounds in spoken words and an understanding of the relationship between sounds and letters (Griffith & Olson, 1992). You can also engage children in emergent writing activities during which preschool children get to use invented spelling to approximate their understanding of the sounds they hear in words they want to use in their writing.

> We use many of the skills of reading in a different form when we write.

Language games are a way to focus children's attention on the form of language. Initially you will want to start with activities dealing with large sound units, such as segmenting individual words in a sentence. Children can say the words in a familiar song or rhyme as they engage in a cake walk–type activity, stepping from one block to another as they say the individual words. Similar activities in which children distinguish large sound units can include clapping the syllables in words and comparing the "sound" length of different words. Eventually, they can then make predictions about the relative length of written words based on their spoken forms. As you move towards smaller sound units, children can distinguish between words that begin with the same or different sounds, or between rhyming words. Many of these language games can serve as "sponge" activities to fill short segments of time in the day.

There are many activities specifically targeting young children's development of phonological awareness. We are recommending the following ones that are appropriate for preschool children's developmental level. The activities can be easily integrated into preschool children's daily literacy experiences.

Word Walk

This is a game that we developed based on the popular cake walk game for helping children develop the ability to segment words in a sentence.

1. Select a favorite phrase (or entire sentence) from a story or nursery rhyme that you have recently shared with the children. For example, you can pick the line "ten little monkeys jumping on the bed."

2. Write the phrase on sentence strip paper and read it to the children while pointing to each word as you are reading. Ask the children to join in the reading.

3. Cut up the sentence strip into individual words.

4. Again point to each word and read it slowly, making sure that you stop in between the words.

5. Arrange the words in a circle or a square on the floor and have each child in the game stand on a word.

6. Play music. When the music stops, draw a word used in the same phrase from a box and call out the word.

7. The child standing on that word wins the round.

8. The game can be continued for as long as time allows.

Picture Sort

Picture sort is a powerful activity used by teachers and highly recommended by many literacy educators (e.g., Bear, Invernizzi, Templeton, Johnston, 2004) to develop children's understanding of alliteration and rhyme (i.e., beginning sounds and rhyming words). This can be a small group or individual activity.

Beginning Sound Picture Sort

1. Prepare a set of picture cards with familiar objects that begin with target initial sounds, and then have children name the object on each card.

2. Tell the class that you are going to sort pictures according to their beginning sound. Model how you sort the cards on a board or a pocket chart. For example, you would put the pictures of "candle" and "cake" separate from "ball" and "bat." Tell the children that you put "candle" and "cake" together because they both start with the "/k/" sound and you put "ball" and "bat" together because they both start with the "/b/" sound.

3. Pair children up and give each pair a set of cards. Have them sort the words into different piles according to the same beginning sound.

4. When children have gained more experience in beginning sound sort, you can make it an individual activity.

Rhyming Word Picture Sort

1. Prepare a set of picture cards of familiar objects that rhyme and have children name the object on each card.

2. Tell the class that you are going to sort pictures if they rhyme. Model how you sort the cards on a board or a pocket chart. For example, you would put the pictures of "cake" and "lake" separate from "bat" and "cat." Tell the children that you put "cake" and "lake" together because they end the same, and this is the same reason for you to put "bat" and "cat" together.

3. Pair children up and give each pair a set of cards. Have them sort the words into different piles according to the same rime.

4. When children have gained more experience in rhyming word picture sort, you can make it an individual activity.

Extension: You can collect groups of real concrete objects that start with the same beginning sound and rhyming pattern for use with preschoolers.

Clapping Syllables

Clapping syllables is a popular activity used by many teachers to develop children's awareness of syllables. Cunningham (2000) suggests that we use children's names for this activity because children have a natural infatuation about their names, and they know each other's names by heart too!

1. Tell the class that you are going to play a clapping game with their names.

2. Tell them that some names only have one beat. Use a few children's names as the example. Tell them to clap once when they hear a one-beat name such as "Jake" and "Pam."

3. Proceed to clapping with two-syllable names such as "Adam" and "Erin." Tell them to clap twice when they hear a two-beat name.

4. Proceed to clapping with three-syllable names such as "Emily" and "Kristina." Tell them to clap three times when they hear a three-beat name.

Extension 1: Have children volunteer to clap their names and clap the names of their family members.

Extension 2: Have the class clap their favorite words from the books or stories you've shared with them.

> Clapping syllables is a popular activity used by many teachers to develop children's awareness of syllables.

What Am I Thinking Of?

This guessing game is developed by Yopp (1992) to support children's ability to blend orally spoken sounds into words. The following procedures are adapted from Yopp (1992).

1. Think of a category. It could be anything from clothing to food.

2. Tell the children to listen carefully to the category and the sounds you are going to say. You may say, "The category is food. Here are the sounds /m/-/i/-/el/-/k/. What is the word that I am thinking of?" Be sure to say the sounds and not the letters.

3. Once children correctly produce the word, applaud their attempt and continue the game.

4. As children get better at blending the sounds, you can ask them to take the lead in providing the category and the sounds for their peers to blend.

Let Children Be Sounds

This activity is useful for children to see how sounds can be blended together to make a word. With preschoolers, we recommend that you start with words that have perfect letter-sound correspondence. You can also use the words from children's favorite stories or poems.

1. Select a set of words that are already part of children's oral language. For example, you can use words such as "mom," "dad," or "cheese" used in their daily lives, or words such as "cat" and "hat" from Dr. Seuss's stories.

2. Allow children to decide which sound they want to be.

3. Say the word and have the children who represent the sounds in the word to come up to the front. Line them up in order.

4. Point to each child and say the sound represented by the child. Repeat all the sounds and ask the class to say the word.

ADDRESSING DIVERSITY

Students from some African American and Hispanic communities use vernacular dialects of English. The unique characteristics of all dialects should be respected. Vernaculars such as Chicano English and African

American Vernacular English (a.k.a. Ebonics) do not conform to all phonological and syntactic features used in standard English, because they have their own systematic set of linguistic rules to follow just as in regional dialects of English.

> The unique characteristics of all dialects should be respected.

Teachers working with children speaking English vernaculars should be aware of the major differences in the phonology of the vernacular from that of standard English. Because phonological awareness is about one's understanding of sound, inviting children to identify and manipulate sounds in the words of the vernacular they speak could serve as a springboard to developing phonological awareness in standard English.

American schools have witnessed a rapid increase in the population of English as second language learners in recent years. Many of these children do not speak English, and this could pose a huge challenge to the teachers who work with them.

Hispanic and Asian children are two of the biggest groups of English language learners (ELL) in today's schools. Because phonological awareness of the English language is critical to ELL children's success in their literacy development in English (Lesaux & Siegel, 2003), it is critical that early childhood teachers acquire basic knowledge of the phonologies used by their ELL students' first languages.

Let's take a minute to look at Juan, the Spanish speaking child we first introduced in Chapter 1. The teacher finds that Juan could not distinguish the vowel sounds in words such as "pet" and "pat." Neither could he distinguish the vowels sounds in "leap" and "lip." This happens because there are only five vowel phonemes in Spanish. Juan also has great difficulty in making contrasts between words such as "sin" and "thin," "dan" and "than," "bet" and "vet." This is rather typical of Spanish speakers because contrasts such as /s/ and /th/, /b/ and /v/, and /d/ and /th/ are not made in Spanish (Troike, 1972).

Many Asian languages such as Mandarin Chinese, Japanese, and Korean consist of single syllable characters/words. More importantly, words in these spoken languages rarely end with a consonant. They typically end with a vowel. Therefore, it can be extremely challenging for young Asian children to have the sensitivity needed to be aware of the ending consonant in many English spoken words. This could put them at a huge disadvantage when it comes to developing phonological awareness because they are not able to hear all the sounds in English spoken words.

In addition to immersing these children in rich language, reading, and writing activities that support mainstream children's development of phonological awareness, it is critical that teachers who work with young ELLs carefully, clearly, and slowly enunciate every single sound for these children. Whenever possible, bring ELL children's attention to the ending sounds and work with them on those sounds. Teachers who have knowledge in these children's first language can also greatly support their phonological awareness by pointing out the contrasts that are not in their first language.

As we mentioned earlier, research is pointing to a connection between vocabulary development and the development of phonological awareness (Goswami, 2002; Troia, 2004). Specifically, phonological awareness develops as a result of lexical restructuring during spoken vocabulary growth. Lexical means word, and our lexicon is our mental dictionary, the place in our brains where words and all the information about them (i.e., meaning, phonology, syntax) are stored. As a child learns a new word, she must make a comparison with other similar-sounding words in order to store the new word in her lexicon. This occurs as a natural and relatively automatic part of vocabulary development. Let us consider the word "cat." Cat has many similar sounding neighbors. For example, "cat" and "rat" are rime neighbors due to sharing the common rime "-at." Likewise "cat" and "calf" are onset-vowel neighbors because they differ only in their final sounds, /t/ and /f/. Finally, "cat" and "kit" are neighbors, differing only by their medial vowel sounds. Now, let us say that a child first learns the word "cat." In order to store similar sounding new words such as "rat," "calf," or "kit," the lexicon has to be restructured to accommodate the slightly different phonological structure of each new word. Lexical restructuring requires the child to deal with the segmental structure of speech as new spoken words are learned. This notion of the tie between phonological awareness and the acquisition of spoken language speaks to the critical importance of a continuing focus on vocabulary development. Teachers should always provide a language-rich environment in which linguistic activities include exposure to literature, particularly literature containing language play characteristics, language games and writing experiences.

> Research is pointing to a connection between vocabulary development and the development of phonological awareness.

Children who experience difficulty acquiring language are also likely to be delayed in their development of phonological awareness, and Figure 3.3 lists some risk factors to watch for. However, we also know that instruction can influence the development of phonological awareness. According to Goswami (2002), early phonological development centers on the phonological units of syllable, onset, and rime (p. 112), and we believe the syllable level is where phonological awareness training should center with at-risk three- and four-year olds. While the type of phonological awareness activities do not vary significantly from those recommended for developmentally on target children, the intensity of the instruction does. Instruction should be purposeful and explicit to help at-risk children focus on the phonological characteristics of words.

We can help special needs children become sensitive to the segmental nature of spoken language by pointing out alliteration and rhyme in text. For example, when reading *Sheep on a Ship* (Shaw, 1989) a teacher might comment, "I just realized sheep and ship both sound alike at the beginning. Just start to say sheep, but don't say it all the way—/sh/. Now do the same thing for ship—/sh/. Can you tell? /sh/, /sh/ sheep. /sh/, /sh/ ship." Saying the two words while exaggerating the initial sound of each word makes explicit how "sheep" and "ship" are related by their initial sound. The teacher can invite the child to say each word, and then later to notice how her mouth feels as she starts to say each word, but does not say them all the way. Sequences such as this will help to focus a child's attention on the sound structure separate from the meaning of a word.

In a similar fashion, a teacher might point out that a text contains a substantial number of rhyming words. Consider this rhyming text from *Sheep Trick or Treat* (Shaw, 1997). "Sheep amble to the dell. They reach the barn and ring the bell." When reading this story, the teacher might say, "Dell. Bell. Did you notice that these words rhyme? /d/ /el/, /b/ /el/ They both sound the same at the end." During subsequent readings of the same story, the teacher can invite the child to fill in the rhyming word.

The activities described above occur in the context of story reading. Other language games involve working with individual words. Word sorts are one example which we described above. Special needs children can engage in similar activities but may need more explicit and repeated instruction. For example, the teacher can ask them to sort pictures (or replicas of actual objects, if available) based on a criterion such as same beginning sound using a set (pictures or replicas) of a man, a dog, a mop, a fish, and a mouse. Then the teacher can reiterate the initial sound of man (/m/, /m/, /m/ man) by asking the children to sort the pictures based on the ones that begin like "man" and the ones that do not.

Segmenting and blending sounds are the phonemic awareness skill used in reading and writing. Children must segment the sounds of spoken words to use letter and sound correspondences to invent spellings for words they do not know. Similarly, they must blend sounds as they use correspondences to "sound out" words. Working at the level of syllables with onsets and rimes, we can begin to develop segmenting and blending abilities. Syllables are the largest units of sound that make up

> Segmenting and blending sounds are the phonemic awareness skill used in reading and writing.

words, and are easy for children to identify. Children enjoy clapping out the syllables in words. As we described earlier, children's names are very meaningful words to them, and are good words to begin with this activity.

Once children can segment a word by syllables, move to segmenting syllables into onsets and rimes. Many young children enjoy activities with puppets. You can introduce Mr. Slow Poke (any puppet will do), who speaks so slowly people have a hard time knowing what he is saying. Using a Mr. Slow Poke puppet, the teacher says words segmented at the onset and rime (e.g., d-og). The child helps Mr. Slow Poke out by translating "d-og" to "dog." Children can also help Mr. Slow Poke learn to push his syllables together (e.g. by translating "roc-ket" to "rocket"). In a variation of this game, the child shows Mr. Slow Poke a picture, such as a picture of a boat, and says, "Now Mr. Slow Poke, if I say b-oat, what do you say?" Mr. Slow Poke responds with "boat."

In addition to reading to children and playing language games, we can help at-risk children understand the segmental nature of language by serving as a scribe for their story dictations. Say each word, elongating its pronunciation, as you write the child's language. As you are writing their words, select one word to make explicit the connection between the spoken word and how that word maps onto letters in print. To illustrate, suppose the child's words are "My dog ran out the gate." While writing the teacher would say, "MMMyyy doog ran, hum ran,/rrr/r/ aaa/a/nnn/n out the gate." "My" and "dog" are elongated pronunciations, but "ran" is actually segmented into its three sounds and each matched with a letter. It is important that the dictation process not take so much time that the child's attention wonders, and with this instructional strategy the teacher has to also be sensitive to the developmental level of the child and to the context.

Shaywitz (2003) makes an important point about remediating the phonological skills of at-risk children. This is to address the phonological weakness while at the same time recognizing the higher-level thinking and reasoning abilities of the child. The point is that when considering a child's literacy development, we must look at the bigger picture and not overlook the child's strengths, which always must be identified and nurtured.

SUMMARY

In this chapter, we discuss what phonological awareness is and the progression of phonological awareness development. Phonological awareness is an umbrella term that refers to one's knowledge of the various aspects of the sound of the language in use. Phonemic awareness is the awareness that English spoken language consists of a stream of individual sounds. Children with well-developed phonological awareness are able to rhyme, blend, manipulate, and segment the sounds in the spoken words. We have provided some assessment methods that you can use as well as instructional activities you can implement in your classroom to monitor and support your students' development in this important area. We have also addressed and offered our advice on issues related to working with children speaking diverse English vernaculars, ELL children, and children with special needs. Equipped with the knowledge of children's development of phonological awareness, you are well on your way to help your students lay a firm foundation for their future success as literacy learners.

Alphabetic Principle

4

Annie's class is studying about our healthy bodies. Today in whole group time Annie's teacher, Mrs. Jones, sat next to a chart tablet resting on an easel to model writing and making good decisions. She listed items she needed to purchase at the grocery store. Her list included pancake mix, milk, bananas, and chocolate candy. As she made the list, Mrs. Jones thought aloud as she was writing. *Hmm, I am going to have to get to the grocery store today otherwise I won't have anything for breakfast in the morning. I better make a list so I won't forget anything. I'll write down some words to help me remember what to buy. I know I need pancake mix. I'll write pancake mix on my list.*

As she began to write pancake, she emphasized the beginning of the word again thinking aloud. */p/ /p/ /p/ is the sound at the beginning of pancake. So I know that pancake is going to begin with the letter [p]. Oh, and milk. I better add milk. I drank the last of my milk this morning.* This time she "rubber-banded" the word as she added milk to her list. */mmmm/ /iiiiilk/. /mmmm/ I am going to write the letter[m] to stand for the /mmmm/ sound. /iiii/. That's going to be an [i]. I will write the letter [i] next. /lk/. Next I am going to write [l] and [k]. Milk has four letters [m], [i], [l], and [k]. Now let's see, I know fruit is very good for me. Maybe I should buy some bananas. I really like bananas. I'll put bananas on my list.*

This time Mrs. Jones enlisted the help of the children, "/b/ /b/ /b/ bananas. Class, help me. What letter will bananas begin with?" She confirmed that bananas did begin with [b] as she added the word to her list. *Let's see, maybe I should purchase some chocolate candy because I really like candy bars. I'll add chocolate candy to my list.* Just as quickly as she wrote "chocolate candy," Mrs. Jones rethought her decision. *Maybe I better take chocolate candy off the list. It's not that good for me. I know. I'll add apples. I really like apples. They're good for me, and if I add apples to pancake mix, that's a sweet treat.*

(Continued)

(Continued)

> Mrs. Jones ended the mini-lesson by showing the children how she had prepared paper in just the right size for making a grocery list. These would be in the writing center for the children who wanted to make a grocery list. Later in the day, Annie and her friend Luis were in the housekeeping center. Luis wrote out a list of items, which he told Mrs. Jones was his grocery list.

WHAT IS THE ALPHABETIC PRINCIPLE AND WHAT IS ITS ROLE IN LITERACY DEVELOPMENT?

As we indicated in Chapter 3, English is an alphabetic language. There is a systematic relationship between the sounds in the spoken version of English and the letters in the written version. Letters stand for sounds! When children grasp this understanding, we can say that they understand the alphabetic principle. This understanding is a major milestone in children's literacy development. Also in Chapter 3, we indicated how the process of word learning occurs as we discussed how the written representations of words become affixed to their spoken counterparts in long-term memory. It is an understanding of the alphabetic principle that enables this process to begin since it leads children to realize that there is a logical relationship between letters and sounds.

> English is an alphabetic language . . . Letters stand for sounds!

Prior to an understanding of the alphabetic principle, children will have no basis for learning to read words except by a process of selective association (Gough & Hillinger, 1980). Children select or pick out something unusual or distinctive about a word that they associate with the written version to help them remember how the word is pronounced. Some examples are to remember "look" because it has "two eyes looking at me." In one first-grade classroom, a student indicated that "something" would be very easy to remember because it was the longest word he knew. The problem with this strategy is that as a child's collection of known words grows, it becomes more and more difficult to learn new words. The "two eyes looking at me" strategy breaks down as the child has to remember "book" and "zoo," and the process of word learning becomes almost impossible.

On the other hand, once children have grasped the alphabetic principle, they can begin to see logical relationships between spellings and pronunciations. To illustrate, the spelling pattern "-at" appears prominently in English words—cat, bat, fat, hat, sat, that, rat, and many others. Children's understandings of these logical relationships will be applied to word learning, both through reading and writing. Figure 4.1 illustrates the developmental path defined by the alphabetic principle.

> Once children have grasped the alphabetic principle, they can begin to see logical relationships between spellings and pronunciations.

WHAT DOES RESEARCH TELL US ABOUT THE ALPHABETIC PRINCIPLE?

The two components of understanding the alphabetic principle are phonemic awareness and letter knowledge. In fact, phonemic awareness and letter knowledge have been identified as the two best predictors of how well children will learn to read in their first two years of school (Ehri, 2004). In addition, children need many opportunities to see the relationship between these elements in written language through print exposure

Prealphabetic Reading and Writing Behaviors

Word learning occurs through selective association.

- Remembering words by features such as length or by unusual characteristics

Writing looks like the print in their environment, but is not readable.

- Writing and drawing not distinguished
- Scribbling with reoccurring movements such as the over and under strokes of adult handwriting
- Letter strings

Alphabetic Reading and Writing Behaviors

Word learning occurs by bonding of a word's spelling with its pronunciation.

- Associating the phonemes in a spoken word with the letters in a written word

Writing becomes readable.

- Beginning and ending sounds represented in written words
- More mature writing with vowels represented

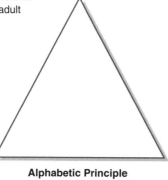

Alphabetic Principle

Figure 4.1   The Developmental Path Defined by the Alphabetic Principle

and use. Mrs. Jones's modeling of list-making is a good example of showing children this relationship.

You may be questioning why knowledge of letters and sounds is so important. In Chapter 3, we discussed phonemic awareness and its link to decoding words using phonics (i.e., converting letters to sounds and blending the sounds to come up with a likely pronunciation for an unfamiliar word). An unfamiliar word may also be read by analogy to a known word (Goswami, 2000; Goswami & Bryant, 1990). To illustrate, by recognizing the common spelling pattern "op" in the word "hop" and blending that with "sh" a child can read the new word "shop." Each of these word recognition strategies requires an easy familiarity with letters and sounds. Some research suggests that children use their knowledge of letter names to learn letter sounds, particularly when the sound occurs in the letter-name (Rathvon, 2004). In higher grades, children continue to use their understanding of the alphabetic principle as they become more sophisticated with reading and writing words. Some ability to focus on the individual sounds in words combined with a modicum of letter naming knowledge allows children's literacy development to begin, and then the process has an upward spiral (Griffith, 1991). As they focus on spelling patterns in words, their ability to remember correct spellings increases through practice.

> Word recognition requires an easy familiarity with letters and sounds.

What are the implications of this information for instruction in early childhood classrooms? The names of letters are part of the language of literacy instruction, and accuracy and speed in naming letters gives children an advantage in learning to read and write words (Strickland & Schickedanz, 2004). At the preschool level, children should be able to recognize at least ten uppercase letters (Strickland & Schickedanz, 2004), and they should leave kindergarten with a solid knowledge of letters and phonemic awareness (Ehri, 2004). In addition, children must be sensitive to speech sounds, as discussed in Chapter 3. Helping children see the relationship between letters and sounds is best approached through multiple and diverse reading and writing activities in a print-rich

> At the preschool level, children should be able to recognize at least ten uppercase letters.

environment. Such experiences should make explicit the process of going from thoughts to saying words to writing them. As they observe and participate, children face head-on the alphabetic principle—the mapping of sounds to letters to written words (Griffith & Olson, 1992).

ASSESSING THE ALPHABETIC PRINCIPLE

Beck (2006) describes the word reading behavior of a child who could read "and" but not "an," "bat" but not "but," and "he" but not "me." This child could not make the simple manipulations involving sounds and letters necessary to read phonemically related words. This is a manifestation of not understanding the alphabetic principle that a first-grade teacher might observe in a child. With younger children, assessment of a child's growing understanding of the alphabetic principle is more validly observed through an analysis of his or her writing.

To illustrate, let's make a try at assessing where Luis is in his understanding of the alphabetic principle (see Figure 4.2). Recall that Luis made his list in the writing center after Mrs. Jones had modeled making a grocery list in large group. Mrs. Jones tries to keep the writing center well-stocked with different writing instruments, and Luis enjoyed using a marker to make his list. Luis has produced strings of letters and letter-like forms, or mock letters. But, there is not any relationship between the letters on the page and the sounds in spoken words. Luis does not yet

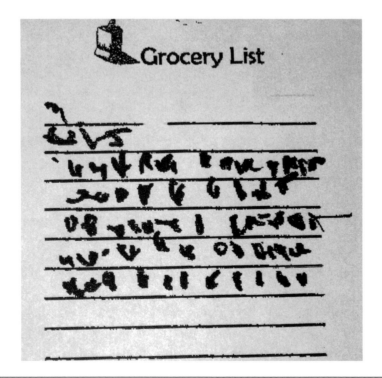

Figure 4.2　Luis's Grocery List

have an understanding of the alphabetic principle. His writing is not readable to anyone, perhaps not even Luis.

However, despite the lack of readability, we can still note some understandings about written language in what Luis has produced. He understands that words are written with letters, and he understands that letters are produced with distinctive strokes, as we see in his mock letters. His horizontal and vertical array of items suggests he is beginning to understand the directional principles of written English. Mrs. Jones noticed that he selected a top left starting position for his writing and that the movement of his writing was left-to-right and top-to-bottom. It is also apparent that Luis has the motor control to write between lines, and that he has attended to the lines. That is unique for children Luis's age. However, what we do not see is any association between letters and sounds. In fact, Luis is not yet writing recognizable letters.

As Luis and Annie have more writing experiences, such as the one we described at the beginning of this chapter in which their teacher models the alphabetic principle as well as opportunities to explore writing on their own terms, their writing will begin to reflect the alphabetic nature of English. Initially, they may represent just the beginning sounds of words, but eventually their spellings will appear more complete. Once we see words in which the beginning, ending, and middle sounds of one syllable words are spelled with letters that reasonably represent the sounds, we can be sure that children are well-grounded in their understanding of the alphabetic principle. We discuss the developmental nature of spelling in more depth in Chapter 5 as we explore writing in early childhood classrooms.

RESEARCH-BASED INSTRUCTIONAL STRATEGIES SUPPORTING UNDERSTANDING OF THE ALPHABETIC PRINCIPLE

As we said above, the components of the alphabetic principle are phonemic awareness and letter-name knowledge. In Chapter 3, we introduced strategies for developing phonological awareness. Among those strategies was an emphasis on teacher read-aloud. We want to revisit teacher read-aloud because of its importance in helping children understand the alphabetic principle through their understanding of the "concept of word."

Concept of Word

Morris and his colleagues (Morris, 1983; Morris, 1993; Morris, Bloodgood, Lomax, & Perney, 2003) have advanced the notion that understanding the "concept of word" is a critical prerequisite for development of phonemic awareness and subsequently understanding the alphabetic principle. Concept of word refers to children's awareness that words in written text are comprised of a set of letters bounded by blank spaces on either side of the word. Rathvon (2004) has called it the understanding that there is a match between spoken and written words when reading words in context. Thus, in the preceding sentence the phrase "concept of word" is composed of three words; the letters do not run together, but instead "concept" has blank spaces at its beginning and ending, as does "of" and "word." When reading "concept of word," we could point to three separate entities each composed of a string of letters representing the three words in the phrase. According to Morris et al. (2003), one of the manifestations of understanding "what is a word" is the ability to finger-point read a sentence. That is, the ability to point to each word in a text as it is read orally by the teacher or child. According to Rathvon (2004), "developing a stable concept of word is a benchmark in reading development that signals the child's ability to integrate several critical literacy skills, including letter recognition, knowledge of initial sounds, initial phoneme segmentation, the ability to identify word boundaries in running text, and the relationship between spoken and written words" (p. 117).

Awareness of beginning consonant sounds in words and an understanding of the concept of a word in written text makes a word "stand still" for a child. Letters that comprise an individual word become evident to the child, and the individual sounds forming the word can begin to be associated with letters. Figure 4.3 presents a likely developmental sequence.

In early childhood classrooms, the concept of a word can be developed through shared reading activities with enlarged text, such as big books.

Alphabet knowledge

Emerging phonemic awareness—initial sounds in words

Understanding of concept of word

Emerging phonemic awareness—ending and the middle sounds in words

Understanding of alphabetic principle—association of letters with sounds in written words

---

Figure 4.3   Developmental Sequence for Understanding the Alphabetic Principle

SOURCE: From Morris, D., Bloodgood, J. W., Lomax, R. G., & Perney, J., Developmental steps in learning to read: A longitudinal study in kindergarten and first grade, *Reading Research Quarterly, 38,* copyright © 2003, pp. 302–328.

The first reading of any book should always emphasize understanding and enjoyment of a new story. Subsequent readings can focus on studying the print for aspects of letter knowledge, concept of word, or sound awareness. During these shared rereadings, the teacher uses a pointer to track the print, word-by-word, as it is read. Sometimes the teacher might focus in on a word by asking a child to frame the word with his hands or by using a word window, first introduced to us by Holdaway (1979). (Figure 4.4 gives directions for making a word window that can be used to isolate a word in text.) Children easily memorize the text of many favorite stories, and these beloved books can be put in the library for independent and partner finger-point reading.

> Concept of word can be developed through shared reading activities with enlarged text.

Letter Knowledge

Clearly, letter knowledge is a vital component of understanding the alphabetic principle. Bradley and Jones (2007) identify four components of letter knowledge: letter-shape, letter-name, letter-sound, and letter-writing. These components are defined in Figure 4.5. Letter knowledge frequently begins with a child's awareness of his or her own first name in print, and particularly the first letter of the name. For many children, their name is the first stable written form that has meaning (Ferreiro & Teberosky, 1982). We can expect four-year-olds who have experiences with the written form of their first names to begin to recognize the letters to their name in the print around them. For instance, Annie incorporated letters from her name into the words she invented for her shopping list. Her mother reported that she recognized some of the letters from her name in the print on a cousin's tee shirt. Teachers can draw on this interest as they begin to develop children's letter knowledge.

> Letter knowledge frequently begins with a child's awareness of his or her own first name in print.

Mrs. Jones finds ways in her classroom of four-year-olds for the children to see their names in their environment. There is a pocket chart that contains the picture of each child in the class along with a card with each child's name. As children arrive each day, they find their name card and place it next to their picture as a way of signing in. Mrs. Jones makes a point to scramble the name cards each day so that the children have to take a careful look at the cards to find their individual names. On the mornings before sharing time, she also writes each child's name on tag

1. Cut a window in a piece of poster paper. The poster paper should be approximately 5" by 12". The window should be as tall as one line of text in a big book and wide enough to show three to four words.

Example

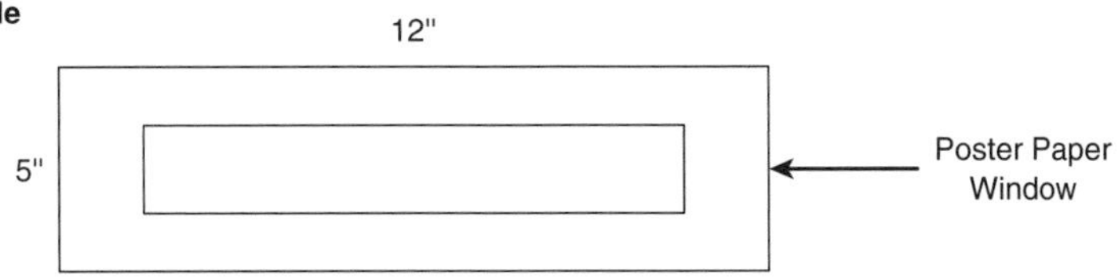

12"

5"

Poster Paper
Window

2. Cut a sliding mask from another piece of poster paper. The mask will be used to open and close the window. The mask should be wider than the window but less than 5" wide. The mask should be about 15" long.

3. Fasten a strip to the back of the word window. Taping the edges of the strip to the poster paper window will make the sliding mask steadier. Leave a loop the width of the mask. The mask will slide through the loop to open and close the word window.

Example

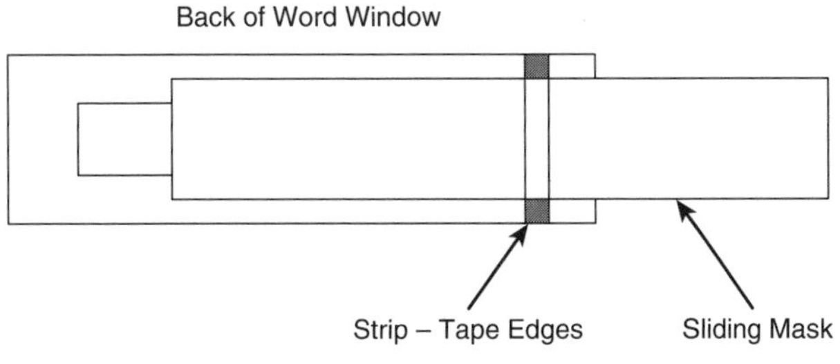

Back of Word Window

Strip – Tape Edges   Sliding Mask

Figure 4.4   Making a Word Window

Letter-Shape Knowledge: The ability to distinguish letters based on key visual features including lines, curves, orientation, and direction.

Letter-Name Knowledge: The understanding that a letter is a symbol, and that each letter-name represents both an upper and lowercase form.

Letter-Sound Knowledge: The understanding that letters represent sounds, and that some letters represent more than one sound.

Letter-Writing Ability: The ability to write letters as compared to producing letter-like forms.

Figure 4.5 Components of Letter Knowledge

SOURCE: Adapted from Bradley, B. A., & Jones, J. (2007). Sharing alphabet books in early childhood classrooms. *The Reading Teacher, 60,* 452–463.

board strips, which she places around the perimeter of the circle time rug. As children arrive in the classroom with something to share, they locate their name and place what they have brought by their name.

At other times, Mrs. Jones and the children develop language experience stories that incorporate the children's names. When seventh graders from an area middle school came to read to the children, Mrs. Jones photographed the event. Later, with Mrs. Jones's help writing the words, each child composed several sentences about a photograph. Each child's picture and dictation became a page in a class book.

Mrs. Jones recognizes that some letters are not so easily learned. She is aware of research indicating that children first learn letters positioned earlier in the alphabet (Justice, Pence, Bowles, & Wiggins, 2006). The research indicates to her that children will learn some letter names without purposeful instruction, and that some of her instruction should be directed at teaching the letters that children might not learn as easily (Justice, Pence, Bowles, & Wiggins, 2006). Mrs. Jones knows that exposure is a key in learning all the letter names, and she has created a classroom environment in which letters are emphasized in many ways.

One way letters are emphasized regularly in Mrs. Jones's classroom is through an alphabet chart she made with the letters of the alphabet in a horizontal array that matches the phrasing of the alphabet song. There were several decisions made here, by Mrs. Jones, that address this stage of understanding the alphabetic principle. First, Mrs. Jones decided to make the chart with the lowercase letters because she knew that the children's experiences with letters outside the classroom were mainly with the uppercase forms (the children have been exposed to capital letters in the writing of their names) (see Figure 4.6). She also knows the terms uppercase and lowercase are abstract to the children, so Mrs. Jones uses the terms "capital" and "small" letters. Another decision is the song—Mrs. Jones thought the alphabet song ideal, since some of the children started school knowing it, and they helped other children learn it. Mrs. Jones keenly did not assume that because children could sing the song that they could also recognize or name the individual letters. The song quickly became a support for the children to use the chart in letter naming activities. As the children sing the alphabet song, Mrs. Jones points to each letter. She does not always start the song at the beginning; instead she frequently focuses towards the middle or end of the song, and has the children sing just one phrase, such as "l, m, n, o, p." Then she asks questions about that phrase, (e.g., "Which one is the n?") as she helps a child finger-point read, using the song to get to the "n."

Letters are also emphasized through the prominent number of books found throughout Mrs. Jones's classroom, and this includes many alphabet books. She has found that reading a book to the children before putting it into a classroom center seems to stimulate their interest in reading the book independently. This is especially true for alphabet books. Sometimes Mrs. Jones reads an alphabet book in its entirety to the class, if she thinks the reading will hold their attention. Other times she only reads

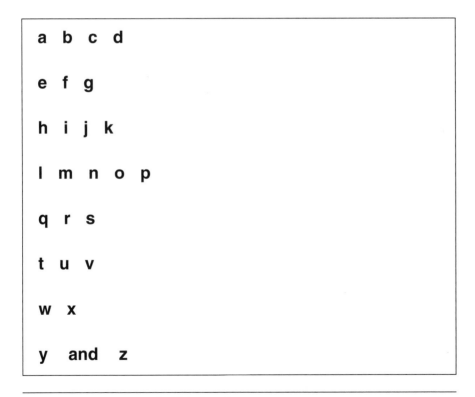

Figure 4.6   Mrs. Jones's Alphabet Chart

a portion of the book. For example, when Mrs. Jones introduced *Alphabatics* by Suse MacDonald (1986) to the class she recognized the potential for the book to stimulate a lot of discussion. Each letter is associated with one word, and in the illustrations we see the transformation of the letter into the word. To illustrate, the two strokes of the letter "h," the stick and the hump, are transformed through a series of illustrations into a house (the hump) with a chimney (the stick). Mrs. Jones did not attempt to read every page. Instead she let several children select a letter that the class explored in the pages of the book. Each time there was a rich discussion of the distinctive features of that letter, and how each feature evolved from the letter into an illustration of the associated word. She then invited the children over the week to read the book with a buddy. Figure 4.7 comprises a list of some of Mrs. Jones's favorite alphabet books. She realizes that within the broad category of alphabet books there are several distinct genres. These include books that

- incorporate alphabet letters as characters in a story
- have elements of language play such as rhyme and alliteration
- engage children in prediction
- present pictures and words associated with each letter

Not every activity with an alphabet book must be directly associated with learning letter names. Mrs. Jones recognizes that children will learn many of the letter names indirectly through their interaction with alphabet books.

Mrs. Jones has also used alphabet books as a springboard for writing activities. Following the genre of pictures and words associated with each letter-name, the children have constructed individual and class books around themes such as animals, friends, and the mall. Each year themes vary based on the class's interests.

There are other ways that Mrs. Jones exposes the children to the alphabet letters. She mounted alphabet cards along one wall at eye level for the children. The writing center contains letter stencils. As children write letters using the stencils, the tracing focuses their attention on the features that make each letter distinctive. To illustrate, uppercase "E" is distinctive from uppercase "F" because it has three horizontal lines to F's two. Figure 4.8 is an example of writing from a child who is exploring letter writing with stencils. There are cookie cutter letter shapes that children can use at the sand table, and for making letter shapes out of clay. Every center has a sign-in sheet, which is one more time children focus on letters as they write their names.

I. Story

Kipper's A to Z: An Alphabet Adventure by Mick Inkpen (Kipper, the puppy, is a series character in many Kipper books, and is a favorite of the children in Mrs. Jones's class.)

Alpha Oops! The Day Z Went First by Althea Kontic (Bob Kolar, illustrator)

The Alphabet Tree by Leo Lionni

Chicka Chicka Boom Boom by Bill Martin Jr. & John Archambault (Lois Ehlert, illustrator)

Shiver Me Letters: A Pirate ABC by June Sobel (Henry Cole, illustrator)

II. Language Play

K is for Kissing a Cool Kangaroo by Giles Andrean (Guy Parker-Rees, illustrator)

Naughty Little Monkeys by Jim Aylesworth (Henry Cole, illustrator)

Animalia by Graeme Base

Click, Clack, Quackity-Quack by Doreen Cronin (Betsy Lewin, illustrator)

Dr. Seuss's ABC by Dr. Seuss

Alphabears: An ABC Book by Kathleen Hague (Michael Hague, illustrator)

Alison's Zinnia by Anita Lobel

Apricot ABC by Miska Miles (Peter Parnall, illustrator)

A Peaceable Kingdom: The Shaker ABECEDARIUS by Alice and Martin Provensen

Max's ABC by Rosemary Wells

III. Prediction

Q is for Duck by Mary Elting and Michael Folsom (Jack Kent, illustrator)

The Z was Zapped by Chris Van Allsburg

IV. Letters and Words/Pictures

Eating the Alphabet: Fruits and Vegetables from A to Z by Lois Ehlert

Alphabatics by Suse MacDonald

Alphabet Explosion: Search and Count from Alien to Zebra by John Nickle

The Construction Alphabet Book by Jerry Pallotta (Rob Bolster, illustrator)

Figure 4.7   Mrs. Jones's Favorite Alphabet Books

Modeling Writing

Writing experiences are among the very best ways for children to see the process of mapping spoken language onto written language. Let's look at how Mrs. Jones emphasized the alphabetic principle as she modeled writing of a grocery list. Thinking-aloud is a strategy for verbalizing thought processes during reading and writing. Mrs. Jones used a think-aloud to make explicit the process of going from thoughts to saying words to writing them.

> Writing experiences are among the very best ways for children to see the process of mapping spoken language onto written language.

Figure 4.8   Exploring Letter Writing With Stencils

She helped children learn the vocabulary of instruction. Children need to understand basic concepts such as word, sound, and letter, and teachers cannot assume that young children have developed these basic concepts. Notice that Mrs. Jones was purposeful in her use of these words as she thought aloud. She did not just say, "I'll make a list." Instead she was careful to say she was writing down words. In the same way, she used the language "sound" and "letter" as she discussed the relationship between the beginning sound of "pancake" and how that sound was represented in print.

Mrs. Jones used several strategies to focus the children's attention on the individual sounds of the spoken word. In emphasizing the initial sound in "pancake," she reiterated the /p/ sound at least three times before beginning to write the word. Another technique was rubber-banding, which she did to help the children be aware of the four sounds comprising the spoken word "milk." Rubber-banding is simply elongating the pronunciation of a word. Sometimes Mrs. Jones has the children engage in this process with her as she uses a rubber band to provide a concrete analogy to the notion of stretching out the sounds in a word. When Mrs. Jones "rubber-banded" the word "milk," she purposefully separated the initial sound, /m/, from the remainder of the word to emphasize the onset and rime of the spoken word "milk." Of course, Mrs. Jones was careful in not overusing any of these strategies because she did not want to lose the children's attention.

ADDRESSING DIVERSITY

We are seeing many children in our schools that come from very different language backgrounds, including languages with nonalphabetic scripts. These children may have less exposure to alphabet letters. It is particularly important to model the writing of individual letters for these children. The sequence and direction for making the lines and circles of a letter cannot be discerned by looking at the already formed letter.

Some suggestions to help children become aware of the distinctive features of the individual letters are listed below:

- Incorporating alphabet games—in which children match letters—and alphabet puzzles in the classroom will give children experiences comparing letters to each other (Schickedanz, 1999).
- Writing each segment with a different color marker when modeling how to write individual letters or when preparing alphabet matching materials further emphasizes distinctive alphabetic features. (Schickedanz, 1999).
- Playing alphabet guessing games with small groups of children by writing one line at a time and having the children make a guess at what the letter might be provides additional opportunities for learning (Schickedanz, 1999).
- Putting alphabet strips on classroom desks will make it easier for children to inspect letters closely.
- Finding opportunities to write children's names every day, spelling aloud the name while writing it, and avoiding Anglicizing the name to make it easier to pronounce, leads to more exposure (Strickland & Schickedanz, 2004).
- Providing opportunities to trace letters in sand and to make letters with clay incorporates tactile experiences that benefit many children.
- Stocking the classroom with alphabet books in languages other than English, and letting children take these books home so their parents can read the books to them honors their culture (Strickland & Schickedanz, 2004).

SUMMARY

To reiterate what we have developed in this chapter, understanding the alphabetic principle means understanding that we write down spoken words by representing the individual sounds in those words with letters.

We have referred to this process at several places in this chapter as mapping sounds onto letters. The components of understanding the alphabetic principle are phonemic awareness, letter knowledge, and many concrete experiences with the mapping process.

Writing

5

Rebecca launched into a vivid discussion about the weed whacker that her father had brought home as she drew a picture of him working in their yard. She imitated the sound of this new equipment, and she brought life and meaning to her drawing as she described how he had used it to "go around the driveway" and "get rid of the grass." Later Rebecca's teacher, Ashley, observed what appeared to be exaggerated speech as she added some letters to the side of her picture—YYR.

HOW ARE READING AND WRITING CONNECTED IN EARLY LITERACY DEVELOPMENT?

Literacy encompasses both reading and writing. Children acquire information about reading and writing before formal instruction begins (Bus, 2002). Frequently, the term "emergent" is joined to literacy to refer to this very beginning process. Teale and Sulzby (1986) helped initiate our thinking about emergent literacy when they wrote, "it is not reasonable to point to a time in a child's life when literacy begins" (p. xix). As the term emergent literacy suggests, reading and writing coexist in their development along a continuum from emergent to conventional behaviors. Clay (2001) confirmed the relationship between reading and writing. "Almost every child learns to read print and write print at the same time (p. 91)."

> Children acquire information about reading and writing before formal instruction begins.

We devote Chapter 2 to language development; however, some points are important to discuss here. We know, from a long series of research studies, the powerful role that vocabulary knowledge plays in reading comprehension. Vocabulary knowledge is a strong predictor of word reading ability at the end of first grade and of reading comprehension in eleventh grade (Juel, 2006). Accomplished authors use their knowledge of word meanings to make their writing more interesting. Dyson (2002) has written about the function of oral language in early writing development. It is a medium for children to invest meaning in the graphics they produce by "naming them or otherwise connecting them to important people or things" (Dyson, 2002, p. 130). To illustrate, Dyson (2002) introduces us to a child who wrote by "telling an elaborate story, blending experiences from the television, the movies, and everyday life to create dramatic, imaginative narratives for anyone who would listen" (p. 128). Thus, we see that reading and writing are tied together through their connection to oral language.

Both reading and writing have their roots in children's exploration of the phonological nature of written language through invented spelling. Invented spelling is a child's attempt to write a word when the spelling of the word is not already known. Invented spellings are phonemically based because children attempt to make a sound-to-letter correspondence when they invent a spelling. Because invented spellings are phonemically based, they are sometimes called phonic spellings. Schickedanz (1999) describes the process as segmenting words into their constituent phonemes and coding each one with an alphabet letter (p. 122). As we will see later in this chapter, invented spellings evolve from simple to more sophisticated and finally to conventional representations for words.

> Both reading and writing have their roots in children's exploration of the phonological nature of written language through invented spelling.

In the chapter on phonological awareness (Chapter 3), we discuss research that pointed to the connection between vocabulary development and phonemic awareness. As the number of spoken words a child learns increases, the greater the child's need to focus on the phonological structure of each new word also increases. This point deserves reiteration here. The roots of reading and writing are in understanding of the alphabetic principle, which leads to a child investigating the phonological structure of words via invented spellings. Figure 5.1 depicts the connections among oral language, phonemic awareness and letter knowledge, the alphabetic principle, invented spelling, and literacy acquisition.

The alphabetic principle is the understanding that written English is phonemically based. Through invented spelling, children explore the sound structure of words by using letters to represent the constituent phonemes in words. Both the understanding of the alphabetic principle and the ability to invent spellings require some level of phonemic awareness, which is grounded in children's oral language. In Figure 5.1, double-headed arrows are used to illustrate the reciprocal nature of the processes. Oral language is depicted as the foundation, or

> Just as oral language contributes to literacy acquisition, so does literacy acquisition contribute back to oral language.

starting point, in the process. However, just as oral language contributes to literacy acquisition, so does literacy acquisition contribute back to oral language. Thus, oral language is both a resource and a beneficiary (Clay, 2001) of language acquisition. Likewise, an understanding of the alphabetic principle contributes to early writing through invented spelling, and as children explore written language through invented spellings their understanding of the alphabetic principle becomes firmly established.

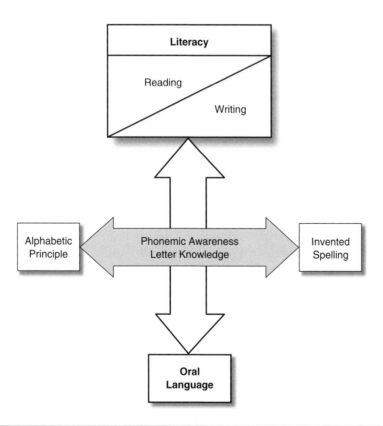

Figure 5.1   The Reciprocal Relationship Between Oral Language and Literacy

WHAT DOES RESEARCH SAY ABOUT
EMERGENT WRITING DEVELOPMENT?

We can divide writing into two major categories: pre-alphabetic and alphabetic. Of course it is important to remember that there can be crossover between the two categories until the child's concept of the alphabetic principle is firmly solidified. By firmly solidified, we do not mean that all skills for alphabetic writing are in place; rather it means that the child has the insight that sounds map onto letters in a systematic way in written English.

Pre-Alphabetic Writing

Initially, children's writing appears as random marks on a page that most adults call scribbling. However, Schickedanz (1999) points out that these early markings are experiments with writing tools—a child's discovery of how lines on a page result from the movement of a pen. Eventually, children begin to distinguish between drawing and writing. Frequent literacy experiences contribute to their ability to make this distinction, including their own experimenting with paper and pen, watching adults as they model writing, and participating in shared reading and writing events.

At age three, Korben produced marks that say "elephant" (see Figure 5.2). Although it is not clear whether the writing/drawing distinction is there, at age four he has clearly made the distinction. He was specific in indicating that Figure 5.3 shows a picture of a Viking. Notice the difference between Figure 5.3 and 5.4. Both were produced on the same day. Korben indicated that his writing in Figure 5.4 said, "We live and we love each other." At the end of kindergarten, he has nicely integrated writing and drawing in a composition for his cousin living in Oklahoma that included, as described by Korben, Pris with her purse, her two dogs, and the ducks in the pond and yard around her house (Figure 5.5). He has included the message "I ♥ you!" We see that he has incorporated characteristics of written language that he has seen in his environment, including rebus writing and punctuation.

Baghban (2007) has written about the importance of drawing in children's writing development. Children use drawing to help organize ideas, construct meaning from experiences, and make sense out of these experiences (p. 21). She indicates that even up to age seven, children may speak in ambiguous ways about whether a drawing is writing or the writing is drawing. She introduces us to Ronald, who at age six asked, "What am I going to write a picture of?" (p. 23). Baghban (2007) advises teachers to

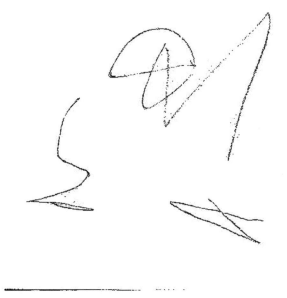

Figure 5.2   Korben, at Age 3, Produced Marks That Say Elephant

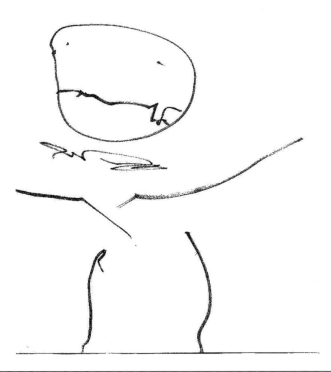

Figure 5.3   Korben, at Age 4, Indicated he Had Drawn a Viking

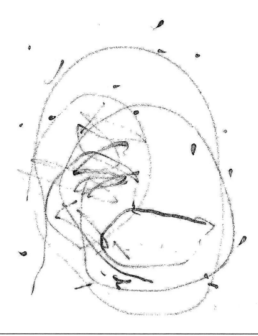

Figure 5.4 Korben's Writing of "We Live and We Love Each Other"

Figure 5.5 Korben's Writing and Drawing for Pris

let the children be the judges about whether their products should be treated as drawing or writing.

As children are sorting out the differences between drawing and writing as separate forms of expression, they make attempts at writing that look like the writing they see in their environment. Ferreiro and

Teberosky (1982) refer to this as reproducing the features of the basic writing form. This phenomenon appears to be cross-cultural. Harste, Woodward, and Burke (1984) reported writing of children from Saudi Arabia and Israel, all of which reflected the unique qualities of Arabic and Hebrew script. Figure 5.6 depicts the writing of Alex, a four-year-old child living in a Midwest state in the United States. Notice how his writing has the recurring, up and down quality of English cursive writing. Before completing the writing in Figure 5.6, Alex and his father were coloring pictures together. When they switched to writing, Alex wrote his name, and then he told his father he did not know how to write a lot of other words so he was going to write some "bumps." In contrast, look at the writing of Junjun in Figure 5.7. Junjun, who lives in China, wrote this on her birthday. Initially when asked to write, she refused, saying she did not know how. However, with some encouragement, she started by writing the character in the middle, and then added more character-like writing. After she finished, she pointed to characters in her writing and said, "Today is my birthday. I give you a birthday cake." Yet another example, Figure 5.8, shows the work of Howard, who is a precocious writer at four years old. Howard sees both English and Chinese writing in his home. He made this list of words he could write in both languages.

Figure 5.6 Alex's Bumps

Figure 5.7   Junjun's Writing on her Birthday

Figure 5.8   Howard's Writing in Chinese and English

Clay (1975) observed several characteristics of early writing. Through an understanding of these characteristics, what may seem to be mere scribbling and misspellings are actually bold explorations of the writing system of language.

> What may seem to be mere scribbling is actually bold explorations of the writing system of language.

- *Recurring patterns including movements with pen that resemble patterns that recur in adult writing.* We observe recurring movements in Alex's writing in Figure 5.6. Also notice that Alex has written a mirror image of his name. Reversed letters are common in the writing of young children, who may not yet have firmly established the notion that orientation matters. Schickedanz and Casbergue (2004) point out that when a child makes the first move in the wrong direction the letter is reversed (p. 23). Although a violation of accepted writing conventions, Alex's mirror image writing shows a good understanding of spacial relations (Schickedanz, 1999).
- *Repeated use of a small set of letters (frequently letters in the child's name) to generate words.* This is evident in Morelia's drawing of a snowman (Figure 5.9). Morelia's teacher has recorded her description of the picture, but we see that Morelia has also written several letter strings that incorporate the letters from her name. Morelia's composition was made on lined notebook paper. Note that in contrast to Luis's writing that we saw in Chapter 4, Morelia gives no notice to the importance to the lines on the page. Rather, her focus is on the drawing of the snowman (during a rare time in Oklahoma City when there was enough snow to build a snowman), labeling the picture, and writing her name.
- *Exploration of the flexibility of letter parts to invent new letters.* Children produce letter-like forms that resemble real letters, yet on close examination we realize they are not letters at all. Schickedanz and Casbergue (2004) call these letter-like forms mock letters, which they point out contain the segments that are the building blocks of real letters (p. 18), lines (horizontal, vertical, and diagonal), and circles or parts of circles. We can see various levels of sophistication in the writing of Korben, Pedro, and Brandon. In Figure 5.10, Korben has written the message "Happy Mother's Day." If we compare this with his writing in Figure 5.4, we see similarities in the large circular motions and the dots, and when we look into the center of Figure 5.10 we see some characters that resemble letters. Figure 5.11 was produced in the fall of prekindergarten

when Pedro was learning to write his name. The horizontal array at the top contains forms that resemble the letters in "Pedro." In addition, we see aspects of the letters in his name throughout the composition. Brandon is in kindergarten (Figure 5.12). He is writing letters and letter-like strings, which is characteristic of the writing of many kindergarten children. It is clear that Brandon has a sense of how words appear in print, both in length and linear arrangement.

- *Contrasts between shapes and word patterns. Clay (1975) has described this as comparing two things that are at the same time similar and different (p. 36).* Clay gives the example of the letters A, H, M, and W, which contrast through lines and angles. In Howard's writing (Figure 5.8), the contrast is with both Chinese characters and English words. Note the Chinese characters in the center of his page. The first two characters represent concepts "up" and "no." However, the contrast is not in meaning but in the appearance of the characters. When the first character (representing "up") is flipped on a horizontal axis and one more stroke added, it becomes the character for "no." Similarly, the fourth, fifth, and sixth characters in his string of Chinese characters also illustrate this principle of contrasts, in that they all incorporate aspects of the fourth character. We also see this contrast in the list of words ending with the letter "o" (to, no, yoo) and in the pairing of "fool" and "Foof."

- *Inventories of known things.* Clay (1975) describes this as children taking "stock of their own learning" (p. 31) by arranging words, letters, numbers, and drawings in sets. Ethan, a kindergartener, produced the work in Figure 5.13. This is a good illustration of an inventory. In this example, the child has titled his work "Alphabet," and then grouped letters in a box, separate from the drawings of people.

Alphabetic Writing

Although prealphabetic writing is the type that will be seen in most prekindergarten classes and at the beginning of kindergarten, it is beneficial for teachers of our youngest children to be familiar with the continuum of spelling development that they may encounter in their classrooms. Invented spelling evolves in recognizable stages (Richgels, 2002).

Figure 5.9   Morelia's Drawing of a Snowman

Figure 5.10 Korben's Writing of Happy Mother's Day

Figure 5.11 Pedro's Early Name Writing

Figure 5.12 Brandon's Writing of Letter-Like Strings

Figure 5.13 Ethan's Inventory of Alphabet Letters

The beginning of invented spelling is very much a tactile-kinesthetic process in which children actually realize how the mouth feels when an individual phoneme is produced. Phonemes begin as air in the lungs moving through the throat and out the mouth. Vowels are made as air moves through the vibrating vocal chords, and the tongue and lips shape the air chamber in the throat. A consonant sound is made by stopping the flow of air in some way using the tongue, lips, teeth, or roof of the mouth. If the vocal chords vibrate, the consonant sound is voiced; otherwise it is voiceless. If the flow of air is directed through the nasal cavity, the consonant is categorized as a nasal (typically /m/, /n/, and /ng/ as in "sing") (Moats, 2000; Pinker, 1994). Juel (2006) has suggested that phonemic awareness may begin with children feeling phonemes in their mouth, thus the term tactile kinesthetic is applied to invented spelling.

Children begin invented spelling through a reliance on letter names (Richgels, 2002), thus the inclusion of letter knowledge along with phonemic awareness in our depiction of the reciprocal relationship between the alphabetic principle and invented spelling in Figure 5.1. Children spell a sound using the letter-name that is closest in pronunciation to the sound. For instance, a very common spelling for "chick" is "hk." Let's analyze the child's logic for this spelling. Begin to say "chick" but do not say it all the way. You will have said the first phoneme in "chick." (You may have included the vowel sound in "chick" as well. Do not worry about that. The phenomenon of coarticulation makes it almost impossible to pronounce the individual sounds in a word. That is, the pronunciation of one sound runs together with the pronunciation of the sounds that surround it.) Having said /ch/, now say the letter-name "H." Notice the common feeling in your mouth as your say the sound, then the letter-name. You should feel your tongue against the roof of your mouth just behind you teeth when you say /ch/ and when you say "H." That is the logic an inventive speller uses to spell "chick" beginning with the letter "H." As you experiment with the pronunciation of "chick," you will also notice that the last sound in this word corresponds to the way the letter-name "K" is pronounced. This spelling process is known as letter-name spelling. Read (1986) first recognized this phenomenon by examining the spellings produced by preschool and kindergarten children by having the Sesame Street puppet Ernie ask children to spell words on a small easel using magnetic uppercase letters. Letter name spelling represents the beginning of an understanding of the alphabetic principle.

Initially, children may represent each syllable in a word with one letter. Ferreiro and Teberosky (1982) have named this the syllabic hypothesis, and they call it a leap forward in children's understandings about writing. Children move from an understanding of a "global correspondence between the written string and the oral expression and progressing to a correspondence between parts of the text (individual letters) and parts of the utterance (syllables)" (pp. 198–199). This is the beginning of their understanding that writing represents sound segments of speech. Eventually they progress to representing the initial and final sounds in a word or syllable and finally to representing the vowel sounds in words. As children begin to notice the print in their environment and in books, they will incorporate the standard spellings of words they see frequently (i.e., high frequency words) as well as information about spelling patterns such as silent letters in words.

Working with pre-alphabetic writers whose literacy environment was Spanish, Ferreiro and Teberosky (1982) recognized that initially children attempted to make their writing correspond to the size of the object or person. They report the request of one child to have the teacher write her name. "You have to make it longer because yesterday was my birthday" (p. 184). One of the authors of this book (Griffith) had a similar experience with a first grader over the spelling of the word "ox." He explained that the spelling "o" and "x" could not say "ox" because an ox is very big. A word with only two letters just was not big enough to stand for such a big animal.

According to Ferreiro and Teberosky (1982), when children write from a print model (as compared to a cursive model), they begin to incorporate a hypothesis that a minimum number of characters are needed to write a word. These researchers suggest that the conflict between the minimum quantity of characters (their theories about how many letters should be in a word) and the syllabic hypothesis (representing each syllable in a word with one letter) may help children advance in their understandings about alphabetic writing.

The examples in Figures 5.14, 5.15, 5.16, and 5.17 are from one kindergarten classroom in Norman, Oklahoma. They illustrate the range of spelling development within one classroom. Austin (Figure 5.14) drew on at least three strategies to produce his list of ways to show someone you love them. His list was written near Valentine's Day, and it appears he is using print from his environment to write love and kiss. In fact, love is within the assignment directions. He has employed the syllabic hypotheses for some of the words he wrote, for example "U" in the expression "I love you" in the first line, and "U" and "B" in the expression "Will you be my friend" in the second line. Finally, Austin is using letter-name spellings for several words, including "mi" for "my," "frd" for "friend," "hg" for "hug," and "hlp" for "help". Also notice the spelling of "ehom" for "them" in line three. This spelling is very close to the elongated pronunciation of "them" one might hear in Oklahoma.

Mayer (2007) discussed how children move forward and backward on a developmental spelling continuum depending on the communication task, and more difficult tasks may result in more emergent forms of writing. We can see Mayer's point illustrated in Austin's writing sample. Let's look at line two. This five-word sentence took quite a bit of effort. Austin

Figure 5.14 Austin's Ways to Show Love

had to remember what he wanted to say and coordinate that with where he was in producing his message. Along with that, he had to work through a sound-to-symbol spelling process to produce a spelling for each word. Each of these tasks, which a proficient adult writer can do automatically, required Austin's conscious attention, and required that he revert to some syllabic spelling in order to preserve the message he was trying to convey.

> Children move forward and backward on a developmental spelling continuum depending on the communication task.

Austin is not consistently representing vowel sounds in his writing, in contrast to Alex D. (Figure 5.15), who is doing so. (In this chapter we show writing from two children named Alex. We point out that one of our Alexs' last name begins with a "D," and that he writes his name "Alexd." However, we will refer to him as Alex D.) With some concentration and knowledge of letter-name strategies (refer to Figure 5.18), it is possible to read Alex D.'s messages. Let's look at line two. He has omitted a consonant in the second word, "wot," his spelling for "want," specifically the "n" before the final consonant "t." In actual pronunciation, this nasal sound is "swallowed" into the vowel (Henderson, 1985). Say "want" yourself and feel what happens in your mouth. Consequently, for a letter-name speller such as Alex D., who may not have seen "want" in print or at least has not taken note of the spelling of the word in print, three letters seem to do the trick for spelling this word. Likewise, "pla" and "wet" seem quite logical spellings for "play" and "with." The long vowel sound in "play" is spelled with the letter-name synonymous with the sound. The word "with" contains three phonemes, all of which have been represented in the spelling "wet." The short "i" vowel sound is represented with the letter-name closest to its pronunciation. Notice that in line three, Alex D. has carried the last letter in his spelling for "clothes" over to the next line. Children must learn to organize their writing on a page. That includes leaving spaces between words, and clustering letters together within words. That is something that will come to Alex D. through teacher modeling of writing and attending to print in books.

Avery (Figure 5.16) uses a strategy that is common among young children to distinguish between words. Line five of Avery's list is "Be nice to [unreadable]." Avery uses dots to separate words, indicating a beginning understanding of the concept of word in written text. In Figure 5.17, Ethan, who produced the inventory in Figure 5.13, is employing a version of Clay's (1975) recurring patterns discussed earlier in this chapter. According to Clay, children who know only a few words may take a short cut, repeating the same words to construct a long message. In this case Ethan used the recurring principle and environmental print to respond to the task at hand.

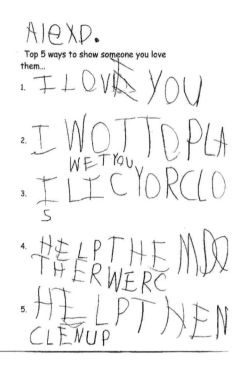

Figure 5.15 Alex D. Incorporates Vowels in His Writing

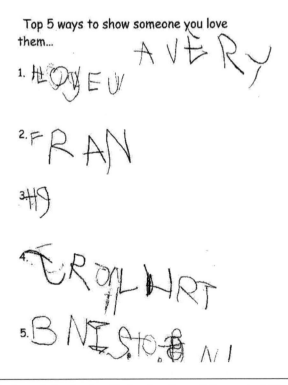

Figure 5.16 Avery's Beginning Understanding of Concept of Word

Ethan

Top 5 ways to show someone you love them...

1. LOVE NRS ISodC

2. LOVE Maggie

3. LOVE JORPAN

4. LOVE AJ

5. LoveALe,xD

Figure 5.17 Ethan Employs the Recurring Principle

ASSESSING WRITING

How can we use children's writing to assess what they are learning about the English writing system? As we think about assessing children's writing, we need to consider progress in four areas: letter knowledge, print concepts, alphabetic principle, and text patterns. Characteristics to look for in children's writing are outlined in Figure 5.19.

> As we think about assessing children's writing, we need to consider progress in four areas: letter knowledge, print concepts, alphabetic principle, and text patterns.

Using the information in Figure 5.19, let's assess some of the children's writing we have seen in this chapter. Observing Rebecca, our child at the beginning of this chapter, we see how important talk was as she conveyed her message about the weed whacker. She labeled her drawing with "YYR." "Y" is a common spelling for the /w/ sound at the beginning of "weed" and "whacker." Rebecca appears to be using syllabic writing, and is at the beginning of understanding the alphabetic

---

Consonants

- The consonant letters "m" and "n" may be left out when they come before another consonant.
- Common syllables found at the end of words, such "ble," "en," "er," "ing" may be spelled with one letter, for example "tchr" for "teacher" and "gatn" for getting.
- "Y" is frequently used to represent the consonant sound /w/, for example "yot" for "want." The logic of this is simple. Start to say "want," but do not say it all the way. The beginning sound of "want" is very much like the pronunciation of the letter name for "y."
- "H" is a common spelling for the /ch/ sound. The logic for this is the same as the "y" spelling for /w/. The sound /ch/ is contained in the letter name pronunciation for "h."
- Consonant blends /tr/ may be spelled with "chr" or "hr," and /dr/ with "jr."

Vowels

- Long vowels are typically spelled with the vowel letter, as in "nis" for "nice."
- Short vowels are spelled with the vowel letter name closest to the pronunciation of the vowel sound.

Short vowel sound	Spelled with	Example/Standard spelling
a	a	cat
e	a	halp/help, gat/get
i	e	wet/with
o	i	hip/hop
u	o or u	op/up

Figure 5.18 Some Tips for Reading Invented Spellings

NOTE: You can hear the pronunciation of each short vowel at the beginning of each of these words—a/apple, e/elephant, i/igloo, o/ostrich, and u/umbrella. Just start to say the word but do not say it all the way, and you will have the pronunciation for the short vowel that begins each word.

principle. Remember in Chapter 3, we observed Rebecca playing with language about monkeys jumping on the bed. We know that she is beginning to focus on the sounds in spoken language, and that insight combined with some letter knowledge has resulted in her label of "YYR" for "weed whacker."

How do we see letter knowledge beginning to develop?

- Korben and Alex incorporate reoccurring patterns from the writing in their environment into their own writing.

Letter Knowledge

- Reoccurring movements resembling writing in environment
- Producing mock letters
- Writing letter strings
- Using letters from own name
- Learning to write own name

Learning about letters is a critical aspect of literacy learning. Mock letters indicate a child attending to distinctive features of individual letters. Producing letter strings are an indication that a child is beginning to notice what individual letters look like. They indicate an attention to the horizontal array of print. Children's names are among the most important pieces of print in their experiences, and one of the first things they will learn to write. Each of these characteristics in their writing indicates the beginnings of letter knowledge.

Print Concepts

- Writing distinguished from drawing
- Organizing writing on a page
- Distinguishing individual words within compositions
- Indicating directionality: top-to-bottom and left-to-right

Print concepts are the arbitrary conventions of writing that children learn through experiences with print. Children must learn that it is the print on the page, not the illustrations, that is read. We can talk about the pictures in various ways from one reading of the text to another, but the pronunciation of the words remains constant. When reading and writing, we typically begin at the top and move across the page from left-to-right and top-to-bottom. While words may run together in spoken utterances, words in print are separated by spaces. We can observe these understandings beginning in children's scribbling.

Alphabetic Principle

- Syllabic writing
- Letter-name spelling
  - ○ Early letter-name spelling with beginning and ending sounds represented
  - ○ Vowel sounds represented

The major linchpin in children's writing development is their understanding of the alphabetic principle. It indicates that children understand how our writing system works. They know that adults use a conventional set of symbols—letters—to represent spoken utterances, and that this representation takes place at the level of individual sounds.

Text Patterns

- Reproducing environmental print in writing
- Using rebus writing
- Attempting to convey a message
- Producing reoccurring sentence patterns
- Knowing that patterns in text vary based on the purpose: stories, information text, letters, poems, lists are among the different patterns

Children have to learn that ideas are organized around patterns based on the message to be conveyed. As young children attempt to convey messages, they employ strategies such as using environmental print, inserting rebuses in their writing, and producing reoccurring sentence patterns.

Figure 5.19 Assessing Children's Writing Development in Four Areas

- Korben, Pedro, and Brandon incorporate some mock letters in their writing. Brandon is writing letter strings that incorporate letter-like forms as well as actual letters. Pedro is learning to write his name.
- Morelia incorporates letters from her name in her snowman composition.
- Ethan shows his letter knowledge through his inventory of the alphabet.

What aspects of print concepts appear in the children's writing?

- Korben, Morelia, and Brandon distinguish between drawing and writing.
- Alex organizes his writing from top-to-bottom across the page. He is aware that writing typically occurs in a horizontal array.
- Avery uses dots to distinguish words within a sentence.
- Howard demonstrates his understanding of directionality with his lists that go from left-to-right and top-to-bottom.

What understanding of the alphabetic principle is demonstrated in the children's writing?

- Austin and Avery move back and forth along a continuum drawing upon syllabic writing, early letter-name spelling, and representing vowels.
- Alex D., whose writing is readable, clearly understands the alphabetic principle.

What aspects of text patterns are appearing in the children's writing?

- At the end of kindergarten, Korben incorporates rebus writing into his composition to convey a message.
- Ethan, Austin, and Alex D. include environmental print in their writing. Ethan attends to the names of children in the class and incorporates them in his writing.
- Ethan uses a reoccurring sentence pattern strategy in his list.

RESEARCH-BASED INSTRUCTIONAL STRATEGIES TO SUPPORT EMERGENT WRITING

In this section, we will focus on two aspects for supporting emergent writing: organizing the environment and organizing instruction. Writing is primarily a social activity. It involves interaction with adults and peers in an environment designed to promote writing experiences in meaningful contexts. This point is at the heart of organizing both the environment and the instruction in a classroom.

Over several decades now there has been much research on how writers work. This research has focused on writing as a process that involves a continuous interplay between three overlapping stages—organizing, drafting and revising, and editing. These stages are depicted in Figure 5.20. Organizing is the stage in which the writer determines the content and develops a plan for writing. For proficient, adult writers this stage may take up to 80 percent of the writing time. It is the stage for research to learn more about the topic, to ponder what to write and how to write it. It is a time of rehearsing ideas and discovering what one has to say. Drafting and revising involve getting ideas down and then making the ideas better through close examination and rewriting. In contrast to the organizing stage when the writer is still discovering and researching, drafting and revising deal with specific content. Editing is the fine-tuning of the document and focuses on mechanics. Now for the caveat, and it is an important one. *We cannot expect our youngest children to have mastered any one of these stages, much less to be able to coordinate all three in their writing.* However, as teachers, it is important to understand the writing process and to expose (through informal modeling) children as young as preschool to each stage. When we discuss organizing instruction, we will explore appropriate ways to involve children in the writing process with teacher support.

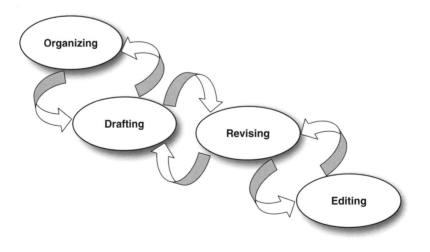

Figure 5.20 Four Overlapping Stages of Writing

Organizing the Environment

Every aspect of the classroom environment should support opportunities for children to engage in literacy activities. Neuman and Roskos (1992) studied the effect of focusing the environment around literacy, including introducing literacy objects into the environment on the literacy play of preschool age children. First, they used print to spatially organize the environment. Items in the environment were identified by print and picture, similar to the way items are organized in a hardware store. Play settings were created in three centers in a way that resembled real-life settings. For example, a kitchen contained actual items one might find in a kitchen: grocery items, cookbooks, coupons, children's books related to the center theme, and writing tools (pencils and paper). The results of their study were that children spent more time in reading and writing activities; they also used language more to communicate with others during literacy-related play.

> Every aspect of the classroom environment should support opportunities for children to engage in literacy activities.

Figures 5.21–5.23 are from Sally Wade's prekindergarten classroom at Lee Elementary School in Oklahoma City. She incorporates literacy in all of the activity centers in her classroom. Figure 5.21 is a music center, and Sally has included a book and writing tools in the basket on the floor. Some centers are more popular than others, and children sign up for their turn. In Figure 5.22, we see the sign-up sheet for the computer. Figure 5.24 is another an example of a sign-up sheet that incorporates children's names for reference. Sally finds meaningful ways for children to practice writing their names. Figure 5.23 is one example where children have indicated how they get to school. This data chart was constructed during a unit on transportation. When children are first learning how their names appear in print it is helpful for them to have models placed throughout the places where they might have to write their names. Books and writing tools are not just in the writing center, but are included in the dramatic center and the block center. Figure 5.25 is a checklist for a literacy-rich classroom that supports writing.

Organizing Instruction

Figure 5.26 depicts a graphic for organizing writing instruction in an early childhood classroom. The core of instruction is writing experiences in meaningful contexts organized around four levels of instructional support (Laframboise, Griffith, & Klesius, 1997). Teacher modeling occurs

Figure 5.21 Literacy in All Centers

SOURCE: Figure 5.21 reprinted with permission from classroom of Sally Wade, Lee Elementary School, Oklahoma City, OK Public Schools.

Figure 5.22 Sign-Up Sheet

SOURCE: Figure 5.22 reprinted with permission from classroom of Sally Wade, Lee Elementary School, Oklahoma City, OK Public Schools.

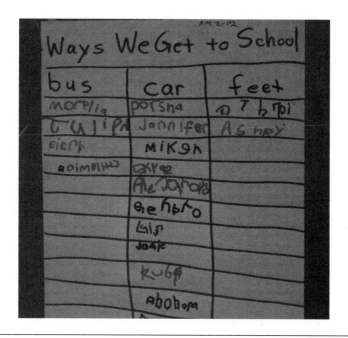

Figure 5.23 Data Chart

SOURCE: Figure 5.23 reprinted with permission from classroom of Sally Wade, Lee Elementary School, Oklahoma City, OK Public Schools.

Alex	Lydia		Roger Rabbit's Restaurant
Betty	Maria		March 26, 2007
Brandon	Mark		1.
Cathy	Pedro		2.
Dingli	Ricky		
Fay	Sara		3.
George	Zoe		4.
Henry	Josue		

Figure 5.24 Model Sign-In Sheet

Checklist for a Literacy-Rich Classroom That Supports Writing

_____ Dramatic play centers contain books related to the current theme.

_____ Alphabet is posted at children's eye level.

_____ Classroom labels contain words and related picture.

_____ A variety (shape, color, texture, purpose) of writing paper is placed across areas of the classroom and in centers.

_____ Many types of writing tools, for example, crayons, markers, pens, and pencils of various styles (pencils with grips, pyramid style, carpenter pencils, and novelty pencils) are placed across the classroom and in centers.

_____ Classroom contains a writing center.

_____ Children's writing is on display in the classroom at the children's eye level.

_____ The classroom contains alphabet puzzles and puzzles with words.

_____ Children include writing in their play.

_____ Adults engage children in modeled and shared writing activities in centers.

_____ Children's names and other environmental print are evident in classroom displays.

_____ Highest interest centers contain sign-up sheets.

Figure 5.25 Checklist for a Literacy-Rich Classroom

when the teacher shows children how to accomplish a writing task through explicit explanation that may include think-aloud talk. This is an opportunity for focused, explicit instruction and for the teacher to model how "expert" writers work. In Chapter 4, Annie's teacher modeled her process for writing a grocery list. Shared writing is an interactive process during which the teacher and student(s) work together to create a meaningful text as the teacher serves as scribe. With the teacher as scribe, the students are freed of the cognitive demands of drafting and can focus on content. A version of shared writing, interactive writing, involves sharing the pen with a child to create a text. Peer collaboration typically occurs in centers as children write together, help each other as they write, and discuss their writing. During peer collaboration, the student is the scribe or children share that role.

> The core of instruction is writing experiences in meaningful contexts.

Figure 5.26 Model for Organizing Writing Instruction

During independent writing, the student is the scribe. Students write individually, although they may use the teacher or other students as a source for inspiration and feedback. Independent writing can occur at any time or place in the classroom.

Let's look at some examples of how this model for organizing instruction might work in a classroom setting. Suppose the children in Rebecca's class have read several books about animals, e.g., *Rosie's Walk* (Hutchins, 1987), *The Rain Forest Counts!* (McCourt, 1997), *Henny Penny* (Galdone, 1968), *The Very Hungry Caterpillar* (Carle, 1987), *Brown Bear, Brown Bear, What Do You See?* (Martin, 1967), *Polar Bear, Polar Bear What Do You Hear?* (Martin, 1991), *Panda Bear, Panda Bear, What Do You See?* (Martin, 2003), *Officer Buckle and Gloria* (Rathmann, 1995), *Who Is the Beast?* (Baker, 1990), *Mrs. Wishy-Washy* (Cowley, 1999), and *The Little Mouse, the Red Ripe Strawberry, and the Big Hungry Bear* (Wood & Wood, 1990). All of these books have been available throughout the classroom or in the classroom library. Rebecca's teacher, Kathi, plans a shared writing activity that will build on their knowledge of animals. She suggests that since the children have been reading books about animals, they could make a list of the animals they know. Kathi is the scribe and writes the names as the children suggest them. Kathi has some of the books listed above available for children to engage in "lookbacks" to remember the names of animals they know. Some children have become very sophisticated in their knowledge about animals, and name some that have "tricky spellings." Kathi uses this to help children understand they can record their ideas with invented spelling. She tells the children, "I am not sure about how to spell that, but I will just give it a try. Later I can edit what I wrote. I might even be able to find the standard spelling by looking in one of our books."

After the recording of all animals is finished, Kathi makes a point to show the children that she is going to change a spelling after checking on it. In fact, she asks some children to find the word that stands for the animal and to tell her the letters in the right order. On another day, Kathi suggests to the children that they might want to revise their chart. They can use their list of animals to make categories based on where each animal might live: in a home, on a farm, in a jungle. Several days later Kathi shows the children a chart she has prepared. She tells the children that this chart (Figure 5.27) will be in the classroom all day, and they can record their name and their favorite animal. Kathi models as she records her name and favorite animal. She tells the children that she will write her name starting with a capital letter. Kathi emphasizes to the children that they can record their favorite animal on the chart with a buddy, if they want to.

Figure 5.28 helps us see how the model for organizing writing instruction is combined with the stages of the writing process in this series of writing activities. The many teacher read-alouds of books about animals provides children with a model of fluent reading, and the discussion around each book has developed children's vocabulary about animals that they apply to their list-making. The actual list-making and the follow-up revision is a drafting and revising activity carried out through shared writing. Kathi models editing when she corrects the spelling of one of the animal names. Finally, Kathi sets up a situation in which children can engage in peer collaboration (or independent writing) to complete a chart about "favorite animals."

ADDRESSING DIVERSITY

In U.S. schools, programs such as Early Reading First have been legislated for the purpose of closing achievement gaps that result from poverty and language diversity with the goal of being sure all children have the knowledge, skills and dispositions for successful school achievement. We know that reading and writing develop concurrently in early literacy development, and that both have their foundation in oral language development. Teachers working with all children, and particularly with children whose home language may be different from that they hear at school, might consider the following points:

Our Favorite Animals	
My Name	*My Favorite Animal*
Kathi	elephant

Figure 5.27 Chart for Favorite Animals

	Organizing	Drafting and Revising	Editing
Teacher Modeling	teacher read-aloud of books		
Student/Teacher Shared Writing		teacher and children draft a list of animals and then revise the chart	teacher edits the spelling of an animal name
Peer Collaboration		children record their ideas on the "favorite animal" chart	
Independent Writing			

Figure 5.28 Organizing Instruction With Writing Process

- *Shared writing activities capitalize on verbal interactions between teacher and child.* That being the case, they provide prime opportunities for children to use their oral language in instructional settings. During shared writing sessions, teachers can employ specific and focused dialogue that will engage children in vocabulary and concept building.
- *It is important for teachers to remember that children need to learn the language of instruction.* We cannot assume that all children, particularly our youngest children, are firm in their understanding of terms such as word, letter, sound, beginning, first, or last.
- *Learning to write is a social process.* When we structure the environment to support peer collaborations, we increase opportunities for children to learn from peers. Peer collaborations increase the amount of time spent in academic engagement and provide immediate feedback from peers (Vaughn, Linan-Thompson, Pollard-Durodola, Mathes, & Hagan, 2006).
- *Environmental print is a key form of literacy information for children who may not have many books in their homes* (Craig & Washington, 2006). In addition, home book programs increase children's access to books. Simple book bags with a book and a suggested follow-up activity for children and parents are an easily achieved home book program.
- *Interactive writing is a form of shared writing that is appropriate in small-group settings (two or three children with the teacher).* Interactive writing is a sharing of the pen between the teacher and a child as they co-construct a text. During a shared writing

experience, the teacher might iterate the beginning sound of a word (e.g., "/t/, /t/, /t/, what sound do you hear at the beginning of 'tell'? What letter will we use to write that sound?"), and then invite a child to share the pen by actually writing

> Environmental print is a key form of literacy information for children who may not have many books in their homes.

the first letter of the word. The teacher can coach this writing by directing the child's attention to an alphabet chart to see how the letter looks, or by guiding the child through explicit steps with language such as "start here," "pull down to make a straight line," or "now push across to finish the 't.'"

SUMMARY

Learning to write is a social process that is developed through writing experiences in meaningful contexts. Reading and writing emerge together as young children explore text in a print-rich environment. When children scribble, they come to understand that they have control over the marks they produce. As they become attune to the writing in their environment, children attempt to make their marks look like the writing they see. An important milestone is for children to distinguish between what is writing and what is drawing. An additional milestone is the discovery of the alphabetic principle, which leads to the use of invented spelling and enables children to write meaningful text.

When planning instruction, teachers have to attend to organizing the environment as well as their instruction. Teachers can create print-rich environments by distributing literacy tools (pencils and paper) throughout the classroom centers. Writing instruction should include opportunities for teacher modeling, shared writing, peer collaboration, and independent writing.

Comprehension: Making Meaning   6

Mr. Gonzalez finished reading *The Very Hungry Caterpillar* (Carle, 1981) with the children in the classroom chiming in as he read about each of the fruits and food the hungry caterpillar had eaten. This book is a favorite of the children so Mr. Gonzalez chose it to reread at the beginning of the unit on healthy eating. "Wow!" he said. "The very hungry caterpillar ate lots of different kinds of foods on his way to becoming a beautiful butterfly. You eat a lot of different foods as well to help you grow big and strong. We're going to start learning about all of the different kinds of foods that we eat and how we can eat healthy. I know that you already know some things about foods that are good for you." He pointed to the KWL (Know—Want to Know—Learned) chart that he had placed on the easel. He told the children that they were going to write down what they knew about foods that will help them grow.

Next, Mr. Gonzalez called on individual children to tell him something they eat that they know will help them to grow strong and healthy. When it was his turn, Juan said, "Yo me gusto los tamales que mi mama hecho. Estos son muy bueno!" Mr. Gonzalez wrote *Tamales are good for you.* As he wrote, he said each word slowly in English. After each child had offered an idea for the K (or Know) part of the chart, Mr. Gonzalez asked the children to close their eyes and think about what they would like to know about foods that will help them grow. He modeled by telling the children that he wanted to know if snacks are "good for you." Several children offered suggestions which he wrote in the W (or Want to know) part of the chart. He told the children that they would put the chart up on the wall to remind themselves of what they want to find out so they can fill in the L (or Learned) part of the chart as they learn the answers.

Mr. Gonzalez then showed the children *Gregory the Terrible Eater* (Sharmat, 1980), the new story related to the unit. He read the title and

(Continued)

(Continued)

> asked the children what they thought the book would be about. Several children responded. Mr. Gonzalez went through the book, pointing out aspects of different pictures on different pages as the children talked about what they thought might be happening. They compared the food that Gregory is eating in the pictures with the food the hungry caterpillar eats. Mr. Gonzalez told the children that they would read the story later in the day in small groups to see if their predictions were correct about what would happen and to find out about the food Gregory eats and why he is a terrible eater. He took out pictures of different foods common to the two books. As the children said the name of the food and if their name started with the same sound as the food, they left the group to go to the center of their choice.

WHAT IS COMPREHENSION?

In the lesson above, Mr. Gonzalez is helping children to comprehend the stories and books that they read together. Comprehending is simply understanding. It is thinking and making meaning. When we talk about literacy, comprehending is building a mental model of what the print says and matching it to what the reader already knows to construct a meaning that makes sense. It is trying to put together the message that an author is trying to communicate. It involves, however, more than the just the words that an author uses. Comprehending includes looking between the lines, seeing how the meaning one is building fits with one's own experiences and with what one knows, thinking about the ideas, and making some sort of judgment about them.

> Comprehension is simply understanding. . . . thinking and making meaning.

Comprehension occurs at different levels. These levels are the literal level, the inferential level, the critical level, the application level, and the appreciative level (Sadoski, 2004, see Figure 6.1). The literal level of comprehension involves understanding the words that are directly said by an author. It does not involve any interpretation of ideas that does not use the exact words of the author in the context that those words are used. Very little comprehension occurs at simply a literal level because authors expect readers to bring some knowledge to a text and to use that knowledge to make interpretations. This type of comprehension, inferential comprehension, is sometimes called reading between the lines. Read the following two sentences: "The boy shook his hat as he came into the house. 'Don't drip on the floor!' his mother scolded as he took off his coat and boots." As a reader, you might infer that it was raining outside and the boy's hat and raincoat were dripping water from his walk in the rain. However, if you live in the northern United States or Canada, your background experience and knowledge might affect your inference and you might infer that the boy was coming inside from playing in the snow.

The next three levels of comprehension are part of responding to a text in some way (Sadoski, 2004). This response involves thinking about what was read, including one's feelings about the text and what it means for one's life. One of these levels of comprehension, the critical level, involves evaluating what was read. This critical comprehension involves making judgments about characters and their actions, about the effectiveness of the story, and about what the author's purpose was in writing the story or informational book and why information was presented in the way it was. Another type of response is application. At this level, a reader uses the knowledge gained from reading to solve a problem. This type of comprehension involves making connections between texts as well as between texts and one's own knowledge and experiences. A last type of response is appreciation. Appreciation is personalizing and becoming part of a text or story. At this level, readers identify with the characters in a story. They enter the story world, making the story come alive in a personal way. When reading informational books, readers might look for personally important facts or ideas.

Literal: understanding what is directly stated in the text by the author. Who was the story about? Where did the story take place?

Inferential: understanding what is implied in the text by using our own knowledge along with the words the author chose. Why was the caterpillar not hungry anymore (after reading what he ate on Saturday)?

Critical: evaluating the ideas in the text. Is this story real or make believe? How do you know?

Application: using the knowledge gained from reading a text in a different situation to solve some sort of problem. If the story continued, what might be the next event?

Appreciation: personalizing and becoming a part of a text. Who is your favorite character in the story? Why? What is the most interesting thing you learned in this book?

Figure 6.1 Levels of Comprehension and Examples of Questions for Each Level

SOURCE: From Sadoski, M. (2004). *Conceptual foundations of teaching reading*, copyright © 2004. New York: The Guilford Press.

Mr. Gonzalez supports all of the levels of comprehension over the course of a day. In the lesson above, he found out about the children's literal comprehension when he asked the children to chime in and tell him what the hungry caterpillar ate on each day as they reread that favorite book. Mr. Gonzalez asked the children to make inferences when he introduced the new book in the group and asked them to predict what might happen in the story using the pictures. Mr. Gonzalez helped the children begin to think at the application level when he asked them to compare the foods eaten by the main characters in the two books. Later, as the children read *Gregory the Terrible Eater* in small groups, Mr. Gonzalez will ask the children if the story is real or make believe. They will discuss why it is make believe and if any parts of it might be true. He will ask the children to choose a favorite part of *Gregory the Terrible Eater* and tell why. They may dramatize the story or connect events to their own lives.

WHAT HELPS CHILDREN COMPREHEND?

Comprehension at each of these different levels does not just happen automatically. Children learn to comprehend as they learn the strategies that good readers use to make meaning. Comprehension is supported as children build up background knowledge about concepts, events, and the structure of different types of text. Comprehension is improved as children understand book and academic language.

> Children learn to comprehend as they learn the strategies that good readers use to make meaning.

Strategies

To comprehend what has been read at all of these levels, good readers use several different strategies, ones that Mr. Gonzalez tries to model and help children begin to use (see Figure 6.2). Good readers use their background knowledge and experiences as well as text cues to predict what might occur in a story or what a piece of informational text might be about. As they read, they either verify their predictions or disprove them and then make more predictions. In stories, the text cues might include pictures, the title of the story, and story details. In informational text, readers use visual cues such as pictures and graphs, and they use headings. Good readers also make connections as they read. They connect information across different books that they have read. They connect what they are reading to their lives and to what they know about how the world works. They make predictions and connections by activating their background knowledge. That knowledge might be about the topic of the story or informational book, or it might be about the setting of a story, or about events they have experienced that might be like the events in a story.

This background knowledge will help a reader to make inferences. Good readers make mental pictures as they read. They imagine in their mind what is happening in a story. Good readers ask questions about a story or a topic. These questions give the reader a purpose for reading. A reader might ask why a character is acting in a particular way or how a character will solve a problem. She might ask questions about a topic she wants to learn more about. As she reads, a good reader summarizes what she has read. For a story, summarizing would include telling the main events. For an informational book, summarizing could include describing the topic in a few sentences. Most importantly, a good reader monitors her understanding. She checks as she reads to make sure that what she is reading makes sense. If it does not make sense, she uses the other strategies to help the story or book make sense.

In the lesson at the beginning of the chapter, Mr. Gonzalez modeled and encouraged the use of several of the strategies that good readers use. He helped them to activate their background knowledge when he asked them what they already knew about food that was good for them and wrote it on the chart. He modeled asking a question he wanted to find an answer to and encouraged the children to come up with their own question. He helped the children predict what the new story might be about using the pictures. He encouraged them to make connections across books as they compared the food eaten by the main characters in the two books.

- Predicting—using cues such as pictures, previous events, ideas to infer what will happen next
- Making connections—connecting knowledge and experiences with what one is reading
- Activating background knowledge—bringing to mind what one already knows about a topic
- Making mental pictures—forming pictures in one's mind as a story is being read
- Making inferences—reading between the lines to form conclusions
- Asking questions—processing questions which one would likely find out the answers as one reads
- Summarizing—identifying the most important information and telling it in a very shortened version
- Monitoring understanding—checking to see if one has understood

Figure 6.2 Strategies Good Readers Use to Make Meaning

Background Knowledge

A key part of comprehension is the background knowledge and experiences that a reader has. Readers have a database of concepts and experiences called schema (Donahue & Foster, 2004; Duchan, 2004). This database helps to organize experiences and ideas. It helps readers remember what they have read and to interpret it. It helps a reader to connect new ideas and experiences with ones that she has had before. According to Duchan (2004), readers have three different types of entries in the database that are important for comprehending what they read. One type of entry in the database helps readers to categorize ideas and concepts. These database entries help a reader identify, for example, when something they see or read about is a food or not a food, or if a particular type of food is a fruit or a vegetable. If, for example, a reader reads about artichokes in a story but has not had experience with an artichoke, she might not recognize that it is a food that a character might eat.

> A key part of comprehension is the background knowledge and experiences that a reader has.

A second type of database entry is those that represent familiar events. These entries include who might participate in the event, what happens during the event, and how the different aspects of the event fit together. For example, someone who lives near the ocean might have a database entry for going to the beach. That entry might include grandparents picking up the family, all of whom are wearing swimming suits and carrying towels, and driving to the ocean. At the seaside, the children take out plastic pails and shovels and run along the sand while the adults set up an umbrella and lay out towels. Then the children build structures out of the sand and play at the edge of the water where the waves come into shore. If a reader has this entry in her database when she reads a story about going to the beach, she will be able to activate that knowledge, visualize what is happening, and make connections, predictions, and inferences about what is happening. If a reader does not have this experience in her database, the story she is reading will be much more difficult to understand.

A third type of entry in the database is especially important to comprehending different types of texts a reader encounters. This type of entry represents the different ways that texts she has encountered in her world can be organized (see Figure 6.3). Stories have a particular organization that includes characters, a setting, a problem, a series of plot events, and a resolution. Informational books have several different ways that they can be organized that are different than stories (Vukelich,

Evans, & Albertson, 2003). One way is where the books describe a concept or idea. Another way is to list events in sequence, or tell how something happened. A third way is to compare and contrast two or more concepts, events, or procedures, noting similarities and differences. A text might present a cause and discuss the effect of that cause, telling why something happened, or present a problem and outline the solution. Finally, informational text can make a statement about an event or an idea and then give reasons for that statement and examples to support those reasons. There are also other texts that readers encounter in everyday life that are organized differently from stories and informational books. These types of text include poetry they read in books or sing as songs, lists, letters and cards, menus, food boxes and cans, billboards and signs, newspapers and newsletters, telephone books, and grocery ads, to name but a few. Each of these types of text is organized in specific ways that indicate its purpose.

Book and Academic Language

Book and academic language is the more formal language found in texts and in school settings. This language is decontextualized from the actions that a child is involved in as the language is being used. This decontextualized language does not have the oral language cues of

---

Stories

> **Characters:** Who is in the story
> **Setting:** Where and when the story takes place
> **Problem:** What motivates the main character to set a goal and start the action
> **Plot events:** Actions taken by the main character to reach the goal
> **Resolution:** Event in which the main character reaches the goal and solves the problem

Informational Books

> **Description:** Tells the reader about a topic
> **Sequence:** Lists facts or events in the order in which they happen
> **Compare and contrast:** Tells about the similarities and differences between ideas
> **Cause and effect:** Explains reasons for why something has happened
> **Problem and solution:** Tells about a problem and how it was solved
> **Reasons and examples:** Gives a main idea and supports it with details and examples

---

Figure 6.3   Structure of Texts

gestures, body language, and real objects. Book language uses verb tenses from the past and the future. The sentence structures may be more complex than in conversation. In some cases, there may be particular conventions that indicate the type of text it is, such as opening a fairy tale with "Once upon a time" and ending a story with "The end."

Academic language is also complicated by the vocabulary that a particular subject matter uses to describe events or concepts. For example, most young children will know about food and be able to name different types of food. In order to understand which foods are healthy foods for growth, a child will also have to understand terms such as fruit, vegetable, grain, meat, protein, dairy, fats, and sugars. She will also need to differentiate between snacks and meals and learn which meals occur at which time period. Mr. Gonzalez supported children's use of book language by encouraging them to chime in with the rereading of the first story. He modeled the use of academic language when he took Juan's more conversational comment about liking his mother's tamales and wrote it more formally on the chart.

ASSESSING COMPREHENSION

Comprehension can be assessed informally as teachers interact with children around a book during whole or small group read-alouds or during individual interactions. During these conversations, a teacher can find out *what* a child has understood in a story or book and *how* that child has gone about constructing that understanding. In assessing the *what* a child has comprehended, a teacher is determining at which levels of comprehension a child is proficient. In assessing the *how*, a teacher wants to discover which strategies a child uses, if the child has the required background knowledge and is using that knowledge, and her understanding of book and academic language.

One effective way to find out about a child's comprehension of a book is to have the child pretend to read a book that has been read to her at least twice before. Begin by asking the child to join you in a quiet place in the classroom. Hand the child the book that you would like for her to pretend to read, saying, "We've read this book together several times. Pretend that I am a friend that has never heard this book before. You can either tell me about the book or pretend to read it to me." If the child is reluctant to start, you can ask her what happened first. Using the checklist in Figure 6.4, a teacher can note the levels of comprehension that are evident. She can note the use of the structure of the text and the use of book and academic language.

Does the child sound like she is reading or telling a story?
Yes_____   **no**_____

If **yes**:
_____story begins with introduction
_____names characters
_____identifies time and/or place
_____identifies goal or problem
_____describes plot events in order
_____identifies solution or goal that has been reached
_____includes story ending

If **no**:
_____labels and comments on pictures
_____sounds like a storyteller telling about the pictures

During the reading:
_____uses conventions like "once upon a time" or "the end."
_____identifies the author
_____makes comments about what is happening

After the reading:
_____can identify a favorite part of the story
_____can make connections from the story to own life
_____can make predictions about what might happen next if the story continues

Figure 6.4   Checklist for Story Rereading

SOURCE: From Sulzby, E., Children's emergent reading of favorite storybooks: A developmental study. *Reading Research Quarterly, 20,* copyright © 1985, pp. 458–481, and Morrow, L. M., & Gambrell, L. B., *Using children's literature in preschool: Comprehending and enjoying books.* Copyright © 2004. Newark, DE: International Reading Association.

A teacher can also assess comprehension through the use of questions. Questions can be open-ended or close-ended. A close-ended question has one answer that is the right answer and can often be answered in just a few words. Close-ended questions often ask for literal comprehensions by asking who, what, when, or where. These questions may ask for children to make inferences such as to identify the cause of an event. An open-ended question has many possible answers and encourages higher levels of thinking. Open-ended questions encourage elaboration. These questions often begin with why or how. Open-ended questions are necessary to find out about the critical, application, and appreciative levels of comprehension. Questioning can occur as part of whole-group book discussion, small-group discussion, or one-on-one as part of a pretend story reading.

RESEARCH-BASED INSTRUCTIONAL STRATEGIES

Teachers can help children to comprehend the stories and informational books that they read to them by doing a few simple things. First, help children activate knowledge and experiences that they might have that will be relevant to the text that will be read. If the children do not have important knowledge or experiences, help them build that knowledge before reading through the use of pictures, manipulatives, and discussion. Include important vocabulary in the discussion. Model your use of different comprehension strategies by thinking aloud as you read to them. Encourage prediction of what might happen next or what the text is about. Ask questions that encourage children to make inferences and connections, be critical, and become involved in the text. Read a text more than once, especially if the text has unfamiliar content.

Directed Listening-Thinking Activity (DLTA)

The Directed Listening-Thinking Activity or DLTA (Morrow & Gambrell, 2004) is a strategy that helps direct children's thinking as they listen to a story and gives them a purpose for listening. The teacher can have many different purposes for using a DLTA, including focusing the children on important details, helping them to remember sequence, interpreting characters' actions, making connections between books or between the story and children's world knowledge or experiences, or predicting outcomes. It can focus on helping children identify story elements or the structure of particular types of texts.

DLTA follows a three-part framework: preparing for listening with discussion and questions, reading the text with few interruptions, and discussing the text. Mr. Gonzalez had begun the DLTA in the lesson at the beginning of the chapter by preparing the children to listen to *Gregory the Terrible Eater.* He has two goals for the DLTA. First, he wants the children to listen for details about the food Gregory eats to build up their vocabulary. Second, he wants the children to make connections between books and their own lives. During the discussion about the pictures, he points out different foods Gregory is eating and asks the children if they have eaten those foods. He uses vocabulary such as "fruit," "vegetable," and "meat." They compare the eating habits of Gregory with the hungry caterpillar and discuss what a terrible eater might be.

The second part of the DLTA will occur in small groups later in the day. Mr. Gonzalez will sit in the library area with four or five children around him and read *Gregory the Terrible Eater* to those children. He will stop only once or twice to comment about different foods or bring up one of the predictions from the large-group time earlier. After the story is over, Mr. Gonzalez will ask the children to tell him all of the different foods that Gregory ate. They will discuss when he ate the foods and if they were foods that would help him stay strong and healthy. They will also discuss why Gregory was considered a terrible eater and if the hungry caterpillar was a good eater or a terrible eater. Finally, they will talk about whether the book was real or pretend, and why.

Book Acting

Book acting (McGee, 2003) is a combination of story retelling and drama. In book acting, a teacher guides the children in a small group in acting out a story that has been read at least twice. Acting out a story helps children make inferences and put story parts together to make a whole. Because the children have to work together, they also have to learn to take on the perspectives of others and collaborate with their peers (McGee, 2003). McGee (2003) lists four steps to implementing book acting in a classroom. First, the teacher must prepare for the activity. This preparation includes selecting a book, deciding on props, and planning how to introduce the story and what vocabulary to emphasize. It is key to choose a storybook that has a strong story line and at least two characters. The story should not be too long or complex but should have dialogue and extend the children's vocabulary. Choosing props will depend on story choice. The props could be pup-pets, pictures, flannel board figures, small objects such as stuffed animals or dolls, or easily put together costumes such as simple masks. Planning how to introduce the story includes planning what strategies the teacher might want to model and what kind of thinking she wants to encourage.

> Acting out a story helps children make inferences and put story parts together to make a whole.

The second step in implementing book acting is to introduce the story to the children and read it multiple times. McGee (2003) suggests that a teacher first introduce the story and read it with the children at group time. This introduction includes discussion of key parts of the story and of important vocabulary. It is important that the story be read and discussed several times, so McGee suggests that further readings be done in small groups to encourage all of the children to talk about the story.

The third step in book acting is introducing the props and guiding the children through their use. This is best done in a small group, but can be done in the large group as well. One way to do this introduction is to show the props and discuss with the children how they are related to the story. Another way is for the teacher to demonstrate the retelling with the props and then pass the props out to the children. The teacher can tell the story, and the child with the appropriate prop can stand up and act out what the teacher is telling. Finally, the teacher can hand out the props, begin the retelling, and then let the children take over.

The final step in book acting is to put the props in a center for independent retelling by the children. The props could be put with several copies of the story in the library center or in a language center. McGee (2003) suggests that the teacher remind children to use the props to retell the story to one of their friends. She recommends that teachers observe the book acting during this independent retelling to note children's use of book and academic language as well as the structure and length of the retelling.

Innovations on a Story or Book

Writing an innovation of a book can be used to support comprehension of either stories or informational books. A book innovation is simply taking the structure of a piece of text and changing key details. For example, after reading *The Very Hungry Caterpillar,* the children could change the main character into another animal. The children could dictate an imaginary story about what that animal ate each day of the week. Writing an innovation helps children to apply what they know about the structure of a particular text to a new text. It helps them to make connections between a text and their own background knowledge.

The first step in writing an innovation is to read and discuss the chosen book with the children. It is best if the book is then reread several times in small groups until the children become very familiar with the structure of the book. Once the book is familiar, the teacher presents a story or sentence frame. For *The Very Hungry Caterpillar,* for example, the story frame could be the following: *The Very Hungry _____.* *On Monday, she ate _____. On Tuesday, she ate _____. On Wednesday, she ate _____. On Thursday, she ate _____. On Friday, she ate _____. On Saturday, she ate _____. She wasn't a very hungry _____ any more. She was a very full _____. So on Sunday, she ate _____.* The small group could construct the story together, dictating each line as the teacher writes one line to a page. Then the children could illustrate the pages to go with the sentence and the page could be bound into a book to be read at group time and placed in the library.

Know, Want to Know, Learned (KWL)

The KWL chart was developed by Ogle (1989) to help children activate background knowledge, ask questions, and set purposes for reading a text or learning about a topic. The chart is divided into three sections. The K section is for what the children already *know* about the topic. The W section is for what the children *want* to know about the topic. The L section is for what the children *learned* about the topic after reading and exploring it.

A KWL chart is a good tool to use at the beginning of the exploration of a new topic in the preschool classroom. The chart serves several purposes for the teacher. First, the children's background knowledge about the topic is activated, making it easier for them to connect new knowledge that they construct to the knowledge that they already have. Second, the teacher can find out what background knowledge the children have about the topic and if they have misconceptions. This information will help the teacher plan how much knowledge she will need to help children build before reading informational books. Third, asking the children what they want to find out helps the teacher meet the needs of the children and to guide her choice of activities and books. The KWL chart should then be revisited periodically throughout the unit. If a book or exploration answers one of the questions on the chart, the teacher can remind the children of the question and they can discuss what they found out to answer that question. The third column of the chart can either be completed as answers to questions are found, or can be completed at the end of the unit. At this time, children can tell what they learned about the topic and determine if their questions were answered. This discussion can help children summarize what they understood.

ADDRESSING DIVERSITY

The children in any preschool classroom come with a variety of experiences and knowledge that will affect their comprehension. A key job for the teacher is to find out what each child brings with him or her, to build up each child's knowledge and language base, and to extend children's thinking by making connections from what they know to new information. For children like Juan who are English language learners, this is especially key since they must not only build knowledge, they must learn the labels for the concepts that they are learning in two languages. Researchers (Barone, Mallette, & Xu, 2005) suggest several strategies that support comprehension development with children with diverse backgrounds.

- *Be aware of differences in cultures about concepts.* For example, a snack for Juan might be a tortilla with butter while for Rebecca it might be an apple or graham crackers.
- *Use books that are predictable and familiar.* Books that are predictable often include repetition or cumulative patterns. Books that are familiar include books about concepts that children know about, books that reflect the cultures of the children, and books that reflect experiences that the children might have had. These books might also be bilingual. Reading multiple books about the same theme or topic makes the concepts more familiar.
- *Read books with clear illustrations and other visuals.* The illustrations should clearly support the text—either the concepts or the story line. Wordless picture books can encourage children to construct their own story or description using their native language or English. They can also lead to discussion about the concepts illustrated in the pictures.
- *Use drama and props to retell stories that have been read several times.* The props provide a concrete visual support for important concepts or parts of the story. By acting out ideas or stories, the children can build up understanding of the concept along with the language.

SUMMARY

In this chapter, we discuss what comprehension is and how to support all of the levels of comprehension. Comprehension is understanding a story or book at several levels. Literal comprehension means understanding the words the author uses in their exact context. Inferential comprehension means reading between the lines. Readers can respond to a story by being critical, applying the knowledge in a new context, or by being appreciative. Good readers use strategies to help them comprehend. They also use their background knowledge of concepts, of events, and of text structures. They use book language and understand academic language to comprehend as well. Teachers can use retellings and questions to assess comprehension. To support comprehension, teachers should build background knowledge, model strategy use, and encourage responding to a story. Good instructional strategies to support comprehension with preschool children include the Directed Listening-Thinking Activity, book acting, innovations on stories and books, and the Know, Want-to-Know, Learned (KWL) chart.

Sharing Books With Children   7

The children in Mrs. Jones's preschool classroom looked at her with great excitement and expectation. Over the past few days, Mrs. Jones had been sharing the book *Brown Bear, Brown Bear, What Do You See?* with her class. She did many activities with the book. On the first day, she read the book aloud to the children, commenting on each animal as she went along. The next day, using a big book, she did a shared reading with the class and invited the children to chime in whenever they wanted while she was reading the book. Many children quickly caught on to the pattern in the book. They giggled and laughed as they chanted the lines. During the next couple of days, Mrs. Jones did several more shared readings of the book, and almost all the children could memorize the whole book.

Mrs. Jones then told the children that she was going to have the class put together a play. Each child was going to take the role of a character in the book. Mrs. Jones used the word character, rather than animal, to reinforce the academic language of books. She had made some stick puppets, and the children took a puppet corresponding to their chosen character. When it came to the role of *the teacher*, Annie could not contain her excitement and shouted "Pick me, pick me!" She thought that being the teacher was the greatest thing in the world. When Mrs. Jones granted Annie's wish, she was so excited that she jumped up and down, clapping her hands until Mrs. Jones had to come over to her and help her sit down on the carpet.

THE IMPORTANCE OF BOOK SHARING FOR CHILDREN'S EARLY LITERACY DEVELOPMENT

Preschool is a critical period in child development. Children's books are important for preschoolers because they can be used to help preschoolers develop cognitively, emotionally, and socially (Morrow & Gambrell, 2004). Young children have a natural affinity for books, in particular those that are fun, humorous, and silly. They learn about the real world through books. Cognitively, books open up doors to valuable knowledge that children need to grow in their thinking and reasoning abilities. High-quality children's books are also ideal for sparking children's imagination and creativity. Emotionally, books help children cope with fears of losing loved ones, being sick, or being abandoned. They alleviate emotional stress accompanying their experience of growing up and being independent. Socially, books help children develop skills for interacting with people. Socially acceptable behaviors can be taught through the reading and discussion of book characters and their behaviors.

> Books open up doors to valuable knowledge that children need to grow in their thinking and reasoning abilities.

Sharing books with preschool children is also critical for their language and early literacy development. Daily read-alouds enable children to experience the wonder of language and the power of words. When young children are enamored with a story and request that the same book be read again and again, they are developing a love for reading that can last for a lifetime.

In the realm of language development, through exposure to storybook read-alouds, preschoolers learn about the sounds of the language, pick up new words to add to their existing vocabulary, and develop their understanding of English syntax, or how words are put together to generate meaningful communication. Books also offer syntactic patterns children may not ordinarily hear in their environment, yet are very important to their language and literacy development. In addition, the discussions and conversations that follow after teachers share books with children help them find personal meaning in reading and provide them with a rich opportunity to learn about the discourse patterns and turn-taking structure that are often used in their formal schooling.

Sharing books with preschool children helps them develop early literacy skills that are necessary if we want them to succeed in their future literacy development. Concepts about print are taught when a teacher specifically points out to children that print has meaning, sentences are made of individual words, and words are made of letters. Through modeling, we teach children to read the print, not the pictures, and directionality principles, including reading a

> Sharing books with preschool children helps them develop early literacy skills that are necessary if we want them to succeed in their future literacy development.

book from front to back and the text from left to right and from top to bottom. In addition, through modeling, we can teach children exceptions to these principles, such as how reading from front to back does not apply when using a dictionary.

When teachers and children enjoy the pleasure of nursery rhymes and poems that include alliteration and rhyming words, they are at the same time developing phonological awareness. Moreover, when we share books with children, they are exposed to the written and spoken word match—a value for understanding the concept of word in written text. They encounter new vocabulary and complex sentence structures that are not part of their spoken vocabulary. And, they exercise their listening comprehension (a foundation for reading comprehension). Klesius and Griffith (1996, p. 553) reviewed research on storybook reading and identified the following benefits:

- Developing knowledge about the world, a sense of how stories are constructed, knowledge about concepts of print, and social behavior that accompanies reading instruction in school.
- Providing practice listening, with oral turn-taking, and observing the comprehension strategies of expert readers.
- Developing oral language including learning word meanings and hearing more complex language patterns that may not be part of their everyday speech.
- Developing phonological awareness as well as an understanding of the symbolic nature of language (i.e., the words and pictures in the book are representations of things in the world).
- Teaching book concepts such as books are for reading, and book events occur outside of real time.
- Helping children become familiar with the decontextualized language of books.

WHAT DOES RESEARCH SAY ABOUT STORYBOOK READING WITH CHILDREN?

Many preschool children who grow up in a print- and literacy-rich environment and have many adult-facilitated interactions with books demonstrate emergent reading behaviors. Storybooks are the most frequently used reading materials during these book-sharing events. The storybook classification scheme developed by Sulzby offers preschool teachers a powerful tool that can be used to guide assessment and inform instruction (Sulzby, 1991). Working with preschool children who were asked to choose their favorite storybook and "read" it, Sulzby documented a developmental pattern in children's knowledge about the nature of written language. The knowledge included an understanding that the syntax, vocabulary, and text structure of books is different from that of oral language. Figure 7.1 provides a summary of Sulzby's scheme, which can be used as an index of children's acquisition of the register of written language.

When using this scheme to assess a child's emergent reading behaviors, the child needs to be allowed to select a favorite storybook for "reading." Typically, favorites are the ones that have been read to the child many times and are of great interest to the child. Adult storybook reading is critical to helping children move from early categories of emergent reading to real and independent reading. Sulzby's scheme illustrates a set of emerging reading behaviors. A significant theme within these behaviors is that children begin to make a distinction between the structure of language that is characteristic of talk and that which is characteristic of written text. They begin to incorporate in their emergent reading behavior the characteristics of written language. Then, at some point, they realize written text represents the specific words of the author. This realization accounts for some children's refusal to read; they know they do *not* know how to read the words. This is a high-level of understanding about written language.

Storybook reading with preschool children typically occurs as interactive storybook reading and shared reading. Interactive storybook reading in a school setting is designed to replicate the lapreading experiences many children experience prior to entering school. Lapreading prepares children to take advantage of formal reading instruction because children learn the social behavior expected in school, such as oral turn-taking skills and understanding that the conversation about a book is controlled by the topic of the book. Interactive storybook reading occurs in small groups of no more than five children (Campbell, 2001; Klesius & Griffith, 1996).

> Interactive storybook reading in a school setting is designed to replicate the lapreading experiences many children experience prior to entering school.

Interactive storybook reading should be accompanied and followed by children's and adults' comments, questions, conversation, and other kinds of social and verbal interactions. In Chapter 2, we introduced a form of interactive storybook reading known as dialogic reading. Dialogic reading procedures are more structured than most interactive reading events.

Klesius and Griffith (1996) distinguish between interactive storybook reading and shared reading. Whereas the focus of interactive storybook reading is language development, shared reading focuses on developing literacy skills. Shared reading originates from the concept of shared book

Emergent Storybook Reading Behaviors	
Focus of Attention	*Reading Behavior*
Focus on Pictures Storybook Reading Sounds Like Conversation	1. The child "reads" by looking at the pictures. The child talks about pictures, but does not form a story across the pages in the book. 2. The child's language sounds like that of a storyteller. There is a story formed by the child. The story can be understood through a combination of listening to the storytelling and looking at the pictures in the book.
Focus on Pictures Storybook Reading Sounds Like Book Language	1. The child is still "reading" by looking at the pictures, however, the child begins to incorporate some characteristics of a written story. For example, the child may incorporate repetitive phrases appearing in the story. There is a combination of storytelling intonation and reading intonation. 2. Even though the child is still focusing on the pictures, the child's speech sounds as though she is actually reading. The listener can follow the story without the aid of pictures.
Focus on Print	1. The child is exploring the print. Various behaviors occur including reading some known words, but skipping over others, or recognizing other words are not known and thus refusing to read. 2. The child reads using conventional strategies. This final level is real reading.

Figure 7.1   Storybook Emergent Reading Behaviors

SOURCES: Summarized from Sulzby, E., Assessment of emergent literacy: Storybook reading. *The Reading Teacher*, 44(7), copyright © 1991, pp. 498–500 and Sulzby, E., Children's emergent reading of favorite storybooks: A developmental study. *Reading Research Quarterly*, 20, copyright © 1985, pp. 458–481.

experience (Holdaway, 1979). Shared reading may occur in a large group setting. The teacher uses a big book as the prop for focused instruction on print concepts such as directionality and the concept of word in written text. During shared reading, the teacher invites the children to chime in during the reading, thus making the reading a shared experience. Many shared readings occur with text that has a predictable sequence, thus facilitating the children and teacher coreading.

SELECTING HIGH-QUALITY CHILDREN'S LITERATURE

It is important that preschool classrooms are stuffed with many high-quality children's books. Several factors deserve careful consideration when building a classroom library. First, the books and the concepts presented must be developmentally appropriate. Books that fit the interests of the children, and those that they can relate to easily, tend to have a better chance for enhancing their cognitive, emotional, and social development. Books about children of their own age, family, real life stories/objects, animals, and insects are usually appealing topics for preschoolers. It is most important to also incorporate books into a classroom library that represent the ethnicities and cultures of the children in the classroom.

> It is important that preschool classrooms are stuffed with many high-quality children's books.

Second, teachers should consider the important features of books such as illustrations, page layout, font style, and size. For books to be attractive to preschoolers, illustration should be carefully considered. Illustration helps to increase comprehension because preschoolers can use the picture cues instead of totally relying on the words on the page to construct meaning about the book. Illustrations also help make a book enjoyable to read. Finally, illustrations help children acquire meanings for words introduced in a story. I (Griffith) recall using the illustrations in *The Napping House* (Wood, 1984) to help a group of kindergarten children connect a collection of new vocabulary (slumbering, snoozing, dozing, dreaming, snoring, and napping) to "sleep," a word the children knew well. Because preschoolers have a short attention span, illustrations should be colorful and concrete with easily recognized objects in order to attract and hold their interest. Page layout should enhance children's ability to follow the text. Layout considerations include large font(s), easily recognized letter style(s), few words on each page, and a left-to-right and top-to-bottom directionality.

Preschoolers enjoy books with a repetitive pattern; that is, with repeated sentences, words, images (e.g., *Rain* by Robert Kalan and *Brown Bear, Brown Bear* by Bill Martin, Jr.); and stories with a clear and easy to follow story structure (i.e., beginning, middle, and end). Characters with funny names, silly plots, and happy endings are also popular among preschoolers (e.g., *Silly Sally* by Audrey Wood) as are books containing sounds and actions that children can imitate (e.g., books by Dr. Seuss).

DEVELOPING CLASSROOM LIBRARIES

A well-stocked classroom library contributes to the building of a literate environment. When developing a classroom library, several things warrant attention. We discuss book formats, genres, and displays.

Various book formats should be included in the classroom library. Some formats to consider are board books, pop-up books, interactive books (with tags that can be pulled or opened/closed to reveal or cover words/pictures), and books on tape. If your classroom has a computer or multiple computers, you may also consider adding to your library electronic books, which include multimedia features and are attractive to young children. Books on tape can be placed in a listening center. Children can sign up to use the computer and listening centers, as seen in Chapter 5.

Classroom libraries should include books from various genres. Although children enjoy picture books of narrative stories (folktales, fairytales, fantasy, realistic fiction, etc.), high-quality informational books, poetry, alphabet books, wordless picture books, and books from other genres also give children opportunities to experience the pleasure of reading. Together, they allow preschoolers to explore and develop language, world knowledge, conceptual vocabulary, and early literacy skills. It is important to remember that not all children enjoy storybooks equally. Some children may enjoy informational books more than narrative stories. Some alphabet books are ideal informational texts for preschoolers. By including a great variety of books in your classroom library, you also ensure that each preschooler can find books that he/she likes to read.

> Classroom libraries should include books from various genres.

Third, the display of books should receive special attention. The books should be easily accessible to the children. Some preschool classrooms have a library corner where books are displayed on bookshelves with front covers facing out, and placed at the children's eye level. Figure 7.2 is of a book display at Lincoln Elementary School in Norman, Oklahoma. This very clever display is constructed from guttering material for houses. If set up correctly, the classroom library can become a favorite place for children. Figure 7.3 features a checklist of points to consider when setting up a classroom library.

Once books are introduced to the children through interactive storybook reading and shared reading, they should immediately be available to children in the classroom. Such books are often the new class

Figure 7.2   Cleverly Crafted Book Display for Young Children

SOURCE: Figure 7.2 reprinted with permission from Kathy Crabtree, Principal, Lincoln Elementary School, Norman, OK.

Checklist for Setting Up A Classroom Library

_____ Defined area in the classroom

_____ Space for 5–6 children

_____ Comfortable area with soft materials for sitting, including chairs and pillows

_____ A ratio of at least 8 books to every 1 child in the classroom

_____ Inviting posters about books on the wall

_____ Books displayed at the children's eye level

_____ Books displayed with the front cover facing out

_____ Listening center with books on tape

_____ Books representing the ethnicities and cultures of all the children in the classroom

_____ In addition to books, magazines, catalogs, newspapers, telephone books, calendars, and any other reading materials interesting to children

_____ Book cards, library stamps, bookmarks, pens, pencils, paper, file folders, and other props to encourage literacy exploration

---

Figure 7.3   Checklist for Setting Up A Classroom Library

favorites. Books should be available in all the center areas, not just the classroom library. For example, alphabet books can be placed in the writing center along with writing tools and materials, books related to weekly or monthly themes can be placed in the dramatic play center, and counting books can be placed in the math center. In Chapter 4, we presented a list of favorite alphabet books, and in the Additional Resources for Teachers section of this book is a list of some books with characters who write. Figure 7.4 offers a list of book genres that might be included in a classroom library, with illustrative titles for each genre. Figure 7.5 is a checklist to help in selecting books for the classroom.

Storybooks

Flower Garden by Eve Bunting (Kathryn Hewitt, illustrator)

The Very Hungry Caterpillar by Eric Carle

Goldilocks and the Three Bears by James Marshall

The Acorn Tree and Other Folktales by Anne F. Rockwell

That's Not My Dinosaur by Fiona Watt

Quick as a Cricket by Audrey Wood (Don Wood, illustrator)

The Napping House by Audrey Wood (Don Wood, illustrator)

Silly Sally by Audrey Wood

Patterned Books

Rain by Robert Kalan (Donald Crews, illustrator)

Brown Bear, Brown Bear, What Do You See? by Bill Martin, Jr. (Eric Carle, illustrator)

Monday, Monday, I Like Monday by Bill Martin, Jr.

Polar Bear, Polar Bear, What Do You Hear? by Bill Martin, Jr. (Eric Carle, illustrator)

The Important Book by Margaret Wise Brown (Leonard Weisgard, illustrator)

Informational Books

Dinosaur Bones by Bob Barner

Freight Train by Don Crews

From Wheat to Pasta by Robert Egan

Alphabet City by Stephen Johnson

On Market Street by Arnold Lobel (Anita Lobel, illustrator)

(Continued)

(Continued)

Wordless Picture Books

My Very First Book of Numbers by Eric Carle

Deep Down Underground by Olivier Dunrea

Changes, Changes by Pat Hutchins

The Red Book by Barbara Lehman

Frog Goes to Dinner by Mercer Mayer

The Great Cat Chase by Mercer Mayer

Picnic by Emily Arnold McCully

School by Emily Arnold McCully

Counting Books

Pigs from 1 to 10 by Arthur Geisert

The Icky Bug Counting Book by Jerry Pallotta (Ralph Masiello, illustrator)

Who's Counting by Nancy Tafuri

Mouse Count by Ellen Stoll Walsh

How Do Dinosaurs Count to Ten? by Jane Yolen (Mark Teague, illustrator)

Nursery Rhymes and Poetry

Read-Aloud Rhymes for the Very Young by Jack Prelutsky (Marc Brown, illustrator)

Richard Scarry's Best Mother Goose Ever by Richard Scarry

Sing a Song of Popcorn: Every Child's Book of Poems edited by Beatrice Schenk de Regniers, Eva Moore, Mary MichaelsWhite, and Jan Carr (Marcia Brown, Leo and Diane Dillon, Richard Egielski, Trina Schart Hyman, Arnold Lobel, Maurice Sendak, Marc Simont, and Margot Zemach, illustrators)

The Real Mother Goose by Blanche Fish Wright

Figure 7.4   Book Genres for the Classroom Library

RESEARCH-BASED INSTRUCTIONAL STRATEGIES FOR SHARING BOOKS WITH CHILDREN

Interactive storybook reading and shared reading are excellent ways to introduce preschoolers into the literacy community and should be an integral part of daily class routine. Several issues about sharing storybooks with children are worthy of special consideration.

First, storybook reading should be an interactive experience. Storybook reading should not be just about reading itself. It should be intertwined

Selecting Books

General Considerations

- The children will be able to sit through a reading of the book.
- The book represents a classroom theme taught during the year.
- Illustrations match and complement the text on the page.
- The text flows from page to page.
- The topic is suitable for preschool or kindergarten age children.
- The book can be used to expand children's vocabulary and general knowledge.

Storybooks

- Children will enjoy the characters and can identify with them.
- The literary components of characters, setting, plot, and theme are used effectively.
- The illustrations complement the theme of the story.
- The children can relate the story to their experiences.
- The book contains dialogue.
- There is a clear beginning, middle, and end to the story.
- Different races, ethnic and religious groups, and cultures are accurately portrayed.
- Women are portrayed as active and successful.

Information Books

- The content is not too complex for the children to understand.
- The information is accurate.
- Illustrations will enhance discussion of the topic.

Variety

Books should represent genres, types, and characteristics listed below.

- Genres
  - Storybooks
  - Pattern books
  - Informational books
  - Alphabet books
  - Wordless picture books
  - Counting books
  - Dictionaries
  - Nursery rhymes and poetry
- Types
  - Board books
  - Books on tape
  - Alphabet puzzles
- Characteristics
  - Rhyme and alliteration
  - Predictable text with repetitions of words, actions, and sentences
  - Humorous events and characters with silly names
  - Range of difficulty levels
  - Award-winning books

Figure 7.5   Classroom Library Checklist for Selecting Books

with children's talk and interactive child-teacher conversations. It is important that the teacher take the role of a facilitator instead of a director. The atmosphere should be warm and conducive to children's exploration of the pictures, words, world knowledge, story structure, and print-related concepts. Some examples of techniques include giving praise; drawing children's attention to pictures, text, and language features; questioning; and scaffolding by expanding on children's comments through explanation, demonstration, and sharing of personal experiences (Klesius & Griffith, 1996).

> Storybook reading should be an interactive experience.

Second, we should encourage student response to the books. As stated in Chapter 6, when we ask children to make predictions about the story by looking at the pictures and later revisit their predictions to confirm or revise them, we are developing their reading comprehension. In addition, it is important that we encourage preschool children to make connections to text. Keene and Zimmermann (1997) describe three types of connections to books. When children compare and contrast the plots in different versions of the three little pigs folktale, they are making *text-to-text connections.* When they talk about what they would do in a similar situation or why they like or dislike the story, they are making *text-to-self connections.* When they discuss what would happen in the real world as compared with the story, they are making *text-to-world connections.* All three types of responses in association with interactive storybook reading and shared reading help lay a solid foundation for preschool children's future development in conceptual knowledge, content knowledge, and reading comprehension.

Third, attention should be given to individual style of storybook reading. Before sharing a storybook with students, a teacher should read through the book at least once, paying attention to the pictures, wording choices, language patterns, and event sequence, so he will be prepared to read the book with accuracy, appropriate speed, intonation, and expression. Sometimes a teacher may even want to practice the oral reading before actually reading the book to children.

Factors that contribute to successful storybook reading with young children include the following:

- Inviting children to read part of the selection
- Letting children fill in predictable words
- Encouraging children to make predictions about the text
- Initiating questions to promote child involvement
- Maintaining eye contact with children

- Reading with expression
- Pointing to meaningful words or pictures while reading (With young children this is particularly important to help them understand the referents of pronouns.)
- Grouping children so that all can see the pictures and hear the story
- Highlighting special words and language features in the story

Although storybooks are the mainstay of reading materials in early childhood classrooms, it is important to remember to use a variety of reading materials when sharing books with preschool and kindergarten children. Research has shown a scarcity of informational books in elementary classrooms, and teachers tend to share fewer informational books with their students (Duke, 2000; Yopp & Yopp, 2000). Yopp and Yopp (2000) propose that teachers use informational alphabet books to support young children's development of vocabulary knowledge and knowledge of informational text structure and features. When preschoolers are exposed to a wide variety of reading materials from various genres at a young age, their understanding of text is broadened, and they are better prepared for the challenges that informational text brings at later grades.

Three specific oral reading techniques are described below.

Interactive Storybook Reading

The primary purpose of interactive storybook reading is to replicate home reading experiences. This type of oral reading should occur in small groups of up to five children, and should include book discussion facilitated by the teacher based on the cues from the children. The teacher should use a small book that is informal and conversational and has a balance of teacher- and student-initiated events. It does not necessarily have to have a predictable sequence but should have a strong emphasis on oral language and negotiating meaning. Some steps for interactive storybook reading adapted from Opitz and Rasinski (1988) and Klesius and Griffith (1996) are listed below:

1. Select a story, poem, or informational text appropriate to the children's interest and maturity.

2. Read the book aloud to children, modeling fluent reading. Also consider changing the voices of different characters and adjusting the volume, tempo, and pitch to enhance enjoyment.

3. Allow the children to interact in an informal way around the topic of the text.

4. Where appropriate, provide scaffolding by helping the children understand the text and expanding ideas during the reading through techniques such as:
   o clarifying information
   o pointing out story structure (characters, setting, problem, resolution)
   o drawing attention to illustrations
   o pointing out text features
   o pointing out new and unusual vocabulary

5. Ask children to listen for meaning. Invite them to read part of the selection, fill in words, make/confirm/disconfirm/predictions, and initiate questions and/or answer teacher questions.

6. At the end of the reading, ask students to make personal responses (text-to-text, text-to-self, text-to-world) to the text.

Shared Reading

Also called shared book experience (Holdaway, 1979), shared reading is a powerful instructional strategy that provides teacher modeling and promotes reading enjoyment and active student engagement. It is also particularly useful for teaching concepts about print including directionality. The following steps are adapted and modified from the model by Holdaway (1979):

1. Select a big book or a book with print large enough for all the children to see. The book should also contain repeated patterns that can be easily followed by the children.

2. Introduce the book to the children. Talk about the title, the name(s) of the author and illustrator. Invite them to make predictions about the book.

3. Point to each word while reading the book aloud to the children. Invite the children to chime in whenever they want to. Comment on print features and draw children's attention to the print. The purpose of shared reading is an intentional focus on developing literacy skills.

4. Encourage children to give personal responses to the story they have heard. Encourage them to read the story on their own or share the story with others.

Echo Reading

Echo reading, also called mirror reading, can give young children an opportunity to echo and participate in fluent reading and maximize their enjoyment of the story. Echo reading is simple to implement and can be incorporated in interactive storybook reading or shared reading. Steps for echo reading are simply to read one line at a time and ask the students to then repeat what the teacher read.

ADDRESSING DIVERSITY

Unlike Rebecca, who has experienced numerous hours of lapreading experience at home, Annie entered preschool with virtually no previous exposure to books. She is not always attentive when stories are read. Annie does not ask questions during the storybook sharing experiences. Only infrequently does she make any personal response about the books read to her. She does not understand the type of discourse expected of children related to storybook reading. It is not unusual for children like Annie to begin school with limited oral language and vocabulary development as well as limited understandings of concepts about print and story structure. Research has found that children with little exposure to books tend to be at risk in their literacy development throughout their formal schooling, if appropriate prevention and intervention are not provided (Snow, Burns, & Griffin, 1998).

To narrow the achievement gap, teachers should provide at-risk children with abundant interactive storybook reading experiences similar to what the children from literate families typically receive. Such read-alouds of high quality children's books need to occur multiple times during the school day.

Oral reading strategies that work well with most children are also useful for children speaking a different vernacular/dialect or for those learning English as a second language. With children speaking an English vernacular/dialect and with ELLs, special attention should be devoted to developing oral language (sound and syntax), expanding vocabulary, improving story comprehension, and also acquiring rules of social interaction that are expected in a school setting. In addition to using books that present a close correlation between pictures and words on the page, those that include repetition are beneficial for ELLs. When presenting concepts and vocabulary that do not exist in the particular dialect or language spoken by the child, the teacher should consider employing strategies such as using gestures, concrete objects, and visual aids. It is also very beneficial that teachers read selected books repeatedly until they can be partly or completely memorized. Such a practice allows children from diverse backgrounds to acquire anchor words and language patterns that they can build upon when they are introduced to other readings.

Some ELLs come from a literate family albeit in their first language. If they have received storybook reading experience in their first language at home, bilingual books that include both English and their native language (e.g., Spanish) can be excellent additions to your classroom library and used for storybook read-alouds. In addition, allowing ELLs to dramatize and act out stories can further enhance the enjoyment of the storybook reading experience, develop oral language, and improve comprehension. Echo reading and choral reading can provide scaffolding for children speaking an English vernacular, ELLs, and students with special needs.

SUMMARY

In this chapter, we discuss the importance of sharing books with preschool children. Reading books to children develops their language and vocabulary, introduces them to print conventions, and helps them develop the social skills they need to take advantage of formal instruction in later school grades. We also address issues related to selecting high quality children's books, describe book selection criteria, and make suggestions for displaying books in the classroom. Several book sharing routines are also provided. These include (a) "interactive storybook reading," which is best implemented in a small-group session and has a strong focus on oral language development, and (b) "shared reading," a routine that is more appropriate for whole-group instruction and has a focus on developing literacy skills. We emphasize these two routines as particularly important to use with children from diverse language backgrounds and children with special needs.

Integrating Literacy Across the Curriculum

8

"Yeoweee!!!! Look at that! It went really really far," Devon exclaims as Juan measures the distance the castle catapult threw a large puffer ball across the playground. Devon, Juan, and two other children grab their papers as they walk off the distance traveled by the ball. Emma's estimate is closest at 5 giant steps. They each record some variation of "Emma" and "5" on their papers. Juan runs off to ask his teacher if "5" is written differently in Spanish. Across the yard, in the sandbox, a group of children are using buckets to mold sandcastles and filling up their moats with water.

Inside, during learning center time, Juan's mother is in the cooking area helping children make "trenchers." During medieval times, thick slices of stale whole-wheat bread, called trenchers, were often used for plates. Juan's class will break from tradition and eat the bread freshly baked. Jenna dances about the castle dramatic play center in a princess gown and puts up a sign she has written saying the drawbridge is up so the castle is closed. Carlos is engrossed in the library center examining a factual book on European castles while Tia tells a story on the magnetic board using the castle pieces Mr. Gonzalez made from magnetic inkjet paper. At the writing center, Diego is serving as scribe for the king and writing a notice telling everyone the banquet will be at 5 o'clock. Olivia uses a scroll to write a note to her mother.

INTEGRATED CURRICULUM

What is going on in Mr. Gonzalez's Head Start classroom? The activities above are a part of an integrated curriculum unit focused on castles. It is called an integrated unit because Mr. Gonzalez uses the castle theme to address all the areas of learning and development appropriate for his class of four-year-old children (Neuharth-Pritchett, Reguero de Atiles & Park, 2003). Literacy concepts are clearly and purposefully included in the unit. However, Mr. Gonzalez also planned learning opportunities focused on social studies, mathematics, and science. In addition, the castle unit allows children to practice fine and gross motor skills and social interactions with peers and adults.

> An integrated unit uses the theme to address all the areas of learning and development.

Mr. Gonzalez decided to implement a unit on castles when he noticed the children playing princess in the dramatic play center and fighting dragons during outdoor play. In addition, he also heard them talking to each other about the castle where the princesses lived with the king and queen. Planning a curriculum unit based on the children's interests is known as emergent curriculum (Jones, Evans, & Rencken, 2001). It fits nicely with the constructivist view of learning described in Chapter 1. It builds on children's interests by providing learning opportunities that challenge their existing thinking, requires problem solving, and involves discovery and reflection. Simply put, an emergent curriculum encourages children to construct their own knowledge. Mr. Gonzalez's castle unit is both emergent and integrated.

One approach to integrated curriculum is the Project Approach described by Lillian Katz (Katz & Chard, 2000). Recent books written specifically for preschool teachers describe how the Project Approach has been used in real classrooms (see Helm & Katz, 2001; Helm & Beneke, 2003). A project typically begins with a field trip and then continues with a variety of classroom activities. These activities are designed to allow the children to investigate the topic and to find answers to questions they have on the topic. Projects allow children to be curious, creative, and self-motivated. Because children can be self-directed in many activities of a project they are well-suited for all children including English language learners and children with special needs.

Projects often occur over an extended period of time (several weeks) as children delve into the topic and engage in investigations that grow in complexity. Through the Project Approach, children learn valuable knowledge within a meaningful context. Often, the concepts addressed represent a surprisingly sophisticated level of knowledge. But in the context of the project, such concepts are meaningful for children and so should not be ignored (Helm & Beneke, 2003). See the resources and Web sites in the Additional Resources for Teachers for help on implementing the Project Approach. These sources also contain descriptions of projects that have been conducted in actual classrooms. "The Lunch Project" (Floerchinger, 2005) in the online journal *Early Childhood Research and Practice* is a good example—one that can give you ideas for implementing your own literacy-rich project. Another good example is Project Katrina, the story of a Baton Rouge, Louisiana, preschool after Hurricane Katrina (Aghayan, Schellhaas, Wayne, Burts, Buchanan, & Benedict, 2005).

The Castle Unit

Since castles are in short supply in the United States, Mr. Gonzalez began the unit with an exploration of castles during a large-group meeting. He found an old calendar with photos of castles in the center's picture file. He mounted several castle photos representing different styles and ages of castles. These photos served as the stimulus for a short discussion of castles. After talking about the castle photos, Mr. Gonzalez led the children in creating a castle KWL chart (see Figure 8.1). He asked questions about the photos to help the children realize what they knew about castles and recorded their responses on chart paper.

Next Mr. Gonzalez asked the children what they wanted to learn about castles. After questions about where the princess sleeps, why the windows are so skinny, and how long ago people lived in castles, the children had trouble coming up with additional ideas. Mr. Gonzalez helped by asking some guiding questions such as "lots of people live in a castle; I wonder who takes care of everything?" A second column was created on the chart paper and used to record what the children wanted to learn. As described in Chapter 6, Mr. Gonzalez rephrased children's comments to represent academic language, saying the words out loud as he wrote them on the chart. The KWL chart was then posted in the classroom for the duration of the castle unit. After the KWL discussion, Mr. Gonzalez studied the children's questions and realized that they focused on an investigation of castle life. At the end of the unit, Mr. Gonzalez will guide the children in creating the final portion of the KWL describing what they learned about castles, and in particular castle life.

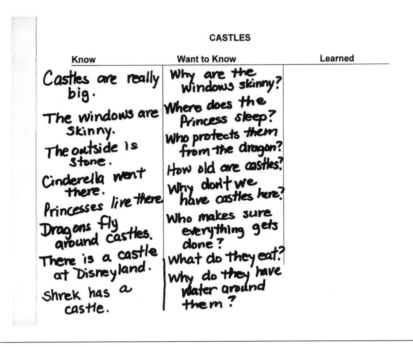

CASTLES

Know	Want to Know	Learned
Castles are really big.	Why are the windows skinny?	
The windows are skinny.	Where does the Princess sleep?	
The outside is stone.	Who protects them from the dragon?	
Cinderella went there.	How old are castles?	
Princesses live there	Why don't we have castles here?	
Dragons fly around castles.	Who makes sure everything gets done?	
There is a castle at Disneyland.	What do they eat?	
Shrek has a castle.	Why do they have water around them?	

Figure 8.1   Castles

Before KWL discussion with the children, Mr. Gonzalez had brain-stormed possible things to learn about castles, vocabulary words to introduce, and ideas for learning centers. His initial notes can be seen in Figure 8.2. Mr. Gonzalez's planning process became more focused after the initial KWL discussion with the children. He used their ideas and questions, as well as his knowledge of their current skills, to plan the unit. He focused his plans more specifically on castle life. He decided what activities to include in learning centers and outdoor play, as well as the content of large- and small-group sessions. He recorded goals and standards met by the activities planned for the castle unit, making adjustments as needed to include a variety of academic disciplines as well as all areas of development. Figure 8.3 shows the learning centers Mr. Gonzalez planned along with the standards addressed by each. For example, standards for the dramatic play center included language development, vocabulary development, and functions of print, as well as social and cognitive skills. Standards addressed in the writing center included multiple components of literacy as well as fine motor development and social studies concepts. During the planning process, Mr. Gonzalez continually referred to his assessment information on the children to make sure he included activities that would challenge the children.

Notes on Possible Things to Learn About

Who lives in the castle

Housekeeper or Chatelaine and her
keys

How meals are cooked & served

Where they get their food—grow it
(animals, vegetables, grain)

Making butter, etc. in the creamery

Breadmaking

Make own soap

Knights protect the castle and wear
armor (focus on protection)

Squires help Knights with their
horses and armor

Making tapestries to cover stone walls

Narrow windows because no
heat—only fireplaces

Only a few people know how to write

Scribes write down messages

Use scrolls to write on

Send messages by horse

Carriages—no cars

Pull up the drawbridge when they
don't want people to come
in—can't get across the moat

Lower the gate or portcullis

Used catapult to throw things
(focus on throwing things)

Use water and water wheel for power

Notes on Ideas for Centers, Outside, etc.

Dramatic play: bedroom, kitchen/dining
hall

Big ring of keys for Chatelaine—use
D-ring

Drawbridge

Gate—portcullis

Make armor

Castle journals in dramatic
play & blocks

Scrolls and stamps in writing center

Some kind of tapestry making in art
or fabric collage

Make bread trenchers in cooking area

Vocabulary Words

Tower
Drawbridge
Portcullis
Banquet
Trestle table
Trenchers (used instead of dishes—
made of bread)
Chatelaine (housekeeper)
Knight
Armor
Helm
Squire
Gown
Filmy gown
Scribe
Tapestry
Medieval
Decree
Scroll
Parchment
Moat
Fire pit
Tannery
Roast boar
Carriage or coach
Hearth
Masonry
Bricklayer
Creamery
Pulley
Coat of Arms
Stables
Lute
Jester

Figure 8.2 Brainstorming Castle Words and Possible Things to Learn About Castle Life

Center	Activity	Goals/Standards & Content Knowledge Addressed
Dramatic Play	Castle—entrance with towers from cardboard Big key ring for Chatelaine & cleaning supplies Table for eating Cooking materials Dresses, gowns, scarves	Expressive & receptive language Vocabulary development Functions of print Symbolic thinking through pretend play Creative expression Peer interaction & social problem-solving
Sensory Table	Sand with variety of small plastic containers (cups, food dishes) to build castles, water to create moats, people Or Water table with water wheels, cups, boats	Fine motor Symbolic thinking (pretend) Concept development through exploration of dry and wet sand Language development
Art	Bricks & mortar Hats & crowns Tapestry making (fabric collage or weaving or embroidery) (burlap and blunt yarn needles)	Creative expression Fine motor development Problem solving with materials Language development
Writing	Story starters Pictures of castle life Stamps for decrees (both letters & objects) Castle journals Knight's journals Scrolls (paper wrapped up between towel rods or Tinkertoy sticks)	Writing as communication Alphabetic principle Phonological awareness Social studies–understanding others, respect for diversity, types of houses Social interaction Fine motor
Library	Princess & Pea flannel board Magnet board with figures of knights, horses, and castle towers Books with castle stories Informational books about castles Favorite books including *Paper Bag Princess*, others not related to the theme	Retelling a story Reading for information Concepts about print Story structure Book language Sequencing
Blocks	Large hollow blocks Unit blocks & people Class block journal	Problem solving Spatial awareness Mathematics & physics Social interaction Writing & illustrating

Center	Activity	Goals/Standards & Content Knowledge Addressed
LARGE MOTOR	Climber with drawbridge (long board) to climber	Gross motor Peer interaction & social problem solving
MANIPULATIVES & PUZZLES	Castle puzzles made from pictures of castle calendar pasted on tag board Legos & people Other manipulatives Rhyming game	Language development Academic language Problem solving Spatial awareness Social interaction Fine motor
COOKING	Bread trenchers	Functions of language Fine motor Science—changes in ingredients when baked including appropriate vocabulary (raw, dough, bread, trencher) Math—measurement & measurement words
WOODWORKING	Making armor for the knights (cardboard and foil paper)	Problem solving Math—measurement Peer interaction Vocabulary (knight, armor, helm) Fine motor
MUSIC	Making lutes with boxes and rubber bands, flutes with cardboard tubes	Creative expression Noticing sound—timbre, rhythm, tempo
PROJECT – OUTSIDE	Catapult	Mathematics—nonstandard measurement, estimation Science/physics—weight and distance traveled Literacy—writing
COMPUTER	Castle search Castle sites bookmarked for children ($n = 5$) Paper & colored pencils for children to draw pictures of their favorite castles My favorite castle voting with pictures from computer sites & name card on magnetic board	Reading for information Writing Vocabulary Self concept Letter recognition Social conventions (how voting works)

Figure 8.3   Castle Unit Learning Centers

In addition to this overall planning, Mr. Gonzalez systematically planned how literacy would be addressed throughout the castle unit using Figure 8.4. He made sure multiple reading and writing opportunities were available in all of the learning centers. He planned for large and small group sessions to include literacy experiences. He also thought carefully about the opportunities for conversation and how the castle vocabulary words could be used.

As the castle unit unfolds, Mr. Gonzalez facilitates the children's learning during both the child-directed learning center activities and the teacher-directed activities. Because learning centers provide important opportunities for children to explore and construct knowledge, Mr. Gonzalez pays special attention to this part of the day. He circulates among the centers commenting on the children's activity, asking open-ended questions, helping to extend play. In the dramatic play center, and whenever children are engaged in pretend, there are two key ways to facilitate the play and learning process. One way is by making suggestions to the children regarding their activity or by providing additional materials. This is referred to as "facilitating play outside the play frame." In contrast, "facilitating play inside the play frame" involves joining in the pretend, taking a role, and supporting learning as a participant in the pretend episode (Vukelich, Christie, & Enz, 2002). Thus, Mr. Gonzalez eats many meals and frequently is assigned duties by the Chatelaine.

Accommodating Diversity

As the castle unit is implemented, Mr. Gonzalez is also mindful of things he can do to make the unit a successful experience for the diverse children in his classroom. He provides more specific and directive comments to Ben, who is autistic, than to the other children during learning center activities. Ben often randomly manipulates legos and other building materials without actually engaging in construction. Therefore, Mr. Gonzalez will hand Ben a lego piece and say, "Put this one on top of yours." Or as Ben arranges dishes in the castle dramatic play, Mr. Gonzalez may say, "Ben, serve Olivia some food."

Because there are many ELLs in the class, Mr. Gonzalez makes sure that the library area contains books written in both English and Spanish. The recipe for the bread trenchers and the papers for reporting catapult throws are written in both languages. Print in the learning centers and on the word wall includes both English and Spanish. Pictures accompany much of the print, helping the children connect the meanings with the text.

As he interacts with the children during the day, Mr. Gonzalez makes sure he has conversations with each of the children using vocabulary

Day of Week:

Important concepts to be emphasized:

Literacy Concepts	Activity	Literacy Standards	Targeted Children	Materials
KEY VOCABULARY				
LARGE-GROUP READ-ALOUD BOOKS(S)				
SMALL-GROUP READ-ALOUD BOOKS				
OTHER BOOKS				
LARGE-GROUP EXPLICIT LITERACY LESSONS: COMPREHENSION				
PHONOLOGICAL AWARENESS				
ALPHABET KNOWLEDGE				
PRINT CONCEPTS				
SMALL-GROUP ACTIVITIES: GROUP 1				
GROUP 2				
GROUP 3				
PLANNED CONVERSATIONS TO EXTEND ORAL LANGUAGE USE				
LITERACY BEHAVIORS TO BE IMPLICITLY TAUGHT OR MODELED				

Figure 8.4 Planning for Literacy in the Castle Unit

words from the castle unit as well as from past units. He knows it is especially important to have complex conversations with the children in his class because most come from families living in poverty. These conversations will help build the children's vocabularies. He addresses short descriptive phrases describing the child's own activities to children who are speaking very little English. For example, he describes Theresa's fabric collage saying, "There are lots of blue in your collage, blue, blue, blue, and blue," as he points to the blue fabric pieces. Juan excitedly tells Mr. Gonzalez about the catapult throwing, code switching between English and Spanish. Mr. Gonzalez rephrases the ideas back to Juan in English, modeling the appropriate English rather than correcting his speech. When Juan asks how to write "5" in Spanish, Mr. Gonzalez recognizes that Juan has constructed the knowledge that a concept can look (writing) and sound (speaking) different in the two languages. He explains that the number itself looks the same, but the number *word* looks and sounds different: "five" and "cinco." He writes each of these on Juan's paper: "5," "five," "cinco."

Assessing the Unit

As the castle unit progresses, Mr. Gonzalez spends time reviewing his curriculum to determine how well literacy has been integrated into each. He does this to make sure that the literacy needs of all of the children have been addressed. He knows it is important to build on what the children already know about literacy as well as about the topic they are exploring. First, he makes sure that he has balanced learning about different types of texts, developing oral language, and supporting word and letter level skills and understandings. Next, he checks on opportunities to use print in different contexts and for different purposes. Since many children in his Head Start classroom are ELLs whose parents were originally from Mexico, Mr. Gonzalez works hard to make the curriculum relevant to the cultural background of these children. He intentionally uses Castillo de Chapultepec, a castle in Mexico City, in several class discussions. Finally, he wants to be sure that the curriculum helps children use language and literacy to learn about their world. To help him with this review, Mr. Gonzalez uses Figure 8.5.

> The curriculum helps children use language and literacy to learn about their world.

As Mr. Gonzalez reviews the week and the castle unit so far, he reflects on how involved the children were in the topic. He noticed that girls were the predominate users of the castle dramatic play center. While both boys and girls were actively involved with the catapult and creating a working portcullis, very little pretend occurred during these activities.

	Yes	Somewhat	No
It was a topic children were interested in and wanted to know about.			
There were important concepts about the world that children could learn.			
The topic was relevant to the children's lives and the community around them.			
There were opportunities to use and extend language.			
There were opportunities to interact with print in various contexts and for various purposes.			
The activities in the learning centers built on what the children already knew about the topic.			
The large- and small-group lessons and activities extended what the children already knew.			
There were a variety of genres of books used in lessons and available for the children to interact with during activities and centers time.			
There were opportunities for the children to share their learning.			
Explicit teaching of appropriate literacy standards was integrated into activities.			
Literacy behaviors and standards were modeled by the teacher in activities and during play.			
There were opportunities for children to use their developing literacy skills in play for authentic purposes.			
Key vocabulary was identified and integrated into different activities across each day.			
There was a balance of activities supporting comprehension and learning about different types of texts, activities supporting oral language development, and activities supporting word and letter level skills.			

Figure 8.5   Assessing the Curriculum Unit

Therefore, Mr. Gonzalez now thinks about ways to attract the boys to the dramatic play center and the pretend play and castle vocabulary occurring there. He decides to make some changes in the props and dress-up clothes, pulling in ideas from books the class had read. With a little support from Mr. Gonzalez, the children should be able to reenact some of the castle stories. The changes in the castle dramatic play will support the language learning of all of the children in the class, especially the second language learners and children with special needs. Using books with which they are familiar will allow the children to build on the knowledge they already have.

Mr. Gonzalez also thinks about the opportunities available for children to interact with print. He decides that he needs to be more purposeful about reminding children playing in the block area to record their block castles (and accompanying stories) in the class block journal. The block journal consists of multiple pieces of blank paper stapled between two sheets of construction paper. It is stored with pencils on the block shelf. Mr. Gonzalez will also take digital photos of block constructions that the children could put with their block journal entries. Mr. Gonzalez was pleased with the discussions going on around the catapult outside. The children experimented with the types of materials loaded in the catapult, made predictions, and recorded the results. This activity blended ideas about mathematics and physics with purposeful writing.

Mr. Gonzalez also reviews the large-group literacy sessions for balance of literacy content and opportunities for children to talk about their learning. As he had intended, his vocabulary brainstorming resulted in a focus on vocabulary development and comprehension. He realizes that he had been using mainly modeling and questioning with the children. However, his ongoing assessments of the children indicate a continued need to model how print works. He needs to more explicitly model his thinking about how he makes sense of a story or an informational book to answer questions about castles. He also realizes that he provided poems about castles, but had not used them to expand children's rhyming ability. He decides to include a rhyming game in the manipulative area the next week. He reviews his observations of the children and notes several children he will invite to join him in playing the rhyming game during upcoming learning center time.

Mr. Gonzalez thinks about the children's engagement in the learning centers and during the large- and small-group sessions. The class had made a list of castle words after looking through several nonfiction books on castles. He decides they will continue by making two class castle books, one fiction and one nonfiction. This will allow the children to compare the two books in terms of reality and fantasy as well as structure. As the unit continues, he will invite children to add the words to the class word wall, either in picture or print form, and ultimately to the class word book. The scrolls in the writing center had been a big hit with children writing messages to each other and their families. So, he decides to add scrolls to the dramatic play center so the children can write messages as part of their pretend play as well.

To be purposeful in his teaching, Mr. Gonzalez uses multiple copies of Figure 8.5 as he plans for the following week. He notes the key concepts he wants the children to learn about castles at the top of the form. He chooses one or two castle vocabulary words to use with the children during conversations throughout each day of the week. He identifies a favorite book to reread on three days of the week and other books to either read for the first time or reread and discuss as part of the class book writing project. He thinks about the literacy skills the children will need to see modeled or taught during large-group time in order to complete the two books (fiction and nonfiction) and notes them in the appropriate places on the form. He also decides to have the children sign up for small-group authoring teams to write the class books. The small-group sessions will focus on composing and illustrating the books. Finally, he lists the materials he will need to include in each center to carry out his plans.

Mr. Gonzalez also begins to think ahead to plan the theme he would implement when the castle unit comes to a close. His observations of the children suggest two possible topics for his next unit: types of homes and machines. The children were interested in different types of castles and had talked about the differences between "really really old castles" and "only a little old castles." They had asked him why there were not any castles where they live, leading to a discussion of the types of housing used by Native Americans. But the most enthusiastic interest focused on the primitive mechanical tools found in medieval castles, specifically the portcullis (gate), the drawbridge, and the catapult. Therefore, he decides to start planning a unit on machines. He decides to move beyond machines operated by gravity and pulleys to construction machines. Juan and several other children have been talking about the earth-moving machines at an apartment construction site they pass on the way to the Head Start center. Both boys and girls have been intrigued by how the machines work and what they do, often asking questions or making statements about what they have seen. As Mr. Gonzalez begins to plan the machine unit, he goes through several steps to organize his thinking. You will recognize the process from the description of the castle unit above. Figure 8.6 and the information below describe the process.

---

1. What do children know about the topic? What questions do they have?

2. Concepts about the world children should learn

3. Plan projects and activities for the unit concepts and literacy learning

4. Identify and gather books to support the unit

5. Identify other materials and activities and standards addressed

6. Decide on assessment strategies

7. How will families be involved?

8. Plan activities & gather materials

Figure 8.6   Planning an Integrated Unit

PLANNING AN INTEGRATED UNIT

Step 1: Find Out What the Children Know and What Questions They Have About the Topic

A key to learning is building on what children already know as well as what they would like to find out. Using children's own questions gives them ownership of the learning and helps them make connections to their prior experience. Finding out what children already know helps identify misconceptions and stereotypes and also provides a base of vocabulary and concepts to expand, elaborate, and build on. Mr. Gonzalez did this during the initial KWL session on the castle unit. Now he jots down some of the questions children have asked him about construction machines over the past week. He decides to have planned conversations with small groups of children during the next week to find out what they know so he can identify misconceptions and build on their understandings.

> A key to learning is building on what children already know as well as what they would like to find out.

Step 2: Identify Important Concepts About the World the Children Should Learn

It is especially important that the unit topic chosen be content rich if children are to build up the background knowledge that they will need to comprehend books and learn more complex subjects (Dickinson, McCabe, & Essex,

2006; Neuman, 2006). Content-rich concepts provide opportunities for children to develop knowledge about their world and the language that goes with that knowledge. Exposing children to specific vocabulary of the discipline or academic language helps children construct the concept as well as develop their vocabulary (Freeman & Freeman, 2006). This is important for all children, but especially important for children learning English as a second language. For the construction machine unit, this may include terms such as crane, backhoe, cement mixer, carpenter, and many others. Over the next week, Mr. Gonzalez will begin to write down what the children could learn about construction and construction machines as well as key vocabulary that could be emphasized. This will be a key part of his brainstorming process.

Step 3: Plan Projects and Activities That Integrate Learning of Unit Content and Literacy

Content-rich classrooms provide opportunities for children to learn about print through "literacy in practice" (Neuman, 2006, p. 35). Literacy in practice activities allow children to use their newly developing literacy skills, and understandings about the functions of language and print, to explore new concepts and demonstrate their understanding of the topic. Language and literacy are used in authentic situations for real purposes and practiced in different contexts.

> Content-rich classrooms provide opportunities for children to learn about print through "literacy in practice."

The description of children engaged in activities from the castle unit at the beginning of this chapter is an example of literacy in practice. As Mr. Gonzalez talks to the children throughout the week, he identifies two or three projects for the construction machine unit that could be used to answer questions the children have raised or clear up misconceptions. He also begins to note possible activities that could occur in the learning centers as well as during group times. As he plans the projects and activities, Mr. Gonzalez refers to the literacy standards on pre-kindergarten for his state. He matches appropriate standards to the activities. He determines which standards need to be modeled, or implicitly taught, or practiced. The standards he chooses represent skills, understandings, and literacy concepts that have already been taught through explicit instruction, and also skills the children hadn't mastered, yet were ready to learn. He also notes a few standards representing ideas he wants to introduce to the children by modeling literate behaviors. He identifies which standards will need explicit teaching before the children will be able to engage in the relevant activities. Mr. Gonzalez then determines which standards he will teach to the whole class and which he will teach to selected groups of children during small-group time or as part of learning center activities.

Step 4: Identify and Gather Books That Support Learning About the Unit Concepts

Books, both informational and narrative, introduce children to vocabulary, language structures, and experiences that they may not encounter in their everyday lives. Mr. Gonzalez looks through the books available in the Head Start center for books about machines. He visits the public library to collect books as well. He selects books which use the key vocabulary and concepts he wants to teach. These books will be read to the whole class during large-group times. These books may also be reread in small-group read-alouds or placed in the library or one of the other learning centers after repeated readings. He also decides which books might be small-group read-aloud books with children working on particular projects or who have particular questions about construction and construction machines.

Step 5: Decide on Additional Books and Activities Unrelated to the Unit Theme and Identify the Literacy Standards They Address

Every activity, book, and lesson does not need to directly apply to the unit topic. Children need to have the opportunity to practice the literacy and language skills that they have begun to develop as they explored other topics. Therefore, Mr. Gonzalez will retain a few castle books plus some favorite books which are not related to either unit topic. This will allow the children to use literacy for a variety of purposes and to satisfy their own needs and interests. The familiarity of these books and activities allows the children to focus on their developing literacy skills rather than concentrate on new content. Mr. Gonzalez has noted, through his daily reflections on his curriculum and the results of his instructional activities, which children might need more support or explicit teaching of different literacy standards. He plans for center activities that address the needs of different children and plans which days he will provide those materials and invite particular children to join him in interacting with them. He plans which favorite books to reread with the children and then which to make available for them to reread on their own.

Step 6: Determine How You Will Assess What the Children Learned About the Topic and About Literacy

In order to meet the needs of the children, ongoing assessment of their learning about both literacy and the unit content is essential. This assessment can take the form of jotting down notes about what children say and do as they participate in learning centers, collecting samples of their writing, inviting specific children into a play center to participate in an activity and recording the results on a checklist, or recording children's dictation about the theme under study. Mr. Gonzalez decides to target four children per day to have a conversation with during center time. He will also observe them as they interact with literacy materials and use language in play during the construction machine unit. He identifies the literacy standards and vocabulary on which he will focus with the children. He looks carefully at the literacy standards he will be implicitly teaching and decides to construct a checklist on two of them. He will use the checklist to assess the learning of the four children he focuses on each day. He also decides to construct a checklist that he can use to evaluate the children's learning about machines through the projects they will complete together.

> Ongoing assessment of children's learning about both literacy and the unit content is essential.

Step 7: Decide How to Involve Families in the Integrated Unit

Involving families in the integrated unit supports and extends children's learning of the unit vocabulary and concepts as their learning is carried over into family life. At the beginning of the castle unit, Mr. Gonzalez sent home a newsletter telling families about the planned activities. He provided questions parents could ask to elicit conversation with their children on castles and what they were learning.

Families can also become a valuable source of information about unit topics and materials. One of the parents, Tia's mother, told him about the castle in Mexico City. For the construction unit, Mr. Gonzalez knows that several of the fathers in his class work in the construction business. He plans on inviting them to visit the class to talk about their work. He may ask them about visiting a construction site nearby. He knows that most of the children would be very excited to sit on one of the big machines. Although Mr. Gonzalez is fairly fluent in Spanish, he has never had a need to learn the Spanish words for the big construction machines. He hopes that family members may be able to provide those words. This will allow him to support both English and Spanish vocabulary growth. As he did with the castle unit, Mr. Gonzalez will create a newsletter for families at the beginning of the construction unit telling what the children will be learning and soliciting parent input. This newsletter, in both English and Spanish, will also list some activities the parents and children can do together at home to support their learning.

Step 8: Plan the Day-to-Day Activities and Lessons and Begin to Gather Needed Materials

This last step is to plan for implementing the activities in the classroom. Mr. Gonzalez makes specific plans only a week at a time because he knows he needs to evaluate children's literacy and concept learning each week. The weekly assessments allow him to adjust activities and sequence learning activities in an order that allows the children to practice what they know already, use what they are learning, and demonstrate their understanding of concepts that have been fully explored.

Advantages of Emergent Integrated Curriculum

Teaching an integrated unit based on children's interests is a big undertaking, as seen in Mr. Gonzalez's work. The benefits make the effort worthwhile. Children become actively and enthusiastically engaged in classroom activities. Misbehavior is uncommon as children are interested and productively engaged in the learning environment. Children are able to construct knowledge in ways that allow them to transfer their new understandings to other situations and settings. Finally, as seen in the description at the beginning of this chapter, the experience is fun and meaningful for both children and teachers.

SUMMARY

This chapter describes how to integrate literacy across the curriculum. Emergent curriculum, basing the curriculum on children's interests, allows literacy to be intertwined with all aspects of learning. Using the Project Approach, teachers purposefully plan activities that allow children to learn about their world at the same time they are learning about literacy. The chapter describes how one teacher developed emergent curriculum and how he assessed what the children were learning and what they needed to learn next to maximize literacy learning. How this approach accommodates diverse learners is also discussed with examples. Steps for planning emergent curriculum are described and illustrated, from choosing a topic through determining important concepts and literacy standards, to planning activities, and last but important, involving the family and community.

Literacy in the Real World   9

Juan rushed into the classroom clutching a plastic grocery bag in his hand. He went straight over to the area at the side of the classroom that was labeled "The Grocery Store/La Bodega." The area was set up as a store, with shelves and aisles similar to the neighborhood grocery store the children had visited the week before. Mr. Gomez, the store owner, had shown them around the store, telling them why he put different foods together. He was coming to the classroom that day to help the children organize their store.

Meanwhile, the shelves were already labeled with the different types of foods and had some food packages, cans, and bags on them. Juan opened his bag and began taking out the food wrappers and cans and setting them on the shelves. Juan's teacher, Mr. Gonzalez, joined him in the store. He asked Juan to tell him about the different foods he had brought and why he was putting them in different sections of the store. Mr. Gonzalez knew that Juan's mother used very few prepared foods, relying on cooking the way her own mother in Mexico had taught her to make foods common to her region, so he was not surprised to see that Juan had brought a bag that held *masa* and another labeled *arroz*.

LANGUAGE AND LITERACY IN COMMUNITIES

Mr. Gonzalez knew that the children in his class brought ways of using language and literacy to his classroom that were learned in their families and communities as part of their everyday activities. These ways of using language and literacy are rooted in the culture of the community of which each of their families is a part (Heath, 1983). All cultures have ways of thinking, beliefs, and values that guide the way the members of a

culture act. How language and literacy function in a particular community is part of those ways of thinking.

Reading, writing, and talking are all part of everyday life, although
what part they play may differ in different communities. Heath (1983)
studied and lived with the people of three different communities for nine
years to find out how they used language and literacy. She wanted to find
out why children in two of the communities were not as successful as
other children in learning to read and write. She called the communities
Trackton, Roadville, and Townspeople. She found that each community
had different purposes for their talk, asked preschool children different
types of questions, and used reading and writing differently. Only one of
those communities, Townspeople, used language and literacy in ways that
matched school language and literacy use.

In Trackton, Heath (1983) found that the preschool children were
asked questions about events or people that expected them to make connections to their own experiences. They were also asked questions that
were meant to bring out a story about an event they had seen. Very seldom were the children asked questions that sought information from the
preschool child or questions to which the adult already knew the answer.
The purpose for learning to talk in Trackton was to learn how to interpret
language meanings in different situations and to shift roles depending on
the expectations of adults. Reading was used to accomplish tasks in daily
life such as paying bills or reading signs; to keep up relationships between
family and friends, such as sending cards or reading announcements
about upcoming events; to keep up with news in the community; and to
nourish or confirm beliefs that were already held. Writing was used to aid
one's own memory, take the place of a face-to-face conversation, to keep
track of financial information, and for recording the events and decisions
of the local church. When the children of Trackton came to preschool,
language was used differently. Teachers thought children were not being
polite when they chatted freely to their neighbors during group time. They
thought they were not answering questions properly when they did not
respond to questions to which they knew the teacher already knew the
answer. Since many children had not participated in storybook reading,
they did not know how books and stories worked.

In Roadville, Heath (1983) found that the preschool children were
asked very different types of questions than the children in Trackton were
asked, and had different purposes for learning to talk. In this community,
children were often asked questions to which the adult already knew the
answer and assumed that the child did as well. The children often heard
questions that really weren't questions but statements about what a child
needed to do. For example, a mother might say to a child who had just

tracked mud into the house, "Don't you know that I just mopped that floor?" (Heath, 1983, p. 132), intending the child to interpret the question as an order to wipe up the footprints. Church and reading the Bible were very important in Roadville, so children were expected to learn Bible verses and repeat them exactly, showing that they could "say it right" (p. 144). Reading was used to gain information for daily life, as well as to gain information about events happening in the world or to other people. It was used to confirm or announce facts or beliefs, to keep up social contacts, and for entertainment. Writing was used as a reminder for oneself or someone else, to support an oral message, for financial reasons, and to uphold social contacts. Roadville children were considered polite to adults but teachers often considered them to be misbehaving because they never responded to requests such as, "It's time to clean up and come to the rug." While being able to exactly retell a story was an expectation that was the same at home and at school for these children, they had to learn that it was okay to pretend and make up stories as well.

Heath (1983) found that the Townspeople viewed talking as having conversations. Preschool children were often involved in a conversation with their parents around what they were doing. They were encouraged to tell stories that were imaginary or to share information and to listen quietly to others. Questions were often asked of the children to which the adult already knew the answer, to request clarification, or to tell about events. Reading was used to gain information, for leisure or entertainment, to become more knowledgeable about literature or social causes, and to keep up relationships. Writing was used to remember, to communicate when one needed a record of the communication, to keep up relationships, and for financial reasons. These purposes and ways of talking were very similar to school ways of talking and using reading and writing, so they were more successful in their preschool settings since their ways of using language and literacy matched the models at school.

Children, then, learn from their families what is proper language use in their home and community and what ways of using reading and writing are valued. Recall Halliday's functions of language that were listed in Chapter 2 (see also Table 9.1 in this chapter). Reading and writing can serve all of those functions as well. Different families and cultures use reading and writing mainly for only some of those functions. Remember in Trackton, families used reading and writing to accomplish tasks in daily life (regulatory), get along with others (interactional), and keep up with and record community and church activities (representational) while in Roadville, reading and writing were used for interactional functions, heuristic functions (to find out about the world), and representational functions. In schools, however, teachers ask children to use reading and writing for all of those functions. Because of these differences in how reading and writing are used, there are also differences in how reading and writing are supported in school and in families and how adults and children view proficiency in demonstrating reading and writing behavior (Arzubiaga, Rueda, & Monzó, 2002; Cairney, 2000). This mismatch can lead to children not understanding what they are supposed to be learning or why they do or should participate in different activities.

In some families, some functions of reading and writing are more evident just because of the circumstances of their social and family lives. In Juan's family, written language serves mainly regulatory and representational functions. Juan's parents read the bills that arrive at the home so that they will continue to have electricity in their apartment and so that they will have a place to live. They follow the rules that are indicated by traffic signs. They read the church bulletin to find out about different church services that are available. His mother reads the ads in the fliers that come to their mailbox each week so that she can find out what foods are on sale at nearby stores. In Rebecca's family, however, written language serves instrumental, interactional, personal, heuristic, and imaginative functions as well. Rebecca's parents make holiday lists with her to send to grandparents. They send holiday cards and e-mails to friends and relatives. They encourage Rebecca to ask questions and look up the answers in books. They read a variety of books with her, often rereading favorites many times. Because Rebecca and Juan have participated in and observed very different reasons for reading and writing, they have different ideas about how they should participate in reading and writing activities.

In addition to differences in how language is used and how reading and writing function, there can also be a mismatch between the kinds of print materials that are found at home and at school (Duke & Purcell-Gates, 2003). Table 9.1 lists some examples of print materials that demonstrate the different functions of language that are found in schools and that are found in homes and communities. As you can see, many of the examples from each setting are very different. In classrooms, children see charts, sign-up sheets, lists with rules, journals, storybooks, informational books, labels and name tags, and print materials such as newsletters posted for parents to read. At home and in the community, they might also see storybooks or journals, or perhaps newsletters. They will also see all of the print materials that enable a person to make their way through everyday life. Parents may read newspapers or magazines. They may receive advertisements for food or other types of sales in the mail. Families might buy cards to send to friends, look at catalogs, read religious materials, or fill out sweepstakes forms. In the community, children will see traffic signs, bill-boards or signs on buildings, or menus at fast food restaurants.

Table 9.1   Functions of Written Language

Function	Description	Example School	Example Home or Community
INSTRUMENTAL	To communicate desires, wishes ("I want")	Charts of favorite foods, sign-up for snack	Grocery list, catalog, menu
REGULATORY	To control behavior of others ("Do as I say")	Classroom rules, sign-in sheet	Traffic signs, warning signs, "OPEN" and "CLOSED" signs, bills
INTERACTIONAL	To get along with others ("Me and you")	Name tags, notes to each other or from teacher to parent	Holiday cards, fliers announcing events at church or community center
PERSONAL	To express self and feelings ("Here I come")	Journals, books about self, pictures with captions	E-mail to family members, letter to editor
HEURISTIC	To find out about the world ("Tell me why")	KWL chart, brainstorm list, charts and graphs	Application for job, sweepstakes form
IMAGINATIVE	To create new worlds ("Let's pretend")	Storybooks, poetry	Storybooks, magazines
REPRESENTATIONAL	To communicate content ("I've got something to tell you")	Informational books, dictionary, school newsletter	Ads, billboards, newspaper, church bulletin, telephone book, food labels

SOURCE: From Halliday, M. A. K., *Learning how to mean: Explorations in the development of language*, Copyright ©1975. London: Edward Arnold.

McGee, L. M., & Richgels, D. J. (2003). *Designing early literacy programs: Strategies for at-risk preschool and kindergarten children.* New York: The Guilford Press.

INFUSING HOME AND COMMUNITY LITERACY IN THE CLASSROOM

To support children's learning about reading and writing, it is important that teachers first learn about the community where the children live and the reading and writing practices of the families in that community. The families in those communities have what are known as funds of knowledge (Velez-Ibanez & Greenberg, 2005), which are the bodies of everyday information and practices that families and community members have that help them to make their way successfully through the life of the community, and to successfully complete the important activities of daily life. If the same knowledge, skills, activities, practices, and ideas are incorporated into classrooms, children will see the connections between the different literacies of their lives and be more successful at learning.

One way to bridge classroom and community is to take the children out into the community surrounding the classroom. In the vignette at the beginning of the chapter, Mr. Gonzalez took the children to the neighborhood grocery store, a place familiar to the children in his Head Start classroom. They looked at the print in the store and how it was used. The store owner, Mr. Gomez, talked with them about how he organized the food in the store. In the big machine unit planned in the previous chapter, the children could walk to the construction site to see the machines, talk to the machine operators, and perhaps sit in one of the machines.

Another way to bridge classroom and community is to bring the community into the classroom. This can be accomplished by bringing community members into the classroom as well as by bringing the print found in families and communities into classroom activities. Community members can be invited because they have expertise related to what the children are studying. For example, Mr. Gomez in the opening vignette was going to help the children organize their grocery store. A construction supervisor could help the children set up a construction site in the classroom block center. Family members can be invited to share their expertise. A mother can bring in a favorite snack recipe and help the children cook it, or a father who is a gardener could help the children pick out plants to plant around the school site. Of course, it is important that the parents and community members be given guidance to help them have a successful visit. This guidance should include helping them to plan for the active involvement of the children as well as helping them know what the children know about the topic and what they want to learn.

Besides having community members visit the classroom, print from the community should become a part of the classroom. Vukelich, Christie, and Enz (2002) suggest that environmental print (EP) from the children's lives becomes a key part of the classroom environment. They suggest that preschool classrooms have an EP board that contains food containers, menus from neighborhood restaurants, newspaper ads for grocery stores, or other print the children bring in. Another way to integrate EP that they suggest is to make EP folders or booklets. These small books could be either built around a theme, such as cookies, or could contain logos and labels that the child can read.

To incorporate print into the classroom environment that children might see in the community, Vukelich et al. (2002) suggest taking an EP walk around the neighborhood. The children and teacher can point out the signs they see and talk about what they might say. When the children return to the classroom, they can draw pictures of the print that they saw and dictate a sentence about it. The pages can be put in a class book that the teacher reads aloud and the children can read in the library area. Alternatively, children can be given a disposable camera to take home to take pictures of print in their home and neighborhood as well as of people using reading and writing. Once the pictures have been developed, each child can make his or her own book made up of the pictures and dictated sentences about the pictures.

An important method for linking home and school literacy is to have real life play centers that are set up to resemble a setting with which the children might be familiar in their life. In the vignette at the beginning of the chapter, Mr. Gonzalez has set up a grocery store like the one the children visited. The children were bringing food items that their families might buy at the store. He will add play food for the fresh produce and signs for the various aisles. There will be a checkout stand with magazines, and food coupons will be available for shoppers to use. Research has shown that children who are offered this type of play center use literacy more in play and develop strategies that will help them comprehend print (Neuman & Roskos, 1992, 1997). It is important that the real life play centers provide contexts that the children have had experience with. For instance, in Annie's and Juan's neighborhoods, there are no pizza restaurants, so that would not be an appropriate restaurant to have in the classroom, but in Michael's and Rebecca's classrooms it would. If the children built a bakery in Juan's classroom, it might have traditional Mexican desserts and sweet breads, while the bakery in Michael's classroom might have doughnuts, yeast rolls, loaves of white bread, and cakes.

Key in linking the classroom and community is being aware of languages other than English that are spoken by the children and their parents. Those languages need to also be included in the classroom print. Mr. Gonzalez used both Spanish and English as he labeled the different centers in the classroom and labeled shelves that held different materials.

He encouraged children to bring in environmental print from their homes that used Spanish. As a member of the community in which his classroom was located, Mr. Gonzalez spoke Spanish and participated in community life with the parents of the children in his classroom. He was able to communicate with the parents in their native language. However, not all teachers speak the languages of the parents and community. It is important, then, to bridge the language gap. Teachers should look for community members or parents who speak both English and the language of the parents who don't speak English. They could help with translating the labels and print in the classroom so that both languages enrich the environment. They could also help the teacher locate books in the children's home language and come in and read those books.

SUMMARY

Children come to preschool with diverse language and literacy backgrounds. They have learned how to use language in ways that their own families and communities value. They see reading and writing used in their lives in ways that may be different from the ways that reading and writing are used in classrooms. Teachers need to bridge the gap between the community and the classroom by going out into the community, bringing community members into the classroom, and bringing print from the home and community into the classroom.

Helping Parents Facilitate Children's Literacy at Home

10

"Mommy, mommy, we have to stay. It's Family Night!" Michael bounds up to his mother who has just arrived to take him home. He grabs her around the waist and hugs as he continues, "Please, please, please?" His mother looks tired and conflicted as she thinks about all the things that must be done tonight. "Oh dear, Daddy is waiting in the car and we have to go to Grandma's to pick up Jennifer [his school-age sister], and she has homework, and I need to do laundry and ..." As Michael's face starts to crumble, she continues, "Stay right here while I go talk to your father." She returns quickly with a spring in her step, "Daddy will go get Jennifer and meet us back here."

WHY PARENTS BECOME INVOLVED

Family Night was important enough to both Michael and his family that his parents were willing to change their plans in order to attend. What motivates parents tired from a long workday to make this choice? Michael's child care program had planned the event around the families who were enrolled by providing supper and specific events for both the adults and the children. Clearly, the way in which the program accommodated the working families influenced the decision of Michael's family to attend. But other factors are important as well. Two of these factors are parental beliefs about involvement and invitations to become involved (Hoover-Dempsey & Sandler, 1997; Walker, Wilkins, Dallaire, Sandler, & Hoover-Dempsey, 2005). While the process is not always easy, early childhood programs can have an impact on both of these.

It is important for teachers to realize that parental beliefs are socially constructed (Hoover-Dempsey & Sandler, 1997; Hoover-Dempsey, Walker, Sandler, Whetsel, Green, Wilkins, & Closson, 2005). This means that parents construct their beliefs through past and present experiences. This includes one's own experiences while growing up. Thus, beliefs about parent involvement are long-standing. In addition, beliefs about parental involvement are shaped by, and represent, the values of family members and friends. This means beliefs are difficult to change. There is no magic program or one special strategy that can easily change beliefs about parent involvement. Instead, teachers need to be both patient and persistent as they use a variety of strategies to encourage parents to become engaged in their children's education. Changes in beliefs and parental involvement practices may occur over several years. Thus, the work early childhood teachers do with parents lays the groundwork for future home-school relationships.

PARENTAL BELIEFS

Role Construction

Parents must believe that they are supposed to be involved—that part of the job of parenting is being involved in their child's education. This view of the parental role may be either parent-focused or partnership-focused (see Box 10.1). This means that parents believe they have the major responsibility for their child's education (parent-focused role), or more ideally, that they partner with the school in educating their children (partnership-focused role). In contrast, parents with a school-focused role tend to leave everything up to the school. Programs can help turn school-focused roles into partnerships by helping parents see how their interest and participation helps their child learn. Again, teachers should remember that changing parental role construction is likely to be a slow process.

> Parents must believe that they are supposed to be involved.

Box 10.1 Why Parents Become Involved

BELIEFS ABOUT INVOLVEMENT	**Role Conception**	This describes what parents think they are supposed to do, what their role in their child's education should be.
		Parents who believe they are supposed to be involved have either parent-focused or partnership-focused role conceptions.
		Parents who do not believe they should be involved have school-focused role conceptions. They believe educating children is the job of the school, not the family.
	Perceived Efficacy	This describes how effective parents believe they can be in helping their child's learning.
		Parents who believe they can be effective get involved.
		Parents who do not believe they can be effective are typically not involved.
INVITATIONS	**From School**	Invitations to parents from school and teachers to be involved in their child's education
	From Child	Requests from child to parent to participate in some activity related to the child's learning

SOURCE: Based on the model described by Walker, J. M. T., Wilkins, A. S., Dallaire, J. R., Sandler, H. M., & Hoover-Dempsey, K. V., Parental involvement: Model revision through scale development. *Elementary School Journal, 106,* copyright © 2005, pp. 85–104.

Effectiveness

Parents who are involved also believe they can be effective in helping their children with school and the learning process. Without this feeling of self-efficacy, parents are likely to avoid the school and do little to participate in their child's academic learning, regardless of their parental role construction. Therefore, early childhood programs should consider ways to nurture both types of beliefs (role construction and efficacy) in the families they serve. Given the choice made by Michael's parents, they clearly believe they should be involved and that they can play an important role in Michael's learning. We can make the same conclusion about Rebecca's family. However, the families of Juan and Annie will be more challenging as their past experiences will lead them to avoid contact with the school.

Invitations

Invitations to families asking them to participate in their children's educational experience help engage parents. Invitations give parents something specific to be involved in and let them know they are both welcome and valued. Parents who believe they should be involved and feel they will be effective are likely to respond positively to invitations from the program. Parents who receive many invitations for a wide variety of parent involvement activities are more likely to actually become involved and engaged (Sheldon, 2005). It seems that both the number of invitations received and the variety of activities represented can entice parents to participate.

> Invitations give parents something specific to be involved in and let them know they are both welcome and valued.

Invitations from children are powerful as well, as seen in the example with Michael above (based on a real incident which occurred in an Early Reading First program). In addition to children's spontaneous invitations, teachers can suggest to children that they invite their parents to participate. In fact, Michael's teacher, Ashley, does this consistently. During afternoon snack, she talked about the upcoming Family Night and told children to remind their parents to come.

Building Partnerships

Regardless of parents' role construction or efficacy beliefs, building family-school partnerships is the key to facilitating parental involvement (Hoover-Dempsey et al., 2005). All of the parent involvement strategies described in this chapter reflect current thinking on ways to build positive partnerships with families. Good partnerships are based on the people and programs involved; no two partnerships are the same, for they grow and develop to fit the partners rather than some arbitrary model (Powell, 2006).

> Building family-school partnerships is the key to facilitating parental involvement.

Keeping this individuality in mind, there are general characteristics that appear to be part of productive partnerships (see Box 10.2). Effective partnerships are based on the needs and interests of the families. Control is shared between parents and schools. This means decision making is joint and that both parents and teachers may bring issues and concerns to the table. There is mutual respect between parents and the school, with parents viewed as having valuable expertise and the ability to guide their children's learning. Partnership activities build on family strengths rather than focusing on perceived deficits. (Lopez, Kreider, & Caspe, 2004–2005; Powell, 2006; Tett, 2001). Powell notes this is particularly important for programs focused on family literacy. Parent education content must be responsive to family values, habits, and circumstances. Expecting Annie's mother to engage her daughter in the same way as Rebecca's parents is unrealistic. In this case, strategies designed to fit into the everyday life of a sharecropper are more likely to be adopted. Think about these partnership characteristics and how they can be infused into the parent involvement practices described below.

Box 10.2   Components of Productive Partnerships

Effective School-Family Partnerships:

- Reflect family interests and needs
- Demonstrate mutual respect and trust among the partners
- Contain ongoing communication and dialogue related to child and family experiences
- Build on family strengths

SOURCE: Adapted from Lopez, M. E., Kreider, H., & Caspe, M. (2004–2005, Winter). Co-constructing family involvement. *The Evaluation Exchange, 10*(4), Article 1. Retrieved May 30, 2007, from http://www.gse.harvard.edu/hfrp/content/eval/issue28/winter2004-2005.pdf

TYPES OF PARENTAL INVOLVEMENT

Parents and schools have a shared responsibility for educating children (Patrikakou, Weissberg, Redding, & Walberg, 2005). Research has consistently shown that children do better academically when their parents are involved. However, without invitations and encouragement from schools, parents with low levels of education and few positive school experiences are not likely to do so (Epstein & Sanders, 2002). Parental involvement is doubly important, then, for families living in poverty because it enhances children's learning. When mothers are involved in their children's education, low-income children do just as well on measures of literacy as do middle-class children (Dearing, Kreider, Simpkins, & Weiss, 2006). Since low-income children typically score below middle-income children on literacy assessments (as noted in Chapter 1), it is important for both teachers and parents to understand that parental attention really can make a difference. When teachers help parents become involved in their child's learning, both the teacher and the parents help the child learn. In addition to helping children's literacy learning, parental involvement in high quality early childhood programs can help children avoid other long-term negative consequences of poverty such as failing a grade or not completing high school (Reynolds & Clements, 2005). This means it is extremely important for early childhood programs to help parents become appropriately involved in their child's learning.

> Parental involvement is doubly important for families living in poverty because it enhances children's learning.

Parent Education

Epstein has defined six types of parent involvement (see Box 10.3). Each can be useful for engaging parents in their children's literacy learning. This chapter focuses on the first four types. The first type of parent involvement is called parenting—basic obligations of families. It includes the basic things families do for their children such as providing food, clothing, and shelter and making sure children go to school. Teachers and schools should play supportive and educational roles in this type of parent involvement. Specifically, they can provide information and education to parents designed to help them raise and educate their children.

Box 10.3   Epstein's Six Types of Parental Involvement

Type of Involvement	Function
1. **Parenting: Basic Obligations of Families**	Schools provide information to families on children's learning and development, and ways to support children's learning and development.
2. **Communication: Basic Obligations of Schools**	Schools communicate with families about their children, school events/opportunities.
3. **Volunteering at the School**	Family members provide assistance to teachers in the classroom, or to the school in other settings/situations.
4. **Learning at Home**	Teachers assist parents in supporting their children's learning at home.
5. **Decision Making**	Parents participate on school councils or committees. The goal is to empower parents and bring perspective of families into school decisions and governance.
6. **Collaborating With the Community**	Schools make connections with community resources, inform families of available services, and advocate for families and children in the community.

SOURCE: Based on Epstein, J. L., & Sanders, M. G. (2002). Family, school, and community partnerships. In M. H. Bornstein (Ed.), *Handbook of parenting, 2nd ed. Vol. 5, Practical issues in parenting* (pp. 407–437). Mahwah, NJ: Lawrence Erlbaum.

Michael's child care program did this through the formal Family Night mentioned in the vignette at the beginning of this chapter. The child care program planned the event very carefully with food, child care, and a meaningful parent activity. To spark interest, multiple strategies were used to identify topics of interest to program families. A questionnaire was distributed to parents early in the school year asking about parents' interests in a variety of child reading topics. Teachers provided information on questions they had received from parents and the types of activities they heard parents and children discussing. Finally, teacher's formal and informal assessments of children's skills suggested areas of development that could benefit from parent-child learning activities. Together this information was used to plan the focus of each Family Night held during the year.

To make the Family Night that Michael's family attended a success, the program provided a hot supper for all family members. Through previous experience, the center staff knew that more families would attend if they did not have to go home, get supper, and then return. Activities and adult supervision were also provided for children of all ages. Like Michael's program, an Early Reading First program we worked with routinely planned to have "leftovers" at their Family Nights. They encouraged their low-income parents to take the extra food home so it would not be wasted. The program staff believed that the possibility of leftovers to take home was an added incentive for families to attend.

The Family Night at Michael's child care center featured a workshop on effective ways for parents to read and discuss books with their children. At the end of the workshop, children and parents were brought together so the parents could practice their newly learned skills with their children. All of the strategies used helped make the Family Night appealing to parents and children and helped ensure a good turnout.

Parent-child book reading is only one possibility for parent education meetings. A variety of literacy-related strategies can be used in parent workshops. Possibilities include how to share wordless picture books, ways to make routine family tasks and outings educational, and how parents can model their own uses of reading and writing for their children. Regardless of the content, it is important it fit parent interests and for parents to be actively involved in the learning process (Powell, 2006). Just like children, adults learn by doing, experimenting, and constructing their knowledge (see Chapter 1). This is why Michael's program ended the evening with parents using the strategy taught with their children.

If formal parent education meetings remain a challenge for families to attend, home visits are an alternative. While labor-intensive, they have the value of offering individualized assistance to parents in their own homes. This allows the home visitor to talk with parents about how their family functions and brainstorm ways to infuse learning opportunities into their home and routines. Figuring out how to insert learning strategies into family routines is not necessarily obvious for parents. A respectful open-ended discussion can help parents identify minor adoptions rather than implementing new ways of accomplishing family tasks.

Communication

One-way Communication

The second type of parent involvement identified by Epstein is communication. Communication can be either one-way or two-way. One-way communication means one party (the parent or school) provides information to the other, but does not expect a response. Early childhood programs often use a variety of one-way communication strategies. One-way communication is typically written. Because Spanish is the language spoken in Juan's family and that of several others in Mr. Gonzalez's Head Start program, written materials are always translated into Spanish. A group of three bilingual speakers/readers are available to translate formal program materials such as policy manuals and newsletters. To make sure the translations communicate the original message, one person translates and a second checks the translation. Because not all classrooms have bilingual teaching staff, the translators are also available to help teachers with written materials to and from parents.

Examples of one-way communication include newsletters, bulletin boards with information for parents, and notes home with specific information about the child. These forms of one-way communication are more likely to be used by parents if they see a direct connection to their child. Thus Ashley, Michael's teacher, often includes information on classroom events, quotes from children, or examples of their work. She tells children what is in the class newsletter emphasizing the parent-child activity ideas and urges the children to ask (invite) their parents to do them.

Bulletin boards for parents should be more than static displays. Bulletin boards or displays that have flyers or handouts that parents can pull off the board and take home are more successful than boards designed simply for viewing. Again, making a clear connection to children stimulates parental interest. Bulletin boards in programs serving English language learners should include text in both English and the families' first language. Linking parent bulletin boards to children's literacy learning is a natural combination. For example, a bulletin board on the development of children's writing could include short statements describing the progression of writing from random scribbles, to scribbled lists, to letters and invented spelling. Examples of children's writing illustrating each step could be posted with the statements. A handout with a more detailed version of the information, including ways to encourage children's writing at home, should also be included on the bulletin board (in a pocket or attached in an easily removable way). The board should be checked periodically and handouts replenished as needed.

> Making a clear connection to children stimulates parental interest.

Notes home are another form of valuable communication. Often they are one-way, but can be turned into two-way communication if a parental response is expected. Both Mr. Gonzalez and Ashley send brief "happy grams" to parents about their children's school activities on a regular basis. They keep the tone positive and give parents a peek at their child's day. It is also important to keep track of who receives happy grams in order to make sure that each parent gets one every couple of weeks. This strategy builds rapport with parents. If problems do arise, parents will be more likely to respond to the teacher's concerns in a helpful way because they have built a relationship through routine, positive exchanges. There are many ways to make notes home eye catching, including attaching stickers, using computer graphics and clip art, and purchasing colorful paper or stationery. The happy gram forms in Figure 10.1 and Figure 10.2 were created using standard word processing software on a home computer. In addition, some Internet sites designed for teachers provide forms for free downloading.

Two-Way Communication

One of the easiest ways to build a good relationship with parents is during drop-off and pick-up times. Short conversations between parent and teacher about the child's day provide valuable information for both parties. Other effective strategies include telephoning parents at home. These phone calls should be like verbal happy grams—positive messages about the child. Again, a history of positive contacts helps both parents and teachers discuss more serious matters at other times.

> One of the easiest ways to build a good relationship with parents is during drop-off and pick-up times.

Home visits are another way to build relationships with families while also gaining insight into the family and the child's home experiences. Kathi, Rebecca's preschool teacher, visited each family in their home before the beginning of the school year. She used what she learned during the visits, along with her knowledge of child development and literacy learning, to make curriculum plans for the beginning of the school year. By the time parents came for the mid-year parent-teacher conferences, they had developed a comfortable relationships with Kathi and were ready to dig in and make serious plans for their children.

Annie's teacher, Mrs. Jones, feels it is important for both teachers and parents to prepare for parent-teacher conferences. She sends home a form with two or three questions that prompt parents to think about what they want to discuss at the conference (see Box 10.4 for ideas). She uses the

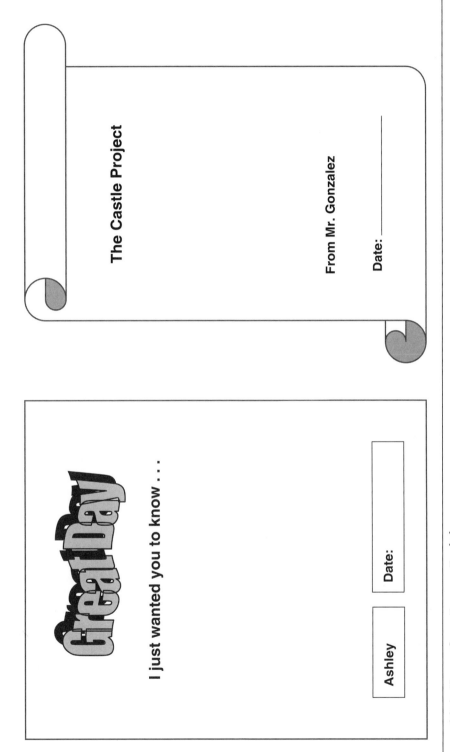

Figure 10.1 Happy Gram Forms—English

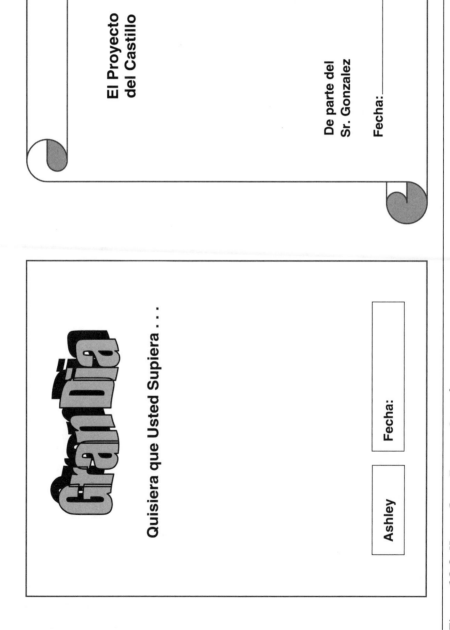

Figure 10.2 Happy Gram Forms—Spanish

sandwich approach as she talks to parents, beginning and ending each conference on a positive note. As she plans to meet with Annie's mother, she decides to start by talking about Annie's recent realization that the words, not the pictures, carry the meaning in picture books. She will also show the mother artifacts from Annie's portfolio and her contribution to a class book. She will then move on to talk about Annie's disruptive group-time behavior. Mrs. Jones hopes that together they can come up with some strategies to help Annie stay calm and focused at group time. Developing a plan to help Annie moves the conference back to a positive tone, completing the sandwich.

Box 10.4	Sample Questions to Prepare Parents for Conferences

Questions for Parents to Consider Before Conferences

It is important for preschool children to learn about both reading and writing at the same time.

- What kinds of writing does your child do at home?
- What questions do you have about this?
- What would you like to know about your child's reading and writing abilities?
- What would you like to know about your child's preschool experience?

Volunteering

Volunteering at school is the most traditional form of parent involvement and is the third type in Epstein's typology. It is important to remember that there are many other ways for parents to be involved. Helping in the classroom may not be the most meaningful form of participation for some parents. That said, parents can play an important role in the classroom. Mrs. Jones asks parents to attend a brief orientation session prior to volunteering in the classroom. This allows her to talk about positive ways to guide children's behavior rather than just saying "no." She also provides a handout on the major goals of each learning center and appropriate things parents can do in the centers to facilitate children's learning.

She has found this information particularly important in the writing and art centers, where she wants adults to encourage children's attempts rather than doing the writing and drawing for them. In addition to helping with ongoing classroom events, Mrs. Jones asks parents to share family traditions with the children. One way she does this is through "Child of the Week" activities. Each family is asked to tell a special family story featuring the child at group time. Parents may visit the class and do this in person, send a note to be read at group time, or verbally give the information to Mrs. Jones so that she may relay it at group time. A digital recorder is available for check out if parents prefer to record their telling of the story. Mrs. Jones makes sure parents understand the story needs to be less than five minutes long.

> Parents attend a brief orientation session prior to volunteering in the classroom.

Mrs. Jones also realizes that many of the parents cannot participate at school due to other family obligations. For those who are interested, she has simple things that can be done outside the class to help. One parent has obtained the cooperation of her employer and uses the materials and equipment there to laminate and spiral-bind classroom books. Another parent is sewing new smocks for children to wear at the water table.

Learning at Home

Helping parents identify ways to facilitate children's literacy learning at home is very important as children really do spend more time at home than at school—even though it sometimes does not seem that way. Learning at home is Epstein's fourth type of parent involvement. Home learning strategies are particularly important for Mrs. Jones's and Mr. Gonzalez's classrooms since they serve families living in poverty. Both teachers know that for these families, parent involvement at home can have a big impact on children's literacy learning (Dearing et al., 2006).

> For families living in poverty, parent involvement at home can have a big impact on children's literacy learning.

Both of these teachers give parents tips on how to have extended, complex conversations with their children. Conversations such as these are very important for children's literacy learning but do not occur very often in families struggling to make ends meet. The teachers explain how complex conversations can occur during routine activities such as clearing up the supper dishes or in the car (see Box 10.5 for ideas).

Box 10.5   Car Games

Literacy Games to Play in the Car

- Find car license plates that contain the first letter of the child's or other family member's name.
- Look for street signs or businesses that contain a specific letter.
- Look for different types of traffic signs—identify and count.
- Make up a story about the people in the next car.
- Look out the window for things that rhyme or start with the same sound.
- Make up rhymes about the houses or businesses you are passing.

Mr. Gonzalez sends home book bags. Each bag contains a book, stuffed animal or plastic figure, and questions and activities regarding the book for parents and children to do together. A favorite book bag activity is the travel journal. Each family is asked to write a page in the journal about their experience with the book and the adventures the stuffed/plastic figure had in their home. This journal entry is then shared with the class at group time when the book bag is returned. Mr. Gonzalez creates his own book bags, making sure to include bags with both English and Spanish language books.

Many resources are available to assist teachers in creating and implementing book bag programs (see the Additional Resources at the end of the book). There are also commercial book bag programs that schools can purchase and use with their families. Raising a Reader is one such program (*What is Raising a Reader?*, n.d.; see Web site for information). Many of the United Way Success by 6 programs, Head Start programs, and public libraries partner with Raising a Reader to provide positive experiences with books to low-income families and their children. The program was designed specifically for families in poverty with parents whose own literacy skills are poor or who have limited English proficiency. Program materials include sturdy book bags, multilingual books, training materials for teachers, and a video (in multiple languages) showing parents how to make the most of the book bag experience with their children.

Returning now to Mr. Gonzalez, another strategy his program uses to engage parents in their children's learning at home is a lending library of children's books. Both English and Spanish books are available.

Mr. Gonzalez emphasizes how important it is for the Spanish-speaking families to read to their children in their native language. This is one thing they can do to help nurture the child's first language. This is a particular concern of Mr. Gonzalez, as a few of the parents have been trying to use only English with their children in an effort to help them be like their English-speaking peers.

Complementing this strategy, Mrs. Jones provides home activities for parents in her classroom to build on what the children learn at school. For instance, she extended a fall unit on leaves by sending home a "Tree Journal" with instructions for use. During the leaf unit, the children were divided into three different groups. Each chose a tree on the playground to watch. They made observations twice a week during the fall and described what the tree looked like. They also took pictures and wrote down descriptive statements. At the end of the unit, Mrs. Jones realized the children were still interested in watching their trees and so the observation and recording activities were continued, but with longer intervals between observations. In addition to watching their trees at school, Mrs. Jones suggested that each family pick a tree or bush to observe near their home. She suggested starting with observations every few days, then progressing to weekly and monthly during the winter and then increasing in frequency again during the spring. She stapled blank white paper inside folded construction paper to make the journals. Each child chose a journal and decorated the outside in class. Then the journals, instructions, and two pencils were sent home providing each family with all the materials needed for the home learning activity.

WHY PARENTAL INVOLVEMENT?

As seen above, participation in the various forms of parental involvement bring the family and early childhood program together. Epstein (Epstein & Sanders, 2002) views home and school as overlapping spheres of influence on children's learning and development. They each influence children's learning and children do best when the home-school relationship is positive. Bronfenbrenner's (Bronfenbrenner & Morris, 2006) theoretical model describes the home-school relationship in a different, but complementary way (see Figure 10.3). According to his theory, children participate in multiple contexts which influence their development. These contexts are called microsystems. Home and the early childhood program are two such microsystems. Within each microsystem, children have many experiences that are repeated over time. These repeated experiences are called proximal processes and are responsible for children's development.

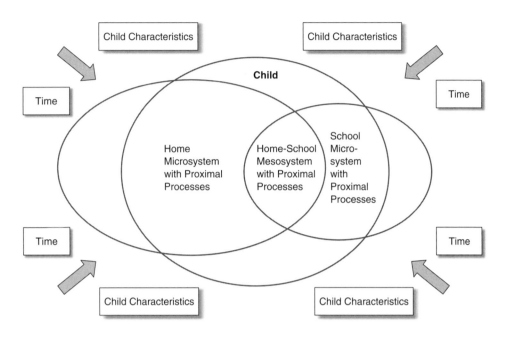

Figure 10.3 Bronfenbrenner's Model Applied To Family-School Relationships

Applying Bronfenbrenner's theory to the home-school relationship indicates mutual respect and cooperation between home and school will benefit children. The experiences of the children featured in this book illustrate various ways in which the proximal processes of home and school can support each other for children's literacy learning. At home, Rebecca experiences many proximal processes that support her literacy learning. Her home is flooded with complex conversations, print is used regularly, and she is expected to perform as a reader and writer.

This is not the case for Annie, though. Her mother comes home from work tired and frazzled. Annie's conversation attempts are greeted with brief responses, and she is not encouraged to continue or expand. There is very little print in the home (no newspapers, books, or magazines); reading occurs rarely and is not brought to her attention. Annie is viewed as a preschool child who has not yet learned anything of significance about reading and writing. Given the dramatic differences in proximal processes in these two home microsystems, it is logical that Annie's literacy development is behind that of Rebecca. Fortunately, Annie experiences more positive proximal processes focused on literacy in Mrs. Jones's classroom.

Mrs. Jones realizes the power of the home environment to influence children's achievement. She also understands that Annie's mother has a school-focused role construction and does not feel confident in her ability to help Annie learn to read. Therefore, Mrs. Jones has worked hard to build a relationship with Annie's mother. Mrs. Jones helps the mother see the progress Annie is making at Head Start and frequently suggests small simple ways in which she can help Annie with language and literacy learning out of school. Mrs. Jones has started with simple strategies such as encouraging her mother to have more extended and elaborated conversations with Annie as they go about family routines such as supper preparation and cleanup, grocery shopping, and riding in the car. Mrs. Jones hopes that eventually, through parent involvement, the experiences Annie has with her family will become more supportive of her literacy learning.

SUMMARY

This chapter explains factors which influence parents' decisions to become involved in their children's education, specifically, parental role construction, beliefs about efficacy, and invitations to become involved. Key features of home-school partnerships that facilitate healthy relationships and active parent involvement are identified. Four types of parent involvement are also explained, along with a variety of strategies for implementing these types. Finally, these parent involvement issues are applied to the children and families featured in this book.

Bringing It All Together

11

Annie walks tentatively into her Head Start classroom on Monday morning. She stops by her cubby and hangs up her coat, brushing her hand over the photo of her family underneath her name. She stops by the sign-in sheet and writes a big "A" next to her name to show that she has arrived. Then Annie surveys the classroom, while chewing on her shirt collar.

Annie's teacher, Mrs. Jones, knows that Monday mornings are often hard for Annie. Getting back into the classroom routine after two days at home seems to be a difficult transition for her. Mrs. Jones says hello to Annie and drapes an arm over her shoulder. "I'm glad you're here today Annie. We have lots of gardening things going on in our room." Gardening is the topic of the integrated unit Mrs. Jones has planned. She hopes that the topic will appeal to Annie as it relates to her family's farming occupation. Annie leans into Mrs. Jones as she looks at the ongoing activities around the room and listens to Mrs. Jones's description of the learning centers. Eventually Annie says "I'm gonna plant beans," and walks off to the sand table where two other children are digging and "planting" colored stones.

PRESCHOOL PROGRAMS MAKE A DIFFERENCE

While preschool programs are beneficial to all children, they are particularly important for children like Annie. Living in poverty is often accompanied by a host of life challenges which are often expressed in low levels of academic achievement and less than optimal development. However, exemplary preschool programs can turn the tide for young children (Shonkoff & Phillips, 2000). High quality preschool programs have been associated with good developmental outcomes for children in general

(Howes & Sanders, 2006). For children in poverty, good preschool programs seem to act as a buffer protecting them from the consequences of poverty and improving their life trajectories (Reynolds & Clements, 2005). These programs also have a positive impact on children's literacy learning (Connor, Morrison, & Slominski, 2006).

This book describes how to create preschool literacy learning environments of the highest quality. Language development, reading, and writing have all been addressed. This chapter describes how to bring all of these ideas together to support children's literacy development. For optimal literacy learning, an exemplary preschool classroom is one that is literacy and language rich. Time and materials are organized so that children have opportunities to use language and literacy for multiple purposes and in multiple settings.

THE PHYSICAL ENVIRONMENT

The previous chapters explained how to teach important literacy concepts to young children in meaningful ways. By now, you should be feeling comfortable with planning for literacy learning. But what does a good classroom look like? What should you do to ensure children obtain the maximum benefit from your literacy curriculum? One place to start is with general principles of program quality shown in Figure 11.1, which highlights key features of good early childhood practice.

The Physical Environment
• Child-sized furniture • Displays are at child eye level • Curriculum materials are rotated to maintain interest • Materials are stored on low shelves near the areas where they are used • Materials are culturally appropriate for the population served • Quiet and active areas of the classroom are separated • Adequate ventilation, heat, cooling • Good lighting • Sound level is moderate—may be enhanced with soft surfaces, such as rugs and cushions, or ceiling and/or wall tiles
Classroom Routines and the Interactional Environment
• Quiet and active periods alternate across the daily schedule • Transitions between activities are relatively smooth and efficient • Structured group times are short—usually twenty minutes or less

- Structured group times include opportunities for movement
- Outdoor play is planned just as carefully and purposefully as indoor play
- The environment and classroom routines encourage children to take responsibility for themselves, make good choices, and engage in autonomous behavior
- Children may choose from a variety of learning activities
- Daily routines are treated as opportunities for learning—mealtime, transitions, attendance
- Teachers and children engage in sensitive interactions that facilitate learning, questioning, and problem solving
- Positive guidance and logical consequences are used instead of punishment or threats

Figure 11.1 General Principles of Program Quality

The physical environment in a quality program is designed around children with child-sized furniture. Displays are posted at children's eye level. The majority of materials displayed are examples of the children's work. Paintings, drawings, and collages are posted around the room. Children's names are written on their work, which often includes dictation from children about their activities. Language experience charts created during group times are posted as well as charts and graphs created during mathematics and science activities. Commercial pictures and posters are culturally appropriate and relate to the unit topic. The classroom is divided into learning centers with quiet areas such as the library and writing centers separated from more noisy centers such as blocks and woodworking. Materials are stored near the area where they are used. For example, next to the writing table in Mrs. Jones's classroom is a low shelf containing a wide variety of papers and writing tools. A sign on the wall beside the sand table says "Bean Field" and is decorated with a parent volunteer's drawing of a bean plant. A pegboard and shelf are located beside the sand table and are used to store the sand tools. Both have outlines with printed labels indicating spaces for shovels, trowels, rakes, and so on.

Books

We move now from the overall environment to a more focused look at the classroom literacy environment. A variety of books should be present, both storybooks and informational books. The storybooks should include predictable books, books with a clear story line, and picture books that only have a few words on each page. Books like these encourage language use and vocabulary development. One of Annie's favorites is *Jump, Frog, Jump!* (Kalan, 1981), a predictable book with few words per page. Annie enjoys saying the "jump frog jump" phrase that is repeated throughout the book. It provides a situation in which her tendency to speak out during group time is appropriate. Mrs. Jones makes sure *Jump, Frog, Jump!* and other favorites are frequently available to help build Annie's sense of competence as a reader.

Informational books in the classroom should include concept books. Examples of concepts books are alphabet or number books, and books about colors or everyday objects. Informational books also include those that can be used to learn about people, places, and things. Mr. Gonzalez depended heavily on informational books during the castle unit (described in Chapter 8). The books showed children a variety of castle configurations found around the world. They also provided information on the castle machines (portcullis, catapult) that so captured the children's interest. Mrs. Jones has placed books on growing vegetables in the library area for the gardening unit. Lois Ehlert's (1994) *Eating the Alphabet* in big book form is displayed on an easel for the children to thumb through and try and identify all of the fruits and vegetables. Several copies of *Growing Vegetable Soup* (Ehlert, 1987), a book read at group time, are available for children to revisit on their own or with friends, and to take to other centers to use as a guide for their own seed planting.

Finally, to encourage language play, the classroom should contain books based on familiar songs, nursery rhymes, or poetry. A favorite book in Ashley's class is based on the song about the old lady who swallowed a fly. In Kathi's class, Rebecca often chooses a nursery rhyme book and then bounces about the classroom chanting the rhymes with modifications to fit her activities. Think back to Rebecca's language play with the "Monkey's on the Bed" rhyme from Chapter 3 and you can imagine what she sounds like.

Finally, classroom books should also reflect the cultures of the children in the classroom and the larger community. Mr. Gonzalez makes sure the books in his classroom include Hispanic and African American characters, as these ethnicities comprise a large proportion of the children in his class. Books with respectful and accurate depictions of cultures unknown to the child are valuable as well (Makin, 2003). Therefore, Mr. Gonzalez also uses books with Native American characters as well as characters from Asia and the Middle East.

Like all classroom materials, books should be displayed within easy reach of children and at their eye level. The library area should be comfortable and inviting. Soft furniture, bean bag chairs, blankets, and pillows encourage children to curl up with a book and a friend (Roskos & Neuman, 2001). But books should not be restricted to a library area. They should also be liberally scattered about the classroom. Books about buildings could be in the block center. Books about the current unit topic should be available in appropriate learning centers. For the castle unit, Mr. Gonzalez placed castle books in the book and writing areas as well as dramatic play and blocks. For the machines unit, he will place some machine books in the manipulative area, the art area, and the block area. His hope is that the books will inspire creative work with Legos and Bristle Blocks in the manipulative area, and with three-dimensional collage materials in the art area. And of course, he hopes the books will inspire some interesting construction play with the large hollow blocks and wooden riding toys.

Print and Literacy Materials

Books are only one form of print that should be available in the classroom. Functional and environmental print should be in all areas of the room. Remember that functional print is print that is a part of everyday activities in a particular setting (Christie, Enz, & Vukelich, 2003). Examples of functional print in a classroom include labels on shelves or cabinets, posters, sign-in sheets, helper charts, charts constructed by the children, lists, and directions.

Functional and Environmental Print

The functional print should be intentionally chosen to support children's emerging understanding of how print and oral language can serve similar functions. The children should be involved in constructing and interacting with the print. For example, a sign-in sheet involves the children in keeping track of who has come to the class and who has not yet arrived. During Mrs. Jones's gardening unit, the children will make a list of items needed to plant seeds. They can then use their lists in the garden store dramatic play. Writing and then using the lists will support the idea that print can be revisited over time. When the children plant seeds during small-group times, the teachers help them through the process by reminding them to look at a chart with directions on how to plant the seeds. These activities help children understand that print can have the function of expanding our knowledge by showing us how to do something.

Environmental print is print that is found in the everyday environment of children. Examples include labels on food containers, newspapers, menus, signs, junk mail, and fast food containers. These types of print help children begin to understand that print has meaning and serves particular functions. Mrs. Jones has included environmental print in her gardening unit. The dramatic play center has been transformed into a garden store containing seed packets, boxes and bags of fertilizer, shopping lists, a price list for seeds, plant food, garden tools, receipts for purchases, and a sign with the store name and hours. The children decided on the store name, "The Green Bean Garden Store," and the hours of operation, "center time" and "after nap." These last two examples allowed the children to create environmental print for the garden store.

Placing environmental print in a classroom brings authenticity to literacy learning as children make connections between literacy in their lives and in school. Functional print has a role as well. Children should see adults interacting with functional print as they remind children to find their own cubby or as the adult uses the labels on shelves to find particular materials, or a telephone list to call the parent of a sick child. Children should help construct functional print as they help make lists or construct charts. Both environmental print, and the materials to construct their own functional print, should be available in play centers. Providing these materials in all play centers leads to more play in which children practice using similar literate behaviors that they see the important adults in their lives use. All of these materials and opportunities allow children to use literacy to make events in their play settings more meaningful (Roskos & Neuman, 2001), as well as more fun.

Materials and Tools

A literacy-rich environment should also contain materials that children can use to construct their own books, charts, lists, etc. These materials encourage children to experiment with reading and writing. It is important to have a comfortable, inviting space in the classroom devoted to writing. To capitalize on the learning potential of the writing center, adults should participate as coplayers with the children. When adults are available as models or to provide assistance, children are more likely to visit the center. When Mrs. Jones visits the writing center in her classroom, she often asks children to read their own writing out loud. By doing so, she emphasizes that the child can compose a message, whether or not the writing is conventional.

One day while Mrs. Jones was in the writing center, Pilar told her, "This says my house is the one with blue windows." Looking at the illustration accompanying Pilar's writing, Mrs. Jones replied, "Did you know there is a special word for those blue things by the windows? The word is 'shutters.' Would you like to see what that word looks like?" After Pilar nodded, Mrs. Jones wrote "shutters" on another piece of paper. Pilar then did some more writing on her paper. As she finished, Pilar tucked Mrs. Jones's sample writing of "shutters" in her pocket saying. "I might need this later" and then left the writing center. Mrs. Jones supported Pilar's emerging understanding about what a word is, and also supported her vocabulary by introducing a rare word that Pilar had probably not heard before. Pilar demonstrated her understanding of the permanence of writing by taking off the word Mrs. Jones had written because it might be useful.

Mrs. Jones routinely stocks her writing center with a variety of writing tools (pencils, markers, colored pencils, stencils, chalk, alphabet stamps, a computer) and things to write on (multiple types, sizes, and colors of paper, small chalkboards or whiteboards, blank booklets, tablets, stationery, and envelopes). The class word wall and an alphabet poster have a prominent place in the center. Shelves in the writing center contain individual alphabet strips and word cards with children's names and other words they have decided are important. "Strawberry" is one word the children have requested for their collection of word cards. Many of their parents, including Annie's mother, work in the commercial strawberry fields native to the area.

Note that there are many representations of the alphabet in Mrs. Jones's writing center. The alphabet is visible in other parts of the classroom as well, including the wall by the sign-in sheet and the library. Centers other than the writing center also include literacy materials. Often these are simply paper and pencils as is the case for the block center. Alphabet letters and sound games are added to the language center. Both environmental and functional print are included in the dramatic play center. Magnetic letters, wooden and rubber alphabet puzzles, alphabet lotto, and matching games are available in the puzzle and manipulative center. Alphabet cookie cutters are in a bin with the playdough tools. These materials are available during learning center times and also used to support more teacher-directed small-group sessions.

Interactive learning centers filled with literacy materials lead to greater use of the centers. The literacy materials extend children's literacy interests and abilities as they use centers time for various purposes (Makin, 2003; Roskos & Neuman, 2001; Yaden et al., 2000).

Roskos and Neuman (2001) assert that children should have the opportunity to explore a variety of familiar settings from their out-of-school lives in the classroom. This means that Mrs. Jones's garden store or themes featuring a doctor's office, grocery store, or fast food restaurant are good choices for dramatic play centers. Roskos and Neuman advise that teachers follow three criteria when choosing materials for a dramatic center: How appropriate is the item to the setting and can it be used safely and naturally by the children? How authentic is the item to the natural environment that is being reproduced in the center? How useful will the item be to the children as they take on adult roles and imitate literate behaviors in those roles? Finally, props should be grouped together in a way that encourages children to make connections with their experiences while building up new knowledge about how literacy and the world work.

THE INTERACTIONAL ENVIRONMENT

The physical environment is only one part of a literacy-rich early childhood program. The way the classroom functions and the opportunities available to children are also critical components of the environment. In fact, the most important feature of the environment is the nature of interactions between teachers and children and between children and children. Specifically, adults should engage children in extended conversations and pose questions that require problem-solving. Dickinson and Smith (2001) have described this as cognitively challenging talk and note that it plays an important role in children's learning. Mrs. Jones used cognitively challenging talk with Annie on the playground, asking about the seed planting activity from small-group time earlier in the day. Mrs. Jones asked Annie to recall the planting process, asked open-ended questions about what to do with the plants at the end of the school year, and used rare words like "germinate" and "seedling."

Conversations

Research has demonstrated the importance of conversations with children for their later literacy development (Dickinson & Tabors, 2001; Yaden et al., 2000). However, it is not just occurrence of conversations that is important. For conversations to be valuable, they must be intellectually challenging for the child, extend the child's topic, and include the use of rare words. Rare words are not those that are most frequently used in daily life. To be intellectually challenging, the conversation must address topics and events that are not happening right now. They should include talk about how the world works, tell the child unknown information, and include words that are not in the child's vocabulary. To extend children's conversations, adults need to ask open-ended questions that encourage elaborations and higher order thinking. These questions might ask for clarification of something the child has said, such as asking why or inviting the child to tell more about the topic. They might ask the child to relate what he is saying to an event that has happened or a concept in their lives.

Conversations need to take place with groups of children during story reading or group time and individually with children during free play. Conversations with groups need to stay focused on the topic but encourage children to use what they know and to listen to each other. Conversations during free play time should be more open and guided by what the child is saying, while expanding both the topic and the sentence structure. A teacher can do that by asking open-ended questions, listening to children's responses, and extending the topic (Dickinson & Smith, 2001). For example, Mrs. Jones might enter the Garden Store as a customer and tell the children there that she wants to make an order for a large number of plants for her garden. She could pull out a list, hand it to one of the children and say, "I'm looking for all of these vegetable plants—tomatoes, lettuce, and eggplant. Do you have any other plants that might work in my garden? Can you tell me about then?" Both conversations in group time and during play time can be spontaneous, but they should also be planned by the teacher to build vocabulary and language skills. Ashley often visits Michael in the block center and asks him to talk about his construction. She follows up with questions such as "Why did you build it that way? How is it like the one you built last week?" Kathi's conversations with Rebecca, on the other hand, are more spontaneous since Rebecca frequently initiates conversations about what she is doing whenever Kathi enters a center in which she is playing.

Routines

A language- and literacy-rich environment includes classroom routines built around practicing and enjoying language and literacy in authentic settings. As mentioned, one routine in Kathi's classroom is the sign-in sheet. When the children arrive at the classroom, they hang up coats and find the "I am here" clipboard. This clipboard has a list of the children's names on it with a blank space beside each name for the children to put their signature. They can write their signatures in any way they would like at the beginning of the year. By the end of the year, Kathi expects each child to be able to sign in using his or her name written correctly.

A routine all of the teachers use is the repeated reading of a favorite story during both small- and large-group times. Repeated reading of favorite stories encourages children to become more involved in the story and helps them learn the different ways stories are put together (story structure). It also provides repeated exposure to vocabulary and language structure. Mrs. Jones's repeated reading of *Jump, Frog, Jump!* in both the large group and in a small group during the unit on ponds pulled Annie into the story. She had seen frogs jumping in the ponds around where she lived, so the story connected to her life. As Mrs. Jones provided repeated exposures to the story, Annie learned the structure and began to explore and read the book on her own during center time.

An important routine in Mr. Gonzalez's classroom is journal writing. Each child has her own journal in the writing center. Mr. Gonzalez encourages each child to write in the journal either during play time at the writing center or at the end of play. The children know that once a week Mr. Gonzalez will ask them to join him in writing about their week if they have not yet done so. After writing in their journal, each child reads the entry to Mr. Gonzalez or the classroom assistant who dates the entry and writes a note describing the entry.

ASSESSING YOUR LITERACY AND LANGUAGE ENVIRONMENT

Mrs. Jones, Kathi, Mr. Gonzalez, and Ashley all understand the importance of ongoing assessment in providing a good early childhood literacy program. Each teacher regularly surveys their classroom to make sure they are providing a variety of materials for the children to use. They also regularly review the activities provided and the routines they have in place. To make sure they are expanding and extending children's language, they reflect on the conversations they have had with the children. The checklist in Figure 11.2 provides a helpful way of keeping track of the environment. Finally, the teachers are systematic and intentional about including literacy throughout the day. The daily schedule chart in Figure 11.3 acts as a useful tool for this process. We hope that you will find these tools useful as well.

1. Take a walk around the classroom. Check off the literacy materials you find in each area of the classroom.

Library
□ picture books
□ predictable books
□ informational books
□ concept books
□ alphabet books
□ big books
□ class written books
□ multicultural books
□ props for acting out books

Writing Center
□ variety of writing tools
□ variety of paper
□ word cards
□ alphabet poster
□ alphabet stamps
□ alphabet stencils
□ journals
□ word books
□ magnetic letters
□ small chalk or white boards
□ blank books
□ sentence strips
□ blank cards
□ cards with words and pictures
□ simple dictionary

Blocks
□ books about theme or building
□ journal or blank books
□ pencils
□ traffic signs
□ labels on shelves

Science Center
□ blank books or journals
□ pencils
□ books about topic
□ posters

Language Center
□ tape player with headsets
□ books on tape with books
□ flannel board stories
□ alphabet games and puzzles
□ rhyming games
□ puppets
□ puzzles with words

Manipulatives/Math
□ labels on shelves
□ puzzles with words
□ books about numbers, shapes
□ pencils, paper, rulers
□ magnetic numbers
□ blank books

Art
□ markers and pencils to write about art work
□ art books
□ labels on shelves of art supplies

Computer Center
□ computer
□ simple software for matching, sorting, concepts

Cooking/Snack Area
□ menu of the day
□ simple cookbooks
□ recipes for snacks

Dramatic Play Center
□ literacy materials appropriate to the theme
□ paper
□ books
□ pencils
□ environmental print
□ functional print

General materials
□ pocket chart
□ chart tablet, markers
□ easels to hold big books

2. Take another look around the room. Which of the following environmental and functional print do you see?

□ names on cubbies
□ charts written together
□ schedule
□ lists or directions

□ labels on shelves
□ messages to parents
□ calendar
□ messages to children

□ sign-in sheet
□ center signs
□ inventory lists of supplies
□ environmental print

3. Think about your daily routines. Which of the following are a part of your day?

□ children sign in or in some way use print to indicate they have arrived
□ rereading of at least one favorite book daily in large group
□ shared reading in large group
□ interactive storybook reading in small group
□ individual journal writing or group interactive writing
□ planned conversation with at least three children

Figure 11.2 Literacy-Rich Environment Checklist

Time of Day	Vocabulary	Reading	Comprehension	ABC Knowledge	Phonological Awareness	Print Concepts
ARRIVAL						
BREAKFAST, LUNCH, SNACK						
LEARNING CENTERS						
LARGE GROUP						
OUTSIDE TIME						
SMALL GROUPS						
REST TIME						
TRANSITIONS						
DEPARTURE						

Figure 11.3 The Daily Schedule and Opportunities for Literacy Learning

PLANNING FULL- AND HALF-DAY PROGRAMS

All of the practices we have described in this book occur within the ongoing context of preschool classrooms. Attention to curriculum, standards, assessments, materials, and activities occur within both full- and half-day programs. There are several key things teachers can do to make the most of their time with children. Think about your daily schedule. Plan it so that children alternate between quiet and active events, between structured and unstructured events, and between child-directed and teacher-directed activities. Alternating in this way helps children better tune into both types of activities. As the children move from one part of the day to another, help them modify their behavior for the new situation. Watch your children for clues that your schedule is working or needs adjustment. If you and the children are consistently frustrated at specific times, then perhaps a change in your routine or schedule will help. Figure 11.4 contains sample schedules that may be helpful for planning.

After an exciting boisterous activity, children need help to calm down for a more sedate activity. Teacher assistance is needed to help children transition from outdoor play to a quiet story time. Help children slow down and calm down as they go inside. Instructions to use "fairy whisper voices," "float like snowflakes," or "tip toe so we don't wake up the elephants" are all fun, fanciful and effective ways to help children slow down their activity level.

While alternating activities is important, the schedule should flow smoothly; too many changes in activities can chop up the day into small unproductive chunks of time. Children need extended and uninterrupted time in rich, stimulating learning centers. A solid one-hour block is ideal for preschool-age children, but forty-five minutes will suffice. This extended time allows children to delve deeply into the learning center activities. Initially children engage in surface level exploration activities as they play (Isenberg & Jalongo, 2006). Short fifteen-minute rotations between centers used by many teachers do not allow enough time for children to move from exploration to deeper knowledge construction. The forty-five- to sixty-minute time frame allows children to move from messing about to real investigation.

Finally, make all of classroom time learning time—including transitions from one activity to another. Instead of simply calling children's names to move them from large group to snack, Ashley makes this transition a learning game. Examples of transitions with literacy content can be seen in Figure 11.5. "The Good Fairy," who touches sleeping children on the head, is a favorite. Ashley also uses her "magic bag" to engage children's enthusiastic participation in the transitions. With great drama she pulls a picture or prop out of her magic bag and uses the item in the transition. Other strategies are extensions of the large-group content in which children record their response or choice to a question that Ashley has asked. The group-time sessions are short, twenty minutes or less, and have movement activities embedded in the middle. This helps children pay attention as breaks in concentrated activity facilitate better concentration after the break (Pellegrini, 2005). Materials and activities for outdoor play are as carefully planned as indoor learning center activities. All of the activities work together to support children's learning and allow them to practice new skills as well as extend their understanding of both literacy and their world.

Sample Full-Day Schedule
• Entrance • Breakfast • Learning centers • Group time • Outside • Small groups followed by limited choice of centers until lunch time • Lunch • Bathroom and transition to nap • Read a book, play quiet music, rub backs as children lay down for nap • Wake up, bathroom, transition to snack • Snack • Outside • Small groups or learning centers • Departure
Sample Half-Day Schedule
• Entrance • Learning centers • Group time • Snack • Outside • Small groups followed by limited choice of centers • Departure

Figure 11.4 Sample Daily Schedules

Transition Activity	Literacy Concept
The Good Fairy: Sing "Are You Sleeping Brother John." Children lay down to sleep. Teacher pretends to be the Good Fairy and wakes up a few children at a time. Use the tune for "This is the Way We Wash our Face" to wake up children. Teacher uses children's names singing "Sleepy Michael you may get up and go to lunch."	Listening comprehension
Use the Magic Bag. Pull pictures or props out of the bag and ask whose name starts with the same sound. Example: "This is a cabbage, whose name starts with the same sound as cabbage?" As children's names are associated with the initial sound they move to the next activity.	Phonological awareness, vocabulary development
Use the Magic Bag. Pull out ABC cards one at a time saying "If your name has this letter in it you can go. . . ." Only place letters included in children's names in the bag.	Alphabetic principle/alphabet knowledge
Create a chart on which children vote for a favorite. Be sure to make it a simple, fast process. Example: Create a chart of children's favorite garden plants. Prepare cards with pictures or stickers with four different plants. Have more cards than children. Call several children at a time to choose a card and tape it to the chart.	Comprehension, vocabulary
Use the Magic Bag. Place flannel board pieces from *The Very Hungry Caterpillar* inside. Move around the group "feeding" two or three children at a time one of the foods from the story. After a quick taste, children move to the next activity and teacher moves on to the next two or three children.	Vocabulary
"If you had oatmeal for breakfast you may go." Continue with other foods such as eggs, toast, cereal, waffles, juice, milk, etc.	Vocabulary, recall of details

Figure 11.5 Transition Activities

SUMMARY

This chapter brings together the content of the previous chapters to describe essential aspects of a preschool classroom environment. The overall quality of classroom environment is key to creating an exemplary preschool classroom. A literacy-rich environment is made up of two important features: the physical environment and the interactional environment. The physical environment in a literacy-rich classroom includes an abundance of books, an assortment of functional and environmental print in all areas of the classroom, and a variety of literacy materials for children to use to write and make their own books. The interactional environment includes opportunities for talk around books, writing, and the children's activities as well as routines that encourage the use of reading and writing for a variety of purposes. Forms are also provided in this chapter to assess your own literacy environment. Finally, organizing the schedule for whole- and half-day programs is discussed, including transition time and focusing on how to make all of the classroom time learning time.

References

Adams, M. J., Foorman, B. R., Lundberg, I., & Beeler, T. (1998). *Phonemic awareness in young children: A classroom curriculum.* Baltimore: Paul H. Brookes Publishing Co.

Aghayan, C., Schellhaas, A., Wayne, A., Burts, D. C., Buchanan, T. K., & Benedict, J. (2005). Project Katrina. *Early Childhood Research and Practice, 7*(2), Article 6. Retrieved September 20, 2006, from http://ecrp.uiuc.edu/v7n2/aghayan.html

Anderson, R. C., Heibert, E. H., Scott, J. A., & Wilkinson, I. A. G. (1985). *Becoming a nation of readers: The report of the commission on reading.* Champaign, IL: Center for the Study of Reading.

Arzubiaga, A., Rueda, R., & Monzó, L. (2002). Family matters related to the reading engagement of Latino children. *Journal of Latinos and Education, 1*(4), 231–243.

Baghban, M. (2007). Scribbles, labels, and stories: The role of drawing in the development of writing. *Young Children, 62*(1) 20–26.

Barone. D. M., Mallette, M. H., & Xu, S. H. (2005). *Teaching Early Literacy.* New York: The Guilford Press.

Bear, D. R., Ivernizzi, M., Templeton, S., & Johnston, F. (2004). *Words their way: Word study for phonics, vocabulary, and spelling instruction* (3rd ed.). Upper Saddle River, NJ: Pearson Merrill Prentice Hall.

Beck, I. L. (2006). *Making sense of phonics: The hows and whys.* New York: The Guilford Press.

Beck, I. L., McKeown, M. G., & Kucan, L. (2002). *Bringing words to life: Robust vocabulary instruction.* New York: The Guilford Press.

Berger, K. S. (2006). *The developing person through childhood* (4th ed.). New York: Worth.

Bradley, B. A., & Jones, J. (2007). Sharing alphabet books in early childhood classrooms. *The Reading Teacher, 60,* 452–463.

Bredekamp, S., & Copple, C. (1997). *Developmentally appropriate practice in early childhood programs* (Revised Edition). Washington, DC: National Association for the Education of Young Children.

Bronfenbrenner, U., & Morris, P. A. (2006). The bioecological model of human development. In W. Damen & R. M. Lerner (Series Eds.), R. M. Lerner (Vol. Ed.), *Handbook of child psychology: Theoretical models of human development* (6th ed., Vol. 1, pp. 793–828). New York: Wiley.

Bus, A. G. (2002). Joint caregiver-child storybook reading: A route to literacy development. In S. B. Neuman & D. K. Dickinson (Eds.), *Handbook of early literacy research* (pp. 179–191). New York: The Guilford Press.

Cairney, T. H. (2000). The construction of literacy and literacy learners. *Language Arts, 77*(6), 496–505.

Calfee, R., Chapman, R., & Venezky, R. (1972). How a child needs to think to learn to read. In L. Gregg (Ed.), *Cognition in learning and memory* (pp. 139–182). New York: Wiley.

Campbell, R. (2001). *Read-alouds with young children.* Newark, DE: International Reading Association.

Chomsky, N. (2002). Language and the mind. In B. M. Power & R. S. Hubbard (Eds.), *Language development: A reader for teachers* (pp. 36–42). Upper Saddle River, NJ: Merrill Prentice Hall.

Christie, J. F., Enz, B., & Vukelich, C. (2003). *Teaching literacy and language: Preschool through the elementary grades* (2nd ed.). Boston: Allyn & Bacon.

Clay, M. M. (1975). *What did I write? Beginning writing behaviour.* Portsmouth, NH: Heinemann Educational Books.

Clay, M. M. (2001). *Change over time in children's literacy development.* Portsmouth, NH: Heinemann.

Clay, M. M. (2002). *An observation survey of early literacy achievement* (2nd ed.). Portsmouth, NH: Heinemann.

Connor, C. M., Morrison, F. J., & Slominski, L. (2006). Preschool instruction and children's emergent literacy growth. *Journal of Educational Psychology, 98,* 665–689.

Craig, H. K., & Washington, J. A. (2006). Recent research on the language and literacy skills of African American student in the early years. In D. K. Dickinson & S. B. Neuman (Eds.), *Handbook of early literacy research* (Vol. 2, pp. 198–210). New York: The Guilford Press.

Cunningham, P. (2000). *Phonics they use: Words for reading and writing.* New York: Longman.

Dearing, E., Kreider, H., Simpkins, S., & Weiss, H. B. (2006). Family involvement at school and low-income children's literacy: Longitudinal associations between and within families. *Journal of Educational Psychology, 98,* 653–664.

Degen, Bruce. (1983). *Jamberry.* New York: Harper Trophy Book Harper & Row.

Dickinson, D. K. (2001a). Large-group and free-play times: Conversational settings supporting language and literacy development. In D. K. Dickinson & P. O. Tabors (Eds.), *Beginning language with literacy* (pp. 223–256). Baltimore: Paul H. Brookes Publishing Co.

Dickinson, D. K. (2001b). Putting the pieces together: Impact of preschool on children's language and literacy development in kindergarten. In D. K. Dickinson & P. O. Tabors (Eds.), *Beginning language with literacy* (pp. 257–288). Baltimore: Paul H. Brookes Publishing Co.

Dickinson, D. K., & Smith, M. K. (2001). Supporting language and literacy development in the preschool classroom. In D. K. Dickinson, & P. O. Tabors (Eds.), *Beginning language with literacy* (pp. 139–148). Baltimore: Paul H. Brookes Publishing Co.

Dickinson, D. K., & Sprague, K. E. (2001). The nature and impact of early childhood care environments on the language and literacy development of children from low-income families. In S. B. Neuman & D. K. Dickinson (Eds.), *Handbook of early literacy research* (pp. 263–280). New York: The Guilford Press.

Dickinson, D. K., & Tabors, P. O. (Eds.) (2001). *Beginning language with literacy.* Baltimore: Paul H. Brookes Publishing Co.

Dickinson, D. K., McCabe, A., & Clark-Chiarelli, N. (2004). Preschool-based preventions of reading disability: Realities vs. possibilities. In C. A. Stone, E. R. Silliman, B. J. Ehren, & K. Apel (Eds.), *Handbook of language and literacy: Development and disorders* (pp. 209–227). New York: The Guilford Press.

Dickinson, D., McCabe, A., & Essex, M. (2006). A window of opportunity we must open to all: The case for preschool with high-quality support for language and literacy. In S. B. Neuman & D. Dickinson (Eds.), *Handbook of early literacy research* (Vol. 2, Chap. 11–28,). New York: The Guilford Press.

Donahue, M. L., & Foster. S. K. (2004). Social cognition, conversation, and reading comprehension: How to read a comedy of manners. In C. A. Stone, E. R. Silliman, B. J. Ehren, & K. Apel (Eds.), *Handbook of language and literacy: Development and Disorders* (pp. 363–379). New York: The Guilford Press.

Duchan, J. F. (2004). The foundational role of schemas in children's language and literacy learning. In C. A. Stone, E. R. Silliman, B. J. Ehren, & K. Apel (Eds.), *Handbook of language and literacy: Development and disorders* (pp. 380–397). New York: The Guilford Press.

Duke, N. (2000). 3.6 minutes per day: The scarcity of information texts in first grade. *Reading Research Quarterly, 35,* 202–224.

Duke, N., & Purcell-Gates, V. (2003). Genres at home and at school: Bridging the known to the new. *The Reading Teacher, 57,* 30–37.

Dunn, L. (1993). Proximal and distal features of day care quality and children's development. *Early Childhood Research Quarterly, 8,* 167–192.

Dunn, L., & Kontos, S. (2003). Introduction to theme issue on standards and appropriate teacher-directed instruction. *Dimensions of Early Childhood, 31*(3), 3–5.

Dyson, A. H. (2002). Writing and children's symbolic repertoires: Development unhinged. In S. B. Neuman & D. K. Dickinson, (Eds.), *Handbook of early literacy research* (pp. 126–141). New York: The Guilford Press.

Ehri, L. C. (1994). Development of the ability to read words: Update. In R. B. Ruddell, M. R. Ruddell, & H. Singer (Eds.), *Theoretical models and processes of reading* (4th ed., pp. 323–358). Newark, DE: International Reading Association.

Ehri, L. C. (2004). Teaching phonemic awareness and phonics: An explanation of the National Reading Panel Meta-Analysis. In P. McCardle & V. Chhabra (Eds.), *The Voice of Evidence in Reading Research* (pp. 153–186). Baltimore: Paul H. Brookes Publishing Co.

Elkonin, D. B. (1973). USSR. In J. Downing (Ed.), *Comparative Reading* (pp. 551–580). New York: Macmillan.

Epstein, J. L., & Sanders, M. G. (2002). Family, school, and community partnerships. In M. H. Bornstein (Ed.), *Handbook of parenting, 2nd ed. Vol. 5, Practical issues in parenting.* (pp. 407–437). Mahwah, NJ: Lawrence Erlbaum.

Ericson, L., & Juliebo, M. F. (1998). *The phonological awareness handbook for kindergarten and primary teachers.* Newark, DE: International Reading Association.

Ferreiro, E., & Teberosky, A. (1982). *Literacy before schooling.* Portsmouth, NH: Heinemann.

Floerchinger, J. (2005). The Lunch Project. *Early Childhood Research and Practice, 7*(1), Article 6. Retrieved September 20, 2006, from http://ecrp.uiuc.edu/v7n1/floerchinger.html

Freeman, D. E., & Freeman, Y. (2006). Teaching language through content themes: Viewing our worlds as global village. In T. A. Young & N. L. Hadaway (Eds.), *Supporting the literacy development of English learners: Increasing success in all classrooms* (pp. 61–79). Newark, DE: The International Reading Association.

Gee, J. P. (2001). A sociocultural perspective on early literacy development. In S. B. Neuman & D. K. Dickinson (Eds.), *Handbook of early literacy research* (pp. 30–42). New York: The Guilford Press.

Goswami, U. (2000). Phonological and lexical processes. In M. L. Kamil, P. B. Mosenthal, P. D. Pearson, & R. Barr (Eds.), *Handbook of reading research* (Vol. III) (pp. 251–267). Mahwah, NJ: Lawrence Erlbaum Associates.

Goswami, U. (2002). Early phonological development and the acquisition of literacy. In S. B. Neuman & D. K. Dickinson (Eds.), *Handbook of early literacy research* (pp. 111–125). New York: The Guilford Press.

Goswami, U., & Bryant, P. (1990). *Phonological skills and learning to read.* East Sussex, UK: Lawrence Erlbaum Associates.

Gough, P. B., & Hillinger, M. L. (1980). Learning to read: An unnatural act. *Bulletin of the Orton Society, 30,* 179–196.

Griffith, P. L. (1991). Phonemic awareness helps first graders invent spellings and third graders remember correct spellings. *Journal of Reading Behavior, 23,* 215–233.

Griffith, P. L., & Olson, M. W. (1992). Phonemic awareness helps beginning readers break the code. *The Reading Teacher, 45*(7), 516–523.

Griffith, P. L. & Ruan, J. (2003). The missing piece in the standards debate: Teacher knowledge and decision making. *Dimensions of Early Childhood, 31*(3), 34–42.

Hall, K. (2003). Effective literacy teaching in the early years of school: A review of evidence. In N. Hall, J. Larson, & J. Marsh (Eds.), *Handbook of early childhood literacy* (pp. 315–326). London: Sage Publications.

Halliday, M. A. K. (1975). *Learning how to mean: Explorations in the development of language.* London: Edward Arnold.

Halliday, M. A. K. (1996). Relevant models of language. In B. A. Power & R. S. Hubbard (Eds.), *Language development: A reader for teachers* (pp. 36–41). Englewood Cliffs, NJ: Merrill Prentice Hall.

Harste, J. C., Woodward, V. A., & Burke, C. L. (1984). *Language stories and literacy lessons.* Portsmouth, NH: Heinemann Educational Books.

Hart, B., & Risley, T. R. (1995). *Meaningful differences in the early experience of young American children.* Baltimore: Brookes.

Heath, S. B. (1983). *Ways with words: Language, life, and work in communities and classrooms.* New York: Cambridge University Press.

Helm, J. H., & Beneke, S. (2003). *The power of projects: Meeting contemporary challenges in early childhood classrooms—Strategies and solutions.* New York: Teachers College Press.

Helm, J. H., & Katz, L. (2001). *Young investigators: The Project Approach in the early years.* New York: Teachers College Press.

Henderson, E. (1985). *Teaching spelling.* Boston: Houghton Mifflin.

Hickman, P., Pollard-Durodola, S., & Vaughn, S. (2004). Storybook reading: Improving vocabulary and comprehension for English-language learners. *The Reading Teacher, 57,* 720–730.

Hoff, E. (2006). Language experience and language milestones during early childhood. In K. McCartney & D. Phillips (Eds.), *Blackwell handbook of early childhood development.* Malden, MA: Blackwell Publishing.

Holdaway, D. (1979). *The foundations of literacy.* Portsmouth, NH: Heinemann.

Hoover-Dempsey, K. V., & Sandler, H. M. (1997). Why do parents become involved in their children's education? *Review of Educational Research, 67,* 3–42.

Hoover-Dempsey, K. V., Walker, J. M. T., Sandler, H. M., Whetsel, D., Green, C. L., Wilkins, A. S., & Closson, K. (2005). Why do parents become involved? Research findings and implications. *Elementary School Journal, 106,* 106–130.

Howes, C., & Sanders, K. (2006). Child care for young children. In B. Spodek & O. Saracho (Eds.), *Handbook of research on the education of young children* (2nd ed., pp. 375–391). Mahwah, NJ: Lawrence Erlbaum.

Hutchins, Pat. (1976). *Don't Forget The Bacon!* New York: Mulberry Books.

Isenberg, J. P., & Jalongo, J. R. (2006). *Creative thinking and arts-based learning.* Upper Saddle River, NJ: Pearson Merrill Prentice Hall.

Jaffe, J., Beebe, B., Feldstein, S., Crown, C. L., & Jasnow, M. D. (2001). Rhythms of dialogue in infancy. *Monographs of the Society of Research in Child Development, 66*(2), Serial No. 265.

Jones, E., Evans, K., & Rencken, K. S. (2001). *The lively kindergarten: Emergent curriculum in action.* Washington, DC: NAEYC.

Juel, C. (2006). The impact of early school experiences on initial reading. In S. B. Neuman & D. K. Dickinson (Eds.), *Handbook of early literacy research* (Vol. 2, pp. 410–426). New York: The Guilford Press.

Justice, L. M., Pence, K., Bowles, R. B., & Wiggins, A. (2006). An investigation of four hypotheses concerning the order by which 4-year-old children learn the alphabet letters. *Early Childhood Research Quarterly, 21,* 374–389.

Kalan, R. *Rain* (Donald Crews, illustrator). (1978). New York: Mulberry Books, an imprint of William Morrow & Company.

Katz, L. G., & Chard, S. C. (2000). *Engaging children's minds: The Project Approach* (2nd ed.). Westport, CT: Greenwood Publishing Group.

Keene, E. O., & Zimmermann, S. (1997). *Mosaic of thought: Teaching comprehension in a reader's workshop.* Portsmouth, NH: Heinemann.

Klesius, J. P., & Griffith, P. L. (1996). Interactive storybook reading for at-risk learners. *The Reading Teacher, 49*(7), 552–561.

Labov, W., Cohen, P., Robins, C., & Lewis, J. (1968). A study of the nonstandard English of Negro and Puerto Rican speakers in New York City. *Cooperative research report 3288, V(I, II)*. Philadephia: U.S. Regional Survey, Linguistic Laboratory, University of Pennsylvania.

Laframboise, K., L., Griffith, P. L., & Klesius, J. P. (1997). Scaffolding helps students become successful writers. *Florida Reading Quarterly, 33*(3), 12–21.

Lesaux, N. K., & Siegel, L. S. (2003). The development of reading in children who speak English as a second language. *Developmental Psychology, 39*(6), 1005–1019.

Lonigan, C. J., & Whitehurst, G. J. (1998). Relative efficacy of parent and teacher involvement in a shared-reading intervention for preschool children from low-income backgrounds. *Early Childhood Research Quarterly, 13*(2), 263–290.

Lonigan, C. J., Anthony, J. L., Bloomfield, B. G., Fyer, S. M., & Samwel, C. S. (1999). Effects of two shared-reading interventions on emergent literacy skills of at-risk preschoolers. *Journal of Early Intervention, 22*(4), 306–322.

Lopez, M. E., Kreider, H., & Caspe, M. (2004–2005, Winter). Co-constructing family involvement. *The Evaluation Exchange, 10*(4), Article 1. Retrieved May 30, 2007, from http://www.gse.harvard.edu/hfrp/content/eval/issue28/winter2004-2005.pdf

Makin, L. (2003). Creating positive literacy learning environments in early childhood. In N. Hall, J. Larson, & J. Marsh (Eds.), *Handbook of early childhood literacy* (pp. 327–337). London: Sage Publications.

Mayer, K. (2007). Research in review: Emerging knowledge about emergent writing. *Young Children, 62(1)*, 34–40.

McGee. L. M. (2003). Book-acting: Storytelling and drama in the early childhood classroom. In D. M. Barone & L.M. Morrow (Eds.), *Literacy and young children: Research-based practice* (pp. 157–176). New York: The Guilford Press.

McGee, L. M., & Richgels, D. J. (2003). *Designing early literacy programs: Strategies for at-risk preschool and kindergarten children*. New York: The Guilford Press.

Mesmer, H. A. E., & Griffith, P. L. (2005/2006). Everybody's selling it: But just what is explicit, systematic phonics instruction? *The Reading Teacher, 59*, 366–376.

Miller, P. H. (2002). *Theories of developmental psychology* (4th ed.). New York: Worth Publishers.

Moats, L. C. (2000). *Speech to print: Language essentials for teachers*. Baltimore, MD: Paul H. Brookes Publishing Co.

Morphett, M. V., & Washburne, C. (1931). When should children begin to read? *Elementary School Journal, 31*, 496–503.

Morris, D. (1983). Concept of word and phoneme awareness in the beginning reader. *Research in the Teaching of English, 17*, 359–373.

Morris, D. (1993). The relationship between beginning readers' concept of word in text and phoneme awareness in learning to read: A longitudinal study. *Research in the Teaching of English, 27*, 133–154.

Morris, D., Bloodgood, J. W., Lomax, R. G., & Perney, J. (2003). Developmental steps in learning to read: A longitudinal study in kindergarten and first grade. *Reading Research Quarterly, 38*, 302–328.

Morrow, L., & Gambrell, L. (2004). *Using children's literature in preschool: Comprehending and enjoying books.* Newark, DE: International Reading Association.

National Institute of Child Health and Human Development. (2000). *Report of the National Reading Panel: Teaching children to read: An evidence-based assessment of the scientific research literature on reading and its implications for reading instruction: Reports of the subgroups* (NIH Publication No. 00–4754). Washington, DC: U.S. Government Printing Office.

Neuharth-Pritchett, S., Reguero de Atiles, J., & Park, B. (2003). Using integrated curriculum to connect standards and developmentally appropriate practice. *Dimensions of Early Childhood, 31*(3), 13–17.

Neuman, S. (2006). The knowledge gap: Implications for early education. In S. B. Neuman & D. K. Dickinson (Eds.), *Handbook of early literacy research* (Vol. 2, pp. 29–40). New York: The Guilford Press.

Neuman, S. B., & Roskos, K. (1992). Literacy objects as cultural tools: Effects on children's literacy behaviors in play. *Reading Research Quarterly, 27,* 202–225.

Neuman, S. B., & Roskos, K. (1997). Literacy knowledge in practice: Contexts of participation for young writers and readers. *Reading Research Quarterly, 32,* 10–32.

Neuman, S. B., Copple, C., and Bredekamp, S. (2000). *Learning to read and write: Developmentally appropriate practices for young children.* Washington, DC: National Association for the Education of Young Children.

No Child Left Behind Act of 2001, Pub. L. No. 107–110, 115 Stat. 1425 (2002).

Norton, D. (1991). *Through the eyes of a child: An introduction to children's literature* (5th ed.). Columbus, OH: Merrill.

Office of Elementary and Secondary Education. (2003). *Archived Information Reading Excellence Program.* Retrieved March 28, 2007, from http://www.ed.gov/offices/OESE/REA/overview.html

Ogle, D. (1989). The know, want to know, learn strategy. In K. Muth (Ed.), *Children's comprehension of text: Research into practice* (pp. 205–223). Newark, DE: International Reading Association.

Opitz, M. F., & Rasinski, T. V. (1998). *Good-bye round robin: 25 effective oral reading strategies.* Portsmouth, NH: Heinemann.

Patrikakou, E. N., Weissberg, R. P., Redding, S., & Walberg, H. J. (2005). School-family partnerships: Enhancing the academic, social, and emotional learning of children. In E. N. Patrikakou, R. P. Weissberg, S. Redding, & H. J. Walberg (Eds.), *School-family partnerships for children's success* (pp. 1–17). New York: Teachers College Press.

Pellegrini, A. D. (2005). *Recess: Its role in education and development.* Mahwah, NJ: Lawrence Erlbaum.

Pinker, S. (1994). *The language instinct: How the mind creates language.* New York: Harper Perennial.

Powell, D. R. (2006). Families and early childhood interventions. In W. Damen & R. M. Lerner (Series Eds.), K. A. Renninger & I. E. Sigel (Vol. Eds.), *Handbook of child psychology: Child psychology in practice* (6th ed., Vol. 4, pp. 548–591). New York: Wiley.

Puckett, M. B., & Black, J. K. (2005). *The young child: Development from prebirth through age eight* (4th ed.). Upper Saddle River, NJ: Pearson Merrill Prentice Hall.

Rathvon, N. (2004). *Early reading assessment: A practitioner's handbook.* New York: The Guilford Press.

Read, C. (1986). *Children's creative spelling.* Boston: Routledge and Kegan Paul.

Reynolds, A. J., & Clements, M. (2005). Parental involvement and children's school success. In E. Patrikakou, R. P. Weissberg, S. Redding, & H. J. Walbeg (Eds.), *School-family partnerships for children's success* (pp. 109–127). New York: Teachers College Press.

Richgels, D. J. (2002). Invented spelling, phonemic awareness, and reading and writing instruction. In S. B. Neuman & D. K. Dickinson (Eds.), *Handbook of early literacy research* (pp. 142–158). New York: The Guilford Press.

Rogoff, B. (1990). *Apprenticeship in thinking: Cognitive development in a social context.* New York: Oxford University Press.

Romaine, S. (1994). *Language in society.* Oxford: Oxford University Press.

Roskos, K., & Neuman, S. B. (2001). Environment and its influences for early literacy teaching and learning. In S. B. Neuman & D. K. Dickinson (Eds.), *Handbook of early literacy research* (pp. 281–292). New York: The Guilford Press.

Roskos, K. A., Tabors, P. O., & Lenhart, L. A. (2004). *Oral language and early literacy in preschool.* Newark, DE: International Reading Association.

Ryan, R. M., Fauth, R. C., & Brooks-Gunn, J. (2006). Childhood poverty: Implications for school readiness and early childhood education. In B. Spodek & O. Saracho (Eds.), *Handbook of research on the education of young children* (2nd ed., pp. 323–346). Mahwah, NJ: Lawrence Erlbaum.

Sadoski, M. (2004). *Conceptual foundations of teaching reading.* New York: The Guilford Press.

Schickedanz, J. A. (1999). *Much more than the ABCs: The early stages of reading and writing.* Washington, DC: National Association for the Education of Young Children.

Schickedanz, J. A. (2004). A framework and suggested guidelines for prekindergarten content standards. *The Reading Teacher, 58*(1), 95–97.

Schickedanz, J. A., & Casbergue, R. M. (2004). *Writing in preschool: Learning to orchestrate meaning and marks.* Newark, DE: International Reading Association.

Serfozo, Mary. (1988). *Who Said Red?* (Keiko Narahashi, Illustrator). New York: Margaret K. McElderry Books.

Shapiro, A. (2002). The latest dope on research (about constructivism): Part I: Different approaches to constructivism—What it's all about. *International Journal of Educational Reform, 11,* 347–361.

Shaywitz, S. (2003). *Overcoming dyslexia.* New York: Alfred A. Knopf.

Sheldon, S. B. (2005). Testing a structural equation model of partnership program implementation and parent involvement. *Elementary School Journal, 106,* 171–187.

Shonkoff, J., & Phillips, D. (2000). *Neurons to neighborhoods.* Washington, DC: National Academy Press.

Snow, C. E., Burns, S., and Griffin, P. (1998). *Preventing reading difficulties in young children.* Washington, DC: National Academy Press.

Snow, C. E., Tabors, P. O., & Dickinson, D. K. (2001). Language development in the preschool years. In D. K. Dickinson & P. O. Tabors (Eds.), *Beginning language with literacy* (pp. 1–25). Baltimore: Paul H. Brookes Publishing Co.

Stahl, S. A. & Yaden, D. B., Jr. (2004). The development of literacy in preschool and primary grades: Work by the center for the improvement of early reading achievement. *Elementary School Journal, 105*(2), 141–165.

Stanovich, K. E. (2000). *Progress in understanding reading: Scientific foundations and new frontiers.* New York: The Guilford Press.

Strickland, D. S., & Schickedanz, J. A. (2004). *Learning about print in preschool: Working with letters, words, and beginning links with phonemic awareness.* Newark, DE: International Reading Association.

Sulzby, E. (1985). Children's emergent reading of favorite storybooks: A developmental study. *Reading Research Quarterly, 20,* 458–481.

Sulzby, E. (1991). Assessment of emergent literacy: Storybook reading. *The Reading Teacher, 44*(7), 498–500.

Taylor, B. A., Dearing, E., & McCartney, K. (2004). Incomes and outcomes in early childhood. *The Journal of Human Resources, 39,* 980–1007.

Teale, W. H., & Sulzby, E. (1986). *Emergent literacy: Reading and writing.* Norwood, NJ: Ablex Publishing Co.

Tett, L. (2001). Parents as problems or parents as people? Parental involvement programmes, schools and adult educators. *International Journal of Lifelong Education, 20,* 188–198.

Tompkins, G. E. (1998). *Language arts: Content and teaching strategies* (4th ed.). Upper Saddle River, NJ: Pearson Merrill Prentice Hall.

Tompkins, G. E. (2006). *Literacy for the 21st century* (4th ed.). Upper Saddle River, NJ: Pearson Education, Inc.

Trawick-Smith, J. (2006). *Early childhood development: A multicultural perspective* (4th ed.). Upper Saddle River, NJ: Pearson Merrill Prentice Hall.

Troia, G. A. (2004). Phonological processing and its influence on literacy learning. In C. A. Stone, E. R. Silliman, B. J. Ehren, & K. Apel (Eds.), *Handbook of language and literacy* (pp. 271–301). New York: The Guilford Press.

Troike, R. C. (1972). English and the bilingual child. In D. L. Shores (Ed.), *Contemporary English: Change and variation.* Philadelphia: J. B. Lippincott.

U. S. Department of Education. (2007). *Early Reading First.* Retrieved March 28, 2007, from http://www.ed.gov/programs/earlyreading/index.html

Van Laan, Nancy. (1990). *Possum come a-knockin'* (George Booth, Illustrator). New York: Alfred A. Knopf.

Vaughn, S., Linan-Thompson, S., Pollard-Durodola, S. D., Mathes, P. G., & Hagan, E. C. (2006). Effective interventions for English language learners (Spanish-English) at risk for reading difficulties. In S. B. Neuman & D. K. Dickinson (Eds.), *Handbook of early literacy research* (Vol. 2, pp. 185–197). New York: The Guilford Press.

Velez-Ibanez, C., & Greenberg, J. (2005). Foundation and transformation of funds of knowledge. In N. Gonzalez., L. C. Moll., & C. Amanti (Eds.), *Funds of knowledge: theorizing practice in households, communities, and classroom* (pp. 47–70). Mahwah, NJ: Lawrence Erlbaum Association.

Vukelich, C., Christie, J., & Enz. B. (2002). *Helping young children learn language and literacy.* Boston, MA: Allyn and Bacon.

Vukelich, C., Evans. C., & Albertson. B. (2003). Organizing expository texts: A look at the possibilities . In D. M. Barone & L. M. Morrow (Eds.), *Literacy and young children: Research-based practices* (pp. 261–290). New York: The Guilford Press.

Vygotsky, L. (1978). *Mind in society: The development of higher psychological processes.* Cambridge, MA: Harvard University Press.

Walker, J. M. T., Wilkins, A. S., Dallaire, J. R., Sandler, H. M., & Hoover-Dempsey, K. V. (2005). Parental involvement: Model revision through scale development. *Elementary School Journal, 106,* 85–104.

Wasik, B. A., & Bond, M. A. (2001). Beyond the pages of a book: Interactive book reading and language development in preschool classrooms. *Journal of Educational Psychology, 93*(2), 243–250.

Watson, R. (2001). Literacy and oral language: Implications for early literacy acquisition. In S. B. Neuman & D. K. Dickinson (Eds.), *Handbook of early literacy research* (pp. 43–53). New York: The Guilford Press.

Wenger, E. (1998). *Communities of practice: Learning, meaning, and identity.* Cambridge, UK: Cambridge University Press.

West, J., Denton, K., & Germino-Hausken, E. (2000, February). *America's Kindergarteners. Statistical Analysis Report. Early Childhood Longitudinal Study— Kindergarten.* Washington, DC: National Center for Education Statistics. Retrieved May 28, 2007, from http://nces.ed.gov/pubs2000/2000070

What Is Raising a Reader? (n.d.). Fact Sheet. Retrieved May 29, 2007, from http://www.raisingareader.org/pdfs/rar_factsheet.pdf

Whitehurst, G. J., Epstein, J. N., Angell, A. L., Payne, A. C., Crone, D. A., & Fischel, J. E. (1994). Outcomes of an emergent literacy intervention in Head Start. *Journal of Educational Psychology, 86*(4), 542–555.

Yaden, D., Rowe, D., & MacGillivray, L. (2000). Emergent literacy: A matter (polyphony) of perspectives. In M. Kamil, P. Mosenthal, P. D. Pearson, & R. Barr (Eds.), *Handbook of reading research* (Vol. III, pp. 425–454). New York: Longman.

Yopp, H. (1987). *The concept and measurement of phonemic awareness.* Unpublished doctoral dissertation, University of California, Riverside.

Yopp, H. (1988). The validity and reliability of phonemic awareness test. *Reading Research Quarterly, 23,* 159–177.

Yopp, H. (1992). Developing phonemic awareness in young children. *The Reading Teacher, 45,* 696–703.

Yopp, H. (1995). Read-aloud books for phonemic awareness: An annotated bibliography. *The Reading Teacher, 48*(6), 538–543.

Yopp, R. H., & Yopp, H. K. (2000). Sharing informational text with young children. *The Reading Teacher, 53*(5), 410–424.

Young, J., & Beach, S. A. (1997). Young students' sense of being literate: What's it all about? In C. K. Kinzer, K. A. Hinchman, & D. J. Leu (Eds.), *Inquiries in literacy theory and practice: 46th yearbook of the National Reading Conference* (pp. 297–307). Chicago: National Reading Conference.

CHILDREN'S BOOKS REFERENCED

Andrean, G. (2002). *K is for kissing a cool kangaroo.* New York: Orchard Books.

Aylesworth, J. (2004). *Naughty little monkeys.* New York: Scholastic Inc.

Baker, K. (1990). *Who is the beast?* New York: Red Wagon Books Harcourt, Inc.

Barner, B. (2001). *Dinosaur bones.* San Francisco: Chronicle Books.

Base, G. (1986). *Animalia.* New York: Harry N. Abrams, Inc.

Brown, M. W. (1977). *The important book.* New York: HarperCollins.

Bunting, E. (1994). *Flower garden.* Orlando, FL: Harcourt, Inc.

Carle, E. (1987). *The very hungry caterpillar.* New York: Philomel.

Carle, E. (2006). *My very first book of numbers.* New York: Philomel.

Cousins, L. (1989). *The little dog laughed and other nursery rhymes.* New York: E. P. Dutton.

Cowley, J. (1999). *Mrs. Wishy-Washy.* New York: Philomel.

Crews, D. (1978). *Freight train.* New York: Greenwillow Books.

Cronin, D. (2005). *Click, clack, quackity-quack.* New York: Atheneum Books for Young Readers.

De Regniers, B. S., Moore, E., White, M. M., & Carr, J. (Eds.). (1988). *Sing a song of popcorn: Every child's book of poems.* New York: Scholastic.

Dr. Seuss. (1963). *Dr. Seuss's ABC.* New York: Random House.

Dunrea, O. (1989). *Deep down underground.* New York: Macmillan.

Egan, R. (1997). *From wheat to pasta.* Chicago: Children's Press.

Ehlert, E. (1989). *Eating the alphabet: Fruits and vegetables from A to Z.* New York: Harcourt Brace Jovanovich.

Ehlert, L. (1987). *Growing vegetable soup.* New York: Voyager Books.

Ehlert, L. (1994). *Eating the alphabet.* New York: Harcourt Big Books.

Elting, M., & Folsom, M. J. (1980). *Q is for duck.* New York: Clarion Books.

Galdone, P. (1968). *Henny penny.* New York: Clarion Books.

Geisert, A. (1992). *Pigs from 1 to 10.* New York: Houghton Mifflin.

Hague, K. (1984). *Alphabears: An ABC book.* New York: Henry Holt.

Hutchins, P. (1971). *Changes, changes.* New York: Simon and Schuster.

Hutchins, P. (1987). *Rosie's walk.* New York: Scholastic.

Inkpen, M. (2000). *Kipper's A to Z: An alphabet adventure.* New York: Harcourt Inc.

Johnson, S. (1999). *Alphabet city.* New York: Puffin Books.

Kalan, R. (1978). *Rain.* New York: Scholastic Inc.

Kalan, R. (1981). *Jump, frog, jump!* New York: HarperCollins.

Kontic, A. (2006). *Alpha oops! The day Z went first.* Cambridge, MA: Candlewick Press.

Lehman, B. (2004). *The red book.* New York: Houghton Mifflin.

Lionni, L. (1968). *The alphabet tree.* New York: Dragonfly Books, Alfred A. Knopf.

Lobel, A. (1981). *On Market Street.* New York: Mulberry Books.

Lobel, A. (1990). *Alison's zinnia.* New York: Greenwillow Books.

MacDonald, S. (1986). *Alphabatics.* New York: Bradbury Press.

Marshall, J. (1988). *Goldilocks and the three bears.* New York: Penguin Putnam, Inc.

Martin, B., Jr. (1967). *Brown bear, brown bear, what do you see?* New York: Henry Holt.

Martin, Jr., B. (1983). *Monday, Monday, I like Monday.* Austin, TX: Holt, Rinehart & Winston.

Martin, B., Jr. (1991). *Polar bear, polar bear, what do you hear?* New York: Henry Holt.

Martin, B., Jr.. (2003). *Panda bear, panda bear, what do you see?* New York: Henry Holt.

Martin, B., Jr., & Archambault, J. (1989). *Chicka chicka boom boom.* New York: Simon & Schuster.

Mayer, M. (1974). *Frog goes to dinner.* New York: Puffin Books.

Mayer, M. (1974). *The great cat chase.* New York: Scholastic Inc.

McCourt, L. (1997). *The rain forest counts!* Mahwah, NJ: Troll Communications.

McCully, E. A. (1987). *School.* New York: Harper & Row.

McCully, E. A. (2003). *Picnic.* New York: HarperCollins.

Miles, M. (1969). *Apricot ABC.* Boston: Little, Brown.

Nickle, J. (2006). *Alphabet explosion: Search and count from alien to zebra.* New York: Schwartz and Wade Books.

Pallotta, J. (1992). *The icky bug counting book.* Watertown, MA: Charlesbridge Publishing.

Pallotta, J. (2006). *The construction alphabet book.* Watertown, MA: Charlesbridge.

Prelutsky, J. (1986). *Read-aloud rhymes for the very young.* New York: Knopf.

Provensen, A., & Provensen, M. (1978). *A peaceable kingdom: The shaker ABECEDARIUS.* New York: Puffin Books.

Rathmann, P. (1995). *Officer Buckle and Gloria.* New York: G. P. Putnam's Sons.

Rockwell, A. F. (1995). *The acorn tree and other folktales.* New York: Greenwillow Books.

Scarry, R. (1999). *Richard Scarry's best Mother Goose ever.* New York: Golden Books.

Sharmat, M. (1980). *Gregory the terrible eater.* New York: Scholastic.

Shaw, N. (1989). *Sheep on a ship.* Boston: Houghton Mifflin.

Shaw, N. (1997). *Sheep trick or treat.* Boston: Houghton Mifflin.

Sobel, J. (2006). *Shiver me letters: A pirate ABC.* New York: Harcourt, Inc.

Tafuri, N. (1993). *Who's counting.* New York: Harper Trophy.

Van Allsburg, C. (1987). *The Z was zapped.* Boston: Houghton Mifflin.

Walsh, E. S. (1991). *Mouse count.* Orlando, FL: Harcourt Brace and Co.

Watt, Fiona. (2002). *That's not my dinosaur* (Rachel Wells, Illustrator). London: Usborne Publishing Ltd.

Wells, R. (2006). *Max's ABC.* New York: Viking.

Wood, A. (1984). *The napping house.* New York: Harcourt Brace Jovanovich Publishers.

Wood, A. (1992). *Silly Sally.* Orlando, FL: Harcourt, Inc.

Wood, A. (1998). *Quick as a cricket.* Swindon, England: Child's Play (International) Ltd.

Wood, D., & Wood, A. (1990). *The little mouse, the red ripe strawberry, and the big hungry bear.* Singapore: Child's Play.

Wright, B. F. (1988). *The real Mother Goose.* New York: Scholastic Inc.

Yolen, J. (2004). *How do dinosaurs count to ten?* New York: Scholastic Inc.

Additional Resources for Teachers

CHAPTER 1

Charlesworth, R. (2003). *Understanding child development* (6th ed.). Clifton Park, NY: Thompson Delmar.

Mayes, L. C., & Cohen, D. J. (2003). *The Yale Child Study Center Guide to understanding your child: Health and development from birth to adolescence.* New York: Little, Brown.

Schaefer, C. E., & Di Geronimo, T. F. (2000). *Ages and stages: A parent's guide to normal child development.* New York: Wiley

Weitzman, E., & Greenber, J. (2002). *Learning language and loving it: A guide to promoting children's social, language, and literacy development in early childhood settings* (2nd ed.). Hanen Centre: Toronto, Canada.

CHAPTER 2

Jalongo, M. R. (2003). *Early childhood language arts* (3rd ed.). Boston: Pearson Education Group, Inc.

Venn, E. C., & Jahn, M. C. (2004). *Teaching and learning in preschool: Using individually appropriate practices in early childhood literacy instruction.* Newark, DE: International Reading Association.

Vukelich, C., Christie, J., & Enz, B. (2002). *Helping young children learn language and literacy.* Boston: Allyn & Bacon.

CHAPTER 3

Gunning, T. G. (2000). *Phonological awareness and primary phonics.* Boston: Allyn & Bacon.

Wilson, R. M., Hall, M., Leu, D. J., & Kinzer, C. K. (2001). *Phonics, phonemic awareness, and word analysis for teachers: An interactive tutorial.* Upper Saddle River, NJ: Merrill Prentice Hall.

CHAPTER 4

Books to Help Children Understand the Alphabetic Principle

Lionni, L. (1968). *The alphabet tree*. New York: Alfred A. Knopf.
Meddaugh, S., (1992). *Martha speaks*. Boston: Houghton Mifflin.

CHAPTER 5

Children's Books With Characters Who Write

Ahlbert, J., & Ahlbert, A. (1986). *The jolly postman or other people's letters*. Boston: Little, Brown.
Cronin, D. (2004). *Duck for president*. New York: Scholastic Inc.
Cronin, D. (2002). *Giggle, giggle, quack*. New York: Simon and Schuster Books for Young Readers.
Cronin, D. (2000). *Click, clack, moo: Cows that type*. New York: Simon and Schuster Books for Young Readers.
Morgan, M. (2006). *Dear bunny: A bunny love story*. New York: Scholastic.
Teague, M. (2002). *Dear Mrs. LaRue: Letters from obedience school*. New York: Scholastic.
Teague, M. (2004). *Dear Mrs. LaRue: Letters from the investigation*. New York: Scholastic.
Wells, R. (1997). *Bunny cakes*. New York: Puffin Books.

Books for Teachers

McCarrier, A., Pinnell, G. S., & Fountas, I. C. (2000). *Interactive writing: How language and literacy come together, K-2*. Portsmouth, NH: Heinemann.
Rog, L. J. (2007). *Marvelous minilessons for teaching beginning writing, K–3*. Newark, DE: International Reading Association.

CHAPTER 6

Barone. D. M., Mallette, M. H., & Xu, S. H. (2005). *Teaching early literacy*. New York: The Guilford Press.
Laminack, L. L., & Wadsworth, R. M. (2006). *Reading aloud across the curriculum: How to build bridges in language arts, math, science, and social studies*. Portsmouth, ME: Heinemann.
McGee, L. M., & Richgels, D. J. (2003). *Designing early literacy programs: Strategies for at-risk preschool and kindergarten children*. New York: The Guilford Press.
Morrow, L. M., & Gambrell, L. B. (2004). *Using children's literature in preschool: Comprehending and enjoying books*. Newark, DE: International Reading Association.

Owocki, G. (2001). *Make way for literacy! Teaching the way young children learn.* Portsmouth, ME: Heinemann.

Owocki, G. (2003). *Comprehension: Strategic instruction for K–3 children.* Portsmouth, ME: Heinemann.

CHAPTER 7

Anderson, N. A. (2007). *What should I read aloud?* Newark, DE: International Reading Association.

Butler, D. (1998). *Babies need books.* Portsmouth, NH: Heinemann.

Cullinan, B. E. (1992). *Read to me: Raising kids who love to read.* New York: Scholastic Inc.

Gillespie, J. T. (Ed). (1998). *Best books for children: Preschool through grade 6.* Providence, NJ: R. R. Bowker (Greenwood Imprint).

Lipson, E. R. (2000). *The New York Times parent guide to the best books for children.* New York: Three Rivers Press.

Trelease, J. (2006). *The read-aloud handbook* (6th ed.). New York: Penguin Group.

CHAPTER 8

Aghayan, C., Schellhaas, A., Wayne, A., Burts, D. C., Buchanan, T. K., & Benedict, J. (2005). Project Katrina. *Early Childhood Research and Practice*, 7(2), Article 6. Retrieved September 20, 2006, from http://ecrp.uiuc.edu/v7n2/aghayan.html

Floerchinger, J. (2005). The Lunch Project. *Early Childhood Research and Practice*, 7(1), Article 6. Retrieved September 20, 2006, from http://ecrp.uiuc.edu/v7n1/floerchinger.html

Gartrell, D. (2001). *What the kids said today: Using classroom conversations to become a better teacher.* St. Paul, MN: Redleaf Press.

Gronlund, G. (2006). *Making early learning standards come alive: Connecting your practice and curriculum to state guidelines.* Washington, DC: NAEYC.

Helm, J. H., & Beneke, S. (2003). *The power of projects: Meeting contemporary challenges in early childhood classrooms—Strategies and solutions.* New York: Teachers College Press.

Helm, J. H., & Katz, L. (2001). *Young investigators: The Project Approach in the early years.* New York: Teachers College Press.

Hendrick, J. (2003). *Next steps toward teaching the Reggio way: Accepting the challenge to change.* NY: Prentice Hall.

Jacobs, G., Crowley, K. E., K. E., & Hyson, M. (2006). *Play, projects, and preschool standards: Nurturing children's sense of wonder and joy in learning.* Thousand Oaks, CA: Corwin Press.

Jones, E., Evans, K., & Rencken, K. S. (2001). *The lively kindergarten: Emergent curriculum in action.* Washington, DC: NAEYC.

Jones, E., & Nimmo, J. (1994). *Emergent curriculum.* Washington, DC: NAEYC.

Neuharth-Pritchett, S., Reguero de Atiles, J, & Park, B. (2003). Using integrated curriculum to connect standards and developmentally appropriate practice. *Dimensions of Early Childhood*, *31*(3), 13–17.

Wurm, J. P. (2005). *Working in the Reggio way: A beginner's guide for American teachers*. St. Paul, MN: Redleaf Press.

CHAPTER 9

Kirkland, L., Aldridge, J., & Kuby, P. (2006). *Integrating environmental print across the curriculum, PreK–3: Making literacy instruction meaningful*. Thousand Oaks, CA: Corwin Press.

Robb, L. (2003). *Literacy links: Practical strategies to develop the emergent literacy at-risk children need*. Portsmouth, ME: Heinemann.

Roseberry, A. S., McIntyre, E., & Gonzalez, N. (Eds.). (2001). *Classroom diversity: Connecting curriculum to students' lives*. Portsmouth, ME: Heinemann.

CHAPTER 10

Book Bag Resources

Barbour, A. C. (1998–1999). Home literacy bags promote family involvement. *Childhood Education*, *75*(2), 71–75.

Dever, M. T. (2001). Family literacy bags: A vehicle for parent involvement and education. *Issues in Education. Journal of Early Education and Family Review*, *8*(4), 17–28.

Hall, K. (2007). Gator's adventures: A lesson in literacy and community. *The Reading Teacher*, *60*, 491–493.

(Please also see the Raising a Reader Web site listed later in this chapter)

Journal Articles

Burningham, L. (2005). An interactive model for fostering family literacy. *Young Children*, *60*(5), 87–94.

Cline, Z. (2001). Reading parties: Helping families share the joy of literacy. *The Reading Teacher*, *55*, 236–237.

Kauffman, E., Perry, A., & Prentiss, D. (2001). Reasons for and solutions to lack of parent involvement of parents of second language learners. ERIC Document Reproduction Service (ED 458956).

Kieff, J., & Wellhousen, K. (2000). Planning family involvement in early childhood programs. *Young Children*, *55*(3), 18–25.

Koch, P. K., & McDonough, M. (1999). Improving parent-teacher conferences through collaborative conversations. *Young Children*, *54*(2), 11–15.

Lundgren, D., & Morrison, J. W. (2003). Involving Spanish-speaking families in early childhood programs. *Young Children, 58*(3), 88–95.

Olson, M. (2007). Strengthening families: Community strategies that work. *Young Children, 62*(2), 26–33.

Paratore, J. R., & Jordan, G. (2007). Starting out together: A home-school partnership for preschool and beyond. *The Reading Teacher, 60,* 694–696.

Waldbart, A., Meyers, B., & Meyers, J. (2006). Invitations to families in an early literacy support program. *The Reading Teacher, 59,* 774–785.

Walker-Dalhouse, D., & Dalhouse, A. D. (2001). Parent-school relations: Communicating more effectively with African American parents. *Young Children, 56*(4), 75–80.

Books

Diffily, D., & Morrison, K (1996). *Family-friendly communication for early childhood programs.* Washington, DC: NAEYC.

Keyser, J. (2006). *From parents to partners: Building a family-centered early childhood program.* St. Paul, MN: Redleaf Press.

Koralek, D. (2007). *Spotlight on young children and families.* Washington, DC: NAEYC.

Wirtz, P., & Schumacher, B. (2003). *Menu for successful parent and family involvement.* Little Rock, AR: Southern Early Childhood.

CHAPTER 11

Copple, C., & Bredekamp, S. (2006). *Basics of developmentally appropriate practices: An introduction for teachers of children 3 to 6.* Washington, DC: NAEYC.

Epstein, A. S. (2007). *The intentional teacher: Choosing the best strategies for promoting children's learning.* Washington, DC: NAEYC.

Isbell, R., & Exelby, B. (2001). *Early learning environments that work.* Beltsville, MD: Gryphon House.

Gartrell, D. (2004). *The power of guidance: Teaching social-emotional skills in early childhood classrooms.* Clifton Park, NY: Thomson Delmar.

Greenman, J. (1988). *Caring spaces, learning places: Children's environments that work.* Richmond, WA: Exchange Press.

Owocki, G. (2005). *Time for Literacy Centers: How to organize and differentiate instruction.* Portland, ME: Heinemann.

McGee, L. M., & Richgels, D. J. (2003). *Designing early literacy programs: Strategies for at-risk preschool and kindergarten children.* New York: Guildford Publications.

Schickedanz, J. A. (1999). *Much more than ABC's: The early stages of reading and writing.* Washington, DC: NAEYC.

HELPFUL WEB SITES

Books and Children

American Library Association: http://www.ala.org. The American Library Association promotes the high quality library and information services and public access to information.

Caldecott Medal: http://www.ala.org/ala/alsc/awardsscholarships/ literaryawds/caldecottmedal/caldecottmedal.htm. The Caldecott Medal was named in honor of nineteenth-century English illustrator Randolph Caldecott. It is awarded annually by the Association for Library Service to Children, a division of the American Library Association, to the artist of the most distinguished American picture book for children.

Children's Book Council: http://www.cbcbooks.org. The Children's Book Council, Inc., is a nonprofit association of publishers and packagers of books and related materials for children and young adults.

Coretta Scott King Award http://www.ala.org/ala/emiert/corettascot tkingbookaward/CSKwinners/cskawardwinners.htm. The Coretta Scott King award titles promote understanding and appreciation of the culture of all peoples and their contribution to the realization of the American dream. It is given to African American authors and illustrators for outstanding inspirational and educational contributions.

Raising a Reader: http://www.pcf.org/raising_reader/index.html. This is a nonprofit support organization for reading aloud to children.

Reading Rainbow: http://www.pbs.org/rainbow. This Web site contains information about books for children, online games, and downloadable materials.

Child Development

Child Development Institute: http://www.childdevelopmentinfo.com/ index.htm. This Web site contains information on child development, parenting, family life, learning, health and safety, and child psychology and mental health including Attention Deficit Hyperactivity Disorder.

The Consultative Group on Early Childhood Care and Development: http://www.ecdgroup.com/index.asp. This is an inter-agency consortium that focuses on young children (pre-birth to eight years), their families, and communities.

Early Childhood Research and Practice: http://ecrp.uiuc.edu. ECRP is a bilingual Internet journal on the development, care, and education of young children. Each issue contains descriptions of projects to do with children.

EDGATEWAY: Preschool English Learners Page: http://www.edgateway .net/pub/docs/pel/bibliography.htm. The purpose of the English Learning for Preschoolers Project is to provide valuable information based on current research surrounding various aspects of the development, abilities, and everyday experiences of preschool English learners.

Head Start and Early Reading First

Early Childhood Learning and Knowledge Center: http://eclkc .ohs.acf.hhs.gov/hslc. This is the Head Start portal for all early childhood information and resources.

Head Start Bureau: http://www.hsnrc.org/CDI/outcontent.cfm. At this site, you can download The Head Start Path to Positive Child Outcomes.

Curriculum Materials and Teaching Ideas

BrainPOP Jr.: http://www.brainpopjr.com. This Web site contains activities across the curriculum. Some activities are appropriate for precocious preschoolers.

Education World: http://www.educationworld.com/tools_templates/ index.shtml#parent. This site contains downloadable materials for teachers similar to the Happy Grams in Chapter 11.

First-School: http://www.first-school.ws. This site contains lesson plans, learning activities, games, and thematic materials.

Funschool: http://funschool.kaboose.com. This site contains links such as time warp, globe rider, formula fusion, fun blaster arcade, and games for older children. There is also a preschool link with a variety of lesson plans and classroom activities.

Linda's Learning Links: http://www.lindaslearninglinks.com. This site is maintained by Linda McCardle, a kindergarten teacher at Mathew's Elementary School in Columbus, Georgia. There are numerous links to resources and information for teachers.

Literacy Activities for Day Care and Preschool Settings: http://www.ncrel.org/sdrs/areas/issues/content/cntareas/reading/li11k40.htm. This site is supported by the North Central Regional Educational Laboratory. It contains literacy activities appropriate for children in child care and preschool settings, including ideas for daily reading, book talks, language play, dramatic play, and writing.

Literacy Web sites for Preschoolers: http://www.literacy.uconn.edu/pksites.htm. This site is part of The Literacy Web at the University of Connecticut. It contains numerous electronic resources for preschool children.

Preschool Printables: http://www.preschoolprintables.com. This is another site with more downloadable materials for teachers.

Project Approach: http://www.projectapproach.org. This site contains resources to enable teachers to carry out projects with children.

Starfall: http://www.starfall.com. This Web site is offered free as a public service by the creators of the bluemountain.com electronic greeting card site. Children can participate in interactive alphabet and phonemic awareness practice. The site has downloadable materials.

Castle Web sites: http://www.latinamericanstudies.org/chapultepec-castle.htm and http://travel.webshots.com/album/554399962USknPL. Both sites contain pictures of Chapultepec Castle in Mexico City.

School-Family-Community

National Center for Family and Community Connections with Schools: http://www.sedl.org/connections/. This center links people with research-based information and resources that they can use to effectively connect schools, families, and communities.

National Center for Family Literacy: http://www.famlit.org. This organization promotes literacy through an intergenerational approach by building on the family to create ongoing learning.

National Child Care Information Center: http://nccic.acf.hhs.gov/user/providers.html. This site is maintained by the U. S. Department of Health and Human Services Administration for Children and Families. It contains information for child care providers and for parents seeking information about child care.

Harvard Family Research Project: http://www.gse.harvard.edu/hfrp/index.html. This site provides information about Complementary Learning, a project to address the achievement gap through after-school programs, libraries, early childhood programs, and community-based institutions.

Professional Groups and Associations

Association for Childhood Education International: http://www.acei.org. The mission of this association is to promote and support in the global community the optimal education and development of children, from birth through early adolescence, and to influence the professional growth of educators and the efforts of others who are committed to the needs of children in a changing society. This association publishes *Childhood Education.*

Get Ready to Read! http://www.getreadytoread.org/games2/index.html. Get Ready to Read! is a national program to build the early literacy skills of preschool children.

International Reading Association: http://reading.org. The International Reading Association is a professional association for those involved in teaching reading to learners of all ages. The Web site contains links to the association's world-wide projects to promote literacy and to publications and other resources for teachers. Information about *The Reading Teacher* journal can be found at http://www.reading.org/publications/journals/rt/index.html.

National Association for the Education of Young Children: http://www.naeyc.org. This association focuses on the quality of educational and developmental services for children from birth through age eight. The journal *Young Children* can be located at http://www.journal.naeyc.org/; also available from this association are "Beyond the Journal" at http://www.journal.naeyc.org/btj/200705/ and "Early Years Are Learning Years" at http://www.naeyc.org/ece/eyly/.

National Council of Teachers of English: www.ncte.org. The National Council of Teachers of English is a professional association devoted to improving the teaching of language arts at all levels. The Web site contains a link to the association's publications and other resources for teachers.

National Writing Project: www.writingproject.org. The belief of the National Writing Project is that every student deserves a highly qualified teacher of writing. Through a network of nearly 200 local sites at universities across the 50 states, Puerto Rico, Washington, D.C., and the U.S. Virgin Islands, the National Writing Project offers summer institutes for teachers to improve writing instruction in their classrooms.

Southern Early Childhood Association: www.southernearlychild hood.org/parent_pages.asp. This organization is focused on promoting quality care and education for young children. The navigation bar includes links to numerous downloadable items, including parent pages, curriculum ideas, and other resources.

Index

CORWIN PRESS

The Corwin Press logo—a raven striding across an open book—represents the union of courage and learning. Corwin Press is committed to improving education for all learners by publishing books and other professional development resources for those serving the field of PreK–12 education. By providing practical, hands-on materials, Corwin Press continues to carry out the promise of its motto: **"Helping Educators Do Their Work Better."**